The Transcendent Life and Art of Burt Shonberg

By
Spencer Kansa

Copyright © 2017 Spencer Kansa

First Edition 2017

All rights reserved. No part of this work may be reproduced or utilized in any form by any means, electronic or mechanical, including *xerography, photocopying, microfilm,* and *recording,* or by any information storage system without permission in writing from the publishers.

Published by
Mandrake of Oxford
PO Box 250
OXFORD
OX1 1AP (UK)

Also by Spencer Kansa and published by Mandrake
Wormwood Star: The Magickal Life of Majorie Cameron

Contents

	Dedications	4
Chapter 1	Bitsy	5
Chapter 2	Frolicking in Flickerville	27
Chapter 3	Cafe Frankenstein	51
Chapter 4	Firestarter	69
Chapter 5	The Experience	93
Chapter 6	Baphomet	114
Chapter 7	Out (of) Here	135
Chapter 8	Super Chief	155
Chapter 9	Rimbaud of the West Coast	172
Chapter 10	Hollywood Babylon	190
Chapter 11	Mysterian of the Cosmos	205
	Epilogue	231
	Appendix	246
	Acknowledgments	251
	Index	252

Dedications

This book is dedicated to my beloved aunt Barbara Snow Phillips (1951-2015), a lovely, selfless woman, with a heart the size of Africa, who deserved a great deal more love and happiness in her life.

To my dear friends Aya (1932-2016), a warrior poet and priestess, and David Meltzer (1937-2016), an adept of words, music and boundless conversation. Adios amigos.

And to Bowie (1947-Forever), who first transfixed me as a 10-year-old kid in 1980, with his Ashes to Ashes song/video, and kept me spellbound throughout my life, through all his shatteringly beautiful incarnations. His magnificent music and astonishing artistry hit the pleasure-centre like nothing else. He liberated the lives and imaginations of millions, myself included, and though I remain sceptical about God(s) and the supernatural, I always made an exception when it came to him.

Chapter 1
Bitsy

For those fortunate enough to grow up and come of age in the beach town of Revere, Massachusetts, during the 1930s and '40s, life was a golden, all-American existence. Named after Paul Revere, the courageous hero of the American War of Independence, who rode from town to town raising the alarm about the invading British troops, Revere was nestled in a particularly patriotic province of America, steeped in valiant Revolutionary War history.

Located on the coastline, just five miles north of Boston, it had long served as a relaxing resort for summering Bostonians and was originally conceived as New England's answer to Coney Island.

It's fairground and amusement arcades were the stuff of juvenile dreams and, during the depression, older patrons would gather to watch the bandstand concerts or marathon dance contests held in the ballrooms on the pier. Others risked a ride on the dangerous roller coasters, that had, in past years, caused fatalities. (Their propensity for rattling ribs was even exploited to help induce abortions in those carrying unwanted pregnancies.)

The pleasure grounds certainly provided ample thrills and spills for local boy Burton Shonberg, the only son of Louis and Helen Shonberg, who was born in Boston on March 30th, 1933, and blessed with the Hebrew name Ben-Zion (Son of God). Although little is known about the paternal side of the family, his mother's family, the Schreters, were Hungarian immigrants, originally from the town of Sighet in Transylvania, who landed at Ellis Island in the late 19th Century, as part of the European Jewish diaspora that settled in New York.

Helen met and wed Louis after a matchmaking cousin of hers

introduced them, believing they would make a good couple. Born in 1889, Louis was 13 years older than his young bride, and already had a son named Bill from his previous marriage. He was a man of average height, with round, hunched shoulders, who earned a living as a salesman at first, but by the time Burton was four-years-old, he was working night shifts as a carman's helper on the Boston Railroad, where he inspected inbound trains for defects and assisted in the maintenance of the rolling stock in the yard. It was a blue-collar job with perks. For despite never owning a car, Louis could always wangle "free" travel for himself and other family members, and it paid the rent on their ground floor apartment of a triple decker on 22 Arlington Avenue. There, for a brief period, the family was joined by Louis' elderly mother, whom Helen cared for until she passed. Sadly, the marriage proved to be no love match for Helen, and trapped in a passionless relationship, she focused all her affection on her son, whom she called Zindala, meaning "Son that I love." Dolores Schrater, known as Dolly, was the daughter of one of Helen's cousins: "My father owned a luggage store on Boylston Street in Boston, and my parents, David and Nellie, would send money and clothing to New York to help that side of the family, as they were considered poor." [1]

Although technically second cousins, she and Burton related to each other more like brother and sister and being roughly the same age, they went through the public-school system together. Grades one to six were spent at Liberty Elementary Grade School (Helen joined Burton in the second grade after attending a private kindergarten), and grades seven to nine were spent at Garfield Junior High School before they finally transferred to Revere High School for their final three years. "From second grade to sixth grade we'd always have lunch and dinner together after school," Dolly remembers. "Helen was a wonderful Hungarian cook and my Dad, because he was raised on those foods, loved her cooking. When I was sick and had to stay home from school,

Auntie Helen would take care of me. I loved her dearly. She was like a second mother to me. She was a very strong woman, plain and on the stout side, about 5 feet 6 inches, who always had trouble with her feet."

From the age of 9 until his bar mitzvah at 13, Burton also attended the Kadima Hebrew School on Walnut Avenue, three days a week, from 3 pm to 5 pm, where he was tutored by Mr. Keller. "His Jewish faith was part of him and he was proud of his background and his Bar Mitzvah," Dolly confirms. "We went to synagogue and celebrated and observed all the Jewish holidays: Passover, Rosh Hashanah and we fasted on Yom Kippur. Their families spent New Year's Eves together, too, and Dolly and Burton would celebrate by cooking hot dogs and marshmallows with a roasting fork over the flame of the stove. "The public schools were closed on the High Holidays, as the area was mostly a Jewish ghetto in those years, with five hills and three or four main streets, and everyone knew each other. The village raised all of us. You could knock on any door and everyone knew you. Us kids were all very confident because we were never put down. We all did well because it was a protected environment. It was wonderful."

As a boy, Burton's huskiness earned him the ironic but affectionate nickname "Bitsy" from his classmates, who have never forgotten his super-sweet nature, beaming smile, and warm, sparkling eyes. "Burton had the essence of a good person," Dolly asserts. "He was sensitive and smart; not street smart but smart for himself. And he was sociable and outgoing." Even if Burton didn't fancy hitting the beach or the amusement arcades (where one appalling stand, called Hit the Nigger on the Head, gave punters the "opportunity" to strike a black man using three balls, while he poked his head through a hole in a curtain), there was always something pleasurable to do. "We played Monopoly a lot and shot marbles together on the floor; played Fish and other card games. On the radio, we'd listen to *The Shadow* and *Jack Armstrong: The All-American Boy*. The 1939 World Fair actually introduced us to television.

Bitsy's family didn't have one at first, so he would come over to our house to watch it. We'd start a small fire in the field behind my house on Franklin Avenue, and cook baked potatoes under the dirt. In the winter we had sleds and, as we lived on hills, we always went coasting (our term for sledding). I would do some ice skating. Bitsy had skates but he never liked the sport, but he would still go with me to Sam`s Park where the city filled the ground with water so those of us who enjoyed it could skate. Bitsy was not agile or graceful and I would tease him and say, 'Come on Gracie!', sarcastically, because of his gracelessness. He never engaged in any sports, but I remember a group of guys would go fishing in the summer and Bitsy would tag along and draw cartoons of everyone on the boat."

Burton was often accompanied by his best bud Sheldon Weinstein, known as "Monster" to his friends, who lived across the street on Arlington. "The Monster moniker came from people I worked for when I was a soda jerk, because, despite my age, I was the biggest guy on the shift and didn't take no guff from anybody," Weinstein explains. Due to Burton's disinterest in sports, Sheldon attended Red Sox games by himself but, like most boys their age, they bonded over comic books, especially the adventures of *Captain Marvel*, the adult alter-ego of Billy Batson, a homeless, 12-year-old newsboy who, with a bolt of lightning, magically transformed into the superhero by uttering "Shazam!" His battles against the arch-villain Captain Nazi, an imposing, blonde Aryan with a swastika emblazoned across his chest, proved so popular during the war the character even outsold Superman. And when it was turned into a 12-chapter film serial by Republic Pictures, the boys faithfully wended their way to the Crescent Ballroom movie house on the beach to watch it. Oftentimes, they made the trips with Dolly in tow. "My dad had a paid season pass to the movies," she explains, "so we could go free, and, if the movie changed, we'd go each time; sometimes three times a week, back when it cost 10 cents. My folks would let me go because I was accompanied by Burton and Sheldon."

The threesome also sat enraptured by the spine-chilling monster movies served up by Universal Pictures, especially Tod Browning's film version of *Dracula*, starring Bela Lugosi as the menacing Count, which invoked the sepulchral atmosphere of Bram Stoker's gothic novel handsomely, and the bravura performances of Lugosi's theatrical rival Boris Karloff; whether he was transmogrifying into *The Wolf Man* or Burton's favourite miscreation, Frankenstein's monster. Although those original films were made in the early 1930s, contemporary versions, known as the 'Monster Rally' series, were also hitting the screens, with contrived storyline's in which Frankenstein, Dracula, and the Wolf Man all interacted together. Back at school, Burton entertained his classmates with his faultless impressions of these accursed creatures, and also mimicked the creepy, whispering cadence of that other horror stalwart, Peter Lorre.

Inspiration from these monster movies soon began showing up in Burton's drawings, and though chums noticed his aptitude for art, they were not always enamoured of it: "I'd say 60 percent of the time he was drawing or doodling," Sheldon recollects, "but he used to draw lots of gory stuff; monsters going after people." And several surviving pictures from Burton's boyhood seem heavily influenced by his Fawcett Comics reading material, whether it's an *Oriental Demon*, with diamond earrings dangling from its lobes, or the sketch of a Japanese officer with a bloody bullet hole in his head, that seems at least partly inspired by Captain Nippon, Captain Marvel Jr.'s nemesis.

"We did homework together and talked about so many things," Dolly asserts. "We had very deep discussions, between the ages of 12-16, about death and life and sex and family. Bitsy was already ruminating on life's big, unanswerable questions. He'd say, 'What was here before nothing? Because nothing is something!' We could never figure out the creation. We would ponder that as kids. We were believers in ET's and I told him I saw a flying saucer. We both believed strongly in life on other planets, we were of the same mind. I still believe it today, though I don't think I'll live to see it."

One of the instrumental factors that helped shape this mind-set was the vivid imagery left imprinted on their imaginations years earlier, when CBS radio listeners were gripped and hoodwinked by a Halloween hoax sprung from the mischievous mind of the theatrical phenom Orson Welles, who delivered excerpts from H. G. Wells' novel *The War of the Worlds*, chronicling a Martian invasion of Earth, as though it were a breaking news story. To enhance its authenticity, Welles tailored the original story to his American audience, transplanting the location of the alien Armageddon from the home counties of England to the suburbs of New Jersey, with actors from of his Mercury Theater Company adding histrionic eyewitness testimony. "I remember listening to *The War of the Worlds* broadcast with my parents," Sheldon recollects, "and everyone thought it was true. My dad worked in New York, so he knew the places in New Jersey that were being attacked as described by Orson Welles."

The brilliantly conceived stunt caused a media outcry at the time, as it ginned up stories about panicked members of the public, especially those who tuned in after the initial introduction. Although it made his name, Welles bore the brunt of the political firestorm that followed, which came at a time when the country was already anxious over the worrying developments in Europe, following the Munich Agreement a month earlier, a disastrous appeasement that handed Hitler the Sudetenland on a platter.

The chilling concept of Total War in Wells' apocalyptic novel (a rule of warfare that didn't spare the targeting of civilians) would prove eerily prescient as the appalling atrocities of the Second World War began to stack up. Although the youngsters were physically cushioned from the warfare being waged in the European and Pacific Theaters, its pall hung over their lives during those years. Eager to do their patriotic duty, Burton and Dolly initiated their own VFW (Veterans of Foreign Wars) junior Civil Defense group; its ranks swelled by their schoolmates. "We did whatever we could do," Dolly recollects, "collecting tin cans and making sure people followed the blackout rules." While the country was kept abreast of the ongoing conflict overseas by the dramatic newsreel footage that preceded the main features at the movie theatre, as well as the reassuring fireside chats delivered by President Roosevelt via his radio addresses, families waited on tenterhooks for letters updating them on the welfare of their loved ones serving abroad, dreading the appearance of a Western Union messenger turning up at their door with a notice of death telegram.

Bill, Burt's half-brother, was one such enlisted man, and though it's unknown where exactly he was posted during the war, he was mercifully shipped home safely, in one piece, much to the relief of the family. Whatever war stories he may have imparted to his stepbrother have long since been forgotten, but Dolly can clearly remember the stomach-churning firsthand accounts of the Shoah shared by recently emigrated relatives, who spared no detail in describing the ethnic cleansing of the Jews (and others deemed undesirables) in the extermination camps, where some extended family members actually perished.

At the time, Revere was made up of three main ethnic groups: Shirley Avenue was all Jewish, Revere Street was predominantly Italian, and Beach mount was home to the Irish community. Though their children attended separate infant schools, when they entered Garfield Junior High they all mixed in together, without any clash of faiths or division. As one student, Eleanor Oliver (nee Cohen), attests: "We all got along. My mother said, 'You're no better than anybody and no one's better than you.'" She too remembers Burton fondly: "He was the nicest, sweetest, caring person. Nobody ever said anything bad about him. I always wanted him as a friend. We went through infant and middle schools together as well as Garfield Junior High. Even my mother loved him." At Garfield, Dolly earned credit as an assistant editor on the school's newspaper, the *Garfield Echo*, and Burton contributed cartoons. One captured the emotional farewell of the popular English teacher Mr. Murray Satz (who was leaving the school for a new post at Revere High), waving a tearful goodbye to his students gathered at a school window. Though it could be construed as a hokey sentiment, it actually encapsulated the wholesomeness of the time. "We were good kids; never drank or smoked," Oliver confirms. "We had good clean fun. We had junior and senior receptions together, and Burton and I went to dances together. I had a picture of us after the Junior Prom. A group of us drove to Boston, all squeezed in, to have dinner at Blinstrub's nightclub." The trip appears to have inspired another one of Burt's surviving sketches from that time, as it shows a group of schoolmates, wearing their varsity jackets, riding in an open-top Ford Model T jalopy, just like the one owned by Archie Andrews and his gang.

Although they were close friends who spent a great deal of time together, at the arcades and swimming in the ocean, Sheldon admits that he and Burton had other pals they also ran with. Danny Weinstein was a case in point. Though he was a year or two younger than Burton, he got to know him very well after Dolly, his girlfriend, introduced them to each other. "I was 14 or 15. I don't know anyone who didn't like him. He was a gentle boy who was so talented. He was a good student at school and he came up with phenomenal drawings – now you see these things, but not back then. He was 50 years ahead of his time. Revere was a great town to grow up in for kids. We had a two-mile long beach and every town nearby had a section of it. We hung out at a section called Punk's Corner, but, despite the title, we were good kids. To get hold of a beer was a big thing for us. Burton even put in a good word for me with Rochelle, who became my wife." Rochelle Weinstein (nee Gauvin) was vacationing in Revere with her sister Lorraine, from their home in Dorchester, Boston, when they met Burton, who was selling cotton candy and ice creams on the beach. "Burton talked to us for nearly three hours. We discussed paintings and what was going on in town. He was wonderful. A politely mannered, caring, sweetheart guy; a joy, who made everyone happy. Later, I had a party at my house in Dorchester and fixed him up on a date with a girl, but it didn't work out because she was from Dorchester and he was from Revere."

By then, Burton was already attending high school, and getting used to his new home, an upper floor apartment in a two-up two-down clapboard house at 41 Francis Street. His school grades wavered through those teenage years. Though he was a C student in subjects like English, biology and history, he excelled in painting and drawing, and in recognition of his artistic talent, he was invited to contribute illustrations to the graduating yearbook. Following his graduation ceremony, Burton was photographed, still dressed in his robes and mortarboard, at a celebration party at Dolly's parent's house.

But his beaming smile and the affectionate body language displayed in the Shonberg family photographs from this time, do not paint a full or accurate picture. For behind the public show of contentment, there was a markedly different dynamic going on. "Helen was a very fine woman but she loved Bitsy so much it was unhealthy," Dolly explains. "Her attention could be stifling at times. She was very clutching – much worse than a typical Jewish mother. She squelched him. She just wouldn't let him breathe; her whole life was him." As cloyingly close as his mother was, Burton's father, conversely, kept a chilly distance: "Bitsy had no relationship with Louis, and he didn't really have much respect for him, as he was henpecked and not very bright. His father was a quiet, hardworking man, not educated or intelligent, but he was jerky. He'd come home but never talked. I doubt he and Burt ever had one conversation together." One of the few places father and son did cross paths, outside of the family home, was at the Wonderland dog track, where Louis spent an inordinate amount of his free time, blowing his money and chomping on cigars. Burton even got a job there, selling newspapers and walking the greyhounds out to the starting gate.

The money he earned went towards the art supplies he needed, for in September 1951, he enrolled at the School of the Museum of Fine Arts in Boston, whose previous alums included Li'l Abner cartoonist Al Capp and the then unrecognized Cy Twombly. SMFA, as it was known by the students, was an easy commute, and his parents covered all his tuition fees. His attendance lasted two years, with each year was made up of two semesters, each starting in the Fall and Spring. In his first year there, Burton studied a foundation course covering drawing, painting and design. His first semester included classes on sculpture and perspective, but he switched to anatomy and ceramics and frescoes by his second. He studied well and his end of year report states that he excelled in most of his classes and was able to improve in his art history lessons. His second year focused on the more commercial aspects of art, with classes dedicated to advertising and calligraphy. Although he discontinued his art history course, a note on his record indicates that he took an elective "SA," which may have meant a stint working as a studio assistant for a member of the faculty. After two years of study, Burton left SMFA without any accreditations or awards, but if he was disappointed it didn't show, for his mind was occupied elsewhere, on romantic matters. He'd fallen in love with an old friend from high school, Connie Campbell, a comely, coquettish beauty who looked like a young, mini Marilyn Monroe. He was absolutely crazy about her, and they spent many blissful nights together at her home at the Lee Trailer Park on Revere Beach Parkway. "We had an agreement," Dolly explains, "whoever had sex first would tell the other one what it was like, and he had it with Connie at the trailer park and came back and said, "Dolly, it was terrific!" However, when his mother found out about the love affair she refused to sanction it, as Connie wasn't Jewish. At the time, Dolly was also romantically involved with someone from outside her faith, a local Irish-American lad named John McCormack, and Burton played an obliging role in their courtship. "Bitsy and I cared for each other and he provided cover for me. He came to the movies with us and, once we were inside, he'd go sit on his own while we made out in the back row." When Dolly's parents discovered the ethnicity of her beau "they had a fit!", she laughs today, but with a little time, they accepted her choice and, hitched at 18, Dolly settled down and started a family.

Helen, however, was not so understanding when it came to the object of her son's affection, and she made it clear that she would never countenance a marriage taking place between them. During one blistering argument over the issue, she slapped her son hard across the face, and this ugly flashpoint was the moment when Burton finally cut the apron strings. "Bitsy never forgave her for that," Dolly confirms, "and their relationship was never the same. He loved his mother but he resented a lot of her ways."

In the aftermath, Burton hatched a plan that would get him out from under his mother's overbearing control forever, though the solution he came up with was drastic, to say the least: he enlisted in the United States Army.

Although this was not an unusual course of action for a young man coming of age – his pals Sheldon and Danny Weinstein were already serving their country in the armed forces, having joined up right after they left school, and the fact that his half-brother Bill was an established army man, may have been another contributing factor – it did suggest a reckless disregard for his own artistic aspirations. Furthermore, although the Armistice Agreement had brought a cessation to hostilities in the country's difficult, seesawing military campaign against Stalinbacked North Korea, there was no guarantee that another conflict might flare up somewhere else, anytime soon, as America maintained its vigilance against the expansionist policies of global communism. Nevertheless, the twenty-year-old entered the service on July 9th, 1953, and after passing through the reception center at Fort Devens in Middlesex County, he was dispatched to Fort Lewis near Tacoma, Washington. A photo taken there, in September of the following year, shows him leaning out of the flap of a military tent, displaying the unabashed cheeriness he was known for.

During that same Fall, he was transferred to Fort Huachuca, a remote outpost in Southeast Arizona, as part of a Signal Battalion unit, where his MOS (Military Occupational Specialty) entailed working as a radio operator. Fort Huachuca (or rainy mountain to give it its Chiricahua-Apache meaning) was first established in 1877, as a temporary cavalry post to protect mine workers, ranchers and other local settlers against raiding Apaches. In fact, its troops played a major part in bringing about the surrender of the great Apache leader Geronimo. Throughout the 1910s, Huachuca soldiers battled along the border against incursions made by Mexican Federalists, and the 10th cavalry rode from Fort Huachuca as part of General Pershing's Punitive Expedition against the paramilitary forces led by the Mexican revolutionary Pancho Villa. Prior to the country's involvement in WW2, the size and infrastructure of the post were expanded greatly, and it was used to train 27 thousand troops in preparation for their deployment overseas. In 1947, the fort was inactivated, as part of the post-war military cutbacks. But it was reactivated in April 1951, for a two-year period, in order to train Engineer Aviation Units. In January 1954, it became a fully functioning facility again, when it was designated as the U.S. Army Electronic Proving Ground, whose purpose was the development of new electronic technology and communication systems for use in modern warfare. It was equipped with a Computer Center, microwave radio relay antennas, and its desert location provided the perfect environment to test fly radio controlled reconnaissance drones, equipped with surveillance cameras.

The fort was also home to members of the Women's Army Corps, and under the command of Brigadier General Emil Lenzner, it was run as a family-friendly facility with lodgings and schooling provided for the spouses and offspring of both military and civilian personnel. There were plenty of recreational facilities, including swimming pools, a golf course, a baseball team and a service club with ping pong and billiard tables. The movie theatres were a popular source of entertainment, as was the ballroom where variety shows and dances were held. There was even a thrift store next door to the post office. And considering the locale was steeped in frontier history and old Western lore, troops could spend their leave enjoying local excursions to Tombstone, where they could assume the roles of Wyatt Earp and his sidekick Doc Holiday and re-enact the famous gunfight at the O.K Corral, or visit the picturesque village of the Pascua Yaqui Tribe in Tucson to take in their colourful fiesta.

For the first eight months, Burton made the most of his new home base: he disarmed his fellow G.I.s with his celebrity impersonations, painted murals on the walls of the mess hall, and contributed cartoons to the Christmas issue of the *Fort Huachuca Scout* newspaper. He also availed himself of the craft shop, where fine art and commercial art was made and woodwork, ceramics, leather craft, and lapidary were practiced. He was pictured there, demonstrating some of these activities to members of a boy scout troop who lived on the post, in a photograph that revealed just how much weight he'd lost, especially in his face, due to the exercise drills and sweltering heat. But no matter how well he occupied himself, his inclination to "bug out" (leave hastily) was growing.

Unsurprisingly, in what was always going to be an impossible fit, the army's regimental regime was wearing him down, so he plotted an escape route out by feigning mental illness. While he was sequestered in the military hospital for psychiatric observation, Burton struck up a friendship with a fellow inpatient named Ed Fagen, who was himself trying to convince the doctors that he was suffering from an appendicitis. "There were 11,000 men at the post; all signal corps but different functions," Fagen explains. "I was drafted in November 1954, and because I had a master's degree in physics, I was in a privileged group: The Combat Development Department. So, I had no contact with ordinary G.I.s until I met Burton in the hospital. He was certainly a rebel in many ways and he was in because they thought he was crazy. He put his thumb inside his fist and refused to remove it, so he couldn't salute anybody." The quirk earned Burton the nickname "Knuckles." In the week to 10 days they spent in the hospital room together, the two men settled into a comfortable rapport: "We talked about life in the army, or he talked – I listened because he was so different to anyone I'd ever met. He was extraordinary and I still have vivid recollections of him."

When they weren't confabbing, Burton spent the rest of his time sketching. "His drawings were comical and fantastical," Fagen attests, and when it came time to leave the hospital, he gifted his newfound friend with a couple of them. One was a caricature of Fagen dressed as an Indian guru, sat cross-legged and decorated in gemstones, while in an eerie foreshadowing of a future encounter, the other pictured the artist sexually entangled with two longhaired demonesses, in what Fagen describes as "a psycho-horror-drama." Although he was genuinely suffering from bleeding ulcers, Burton's psychological subterfuge also worked its magic and, deemed medically unfit, he was discharged from active military duty on June 2nd, 1955, departed with just his sketchpads and his obligatory National Defense Service Medal.

BURT SHONBERG ➡ OUT THERE

GOOD-BY MR. SATZ

Mr. Murray E. Satz, long a member of the Garfield Jr. High faculty, has left us. We bid him fond farewell. At the Univ. of Michigan, Mr. Satz was awarded the Phi Beta Kappa key which is received only by honor students. At present, he is studying for his doctorate at B.U. Mr. Satz taught English and French here. His classes were always interesting and he was one of the best liked teachers.
All of us wish him the best of luck at the Revere High School.
  —Ruth Parker

Burt's earliest surviving drawing, "Goodbye, Mr. Satz," from the *Garfield Echo*. November 3rd, 1947. (Courtesy of Stephen Schrater.)

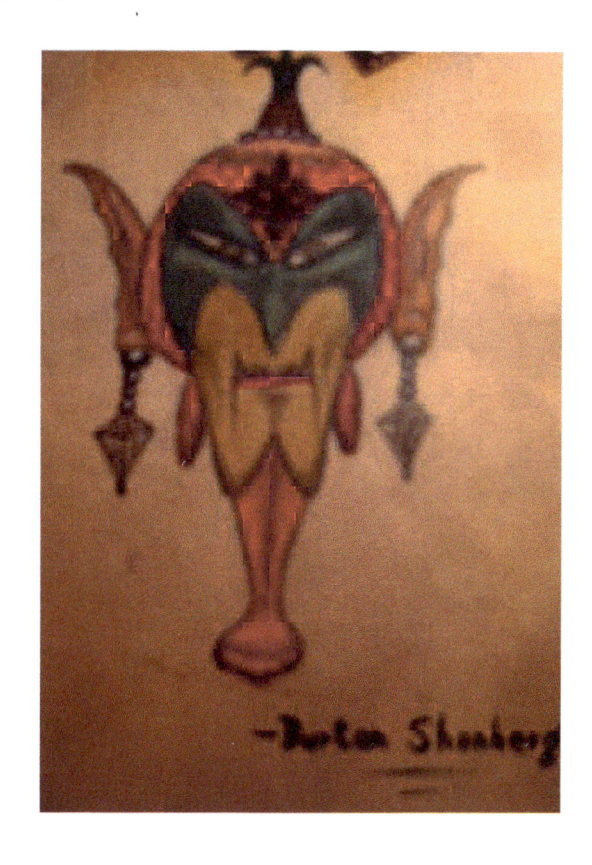

Oriental Demon.
(Courtesy of Stephen Schrater.)

19

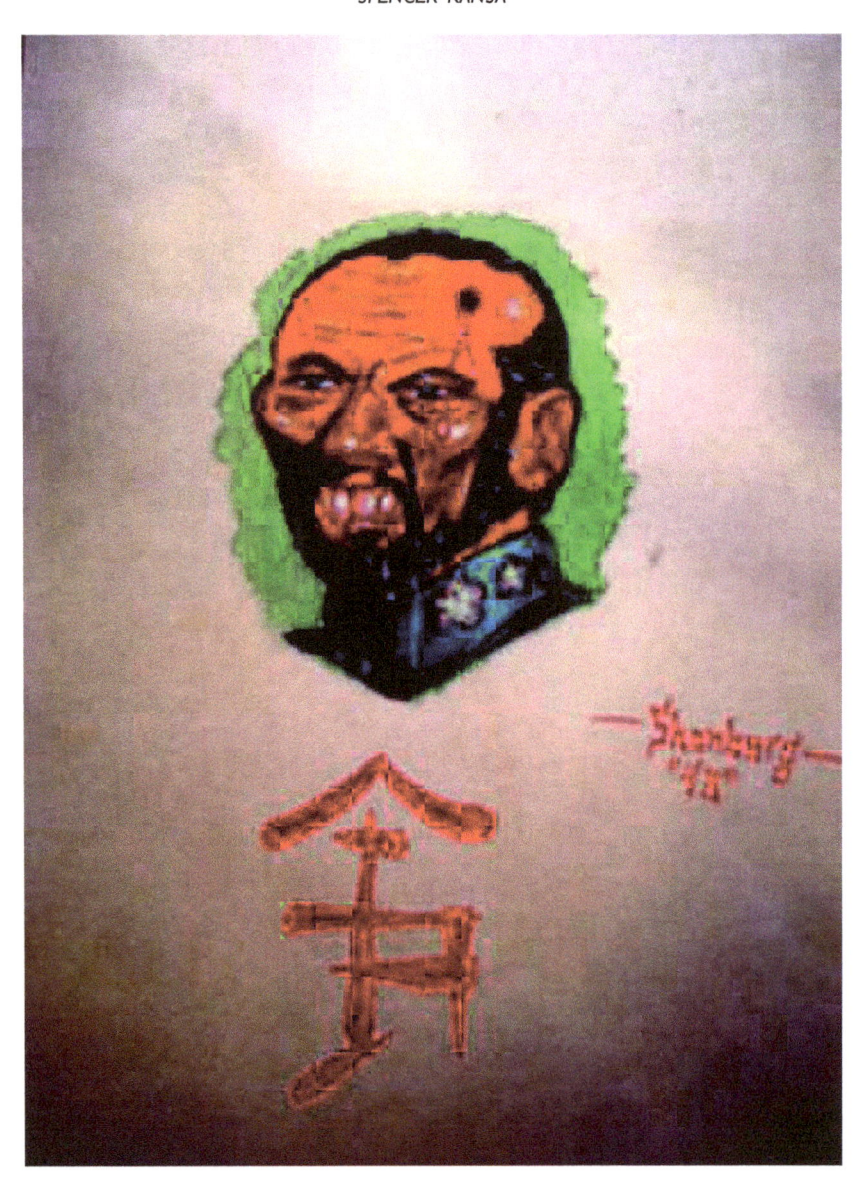

Another comic book-inspired drawing from 1948.
(Courtesy of Stephen Schrater.)

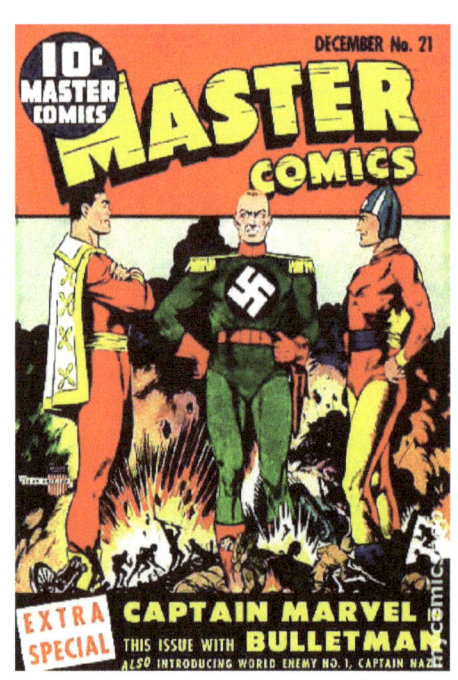

Captain Marvel vs Captain Nazi. 1941.

John McCormack sketch by Burt. Late-1940s. (Courtesy of Steven McCormick.)

BURT SHONBERG ➡ OUT THERE

Dolly's high school photo.

Revere High Joyride. (Courtesy of Stephen Schrater.)

Burt's high school photo inscribed to Sheldon Weinstein. It reads: "To Shelley, a real, sincere lifelong friend and a buddy I know I can always depend on. We've had a lot of fun all through the years of our friendship, both inside and outside of school, and here's hoping nothing ever happens to change it. Always, Bitsy."

Burt with his parents and half-brother Bill. Circa late-40s. (Courtesy of Stephen Schrater.)

Burt's sketch of the new American Teenager. (Courtesy of Stephen Schrater.)

Burt and his parents enjoying themselves at Revere Beach. Late-1940s. (Courtesy of Stephen Schrater.)

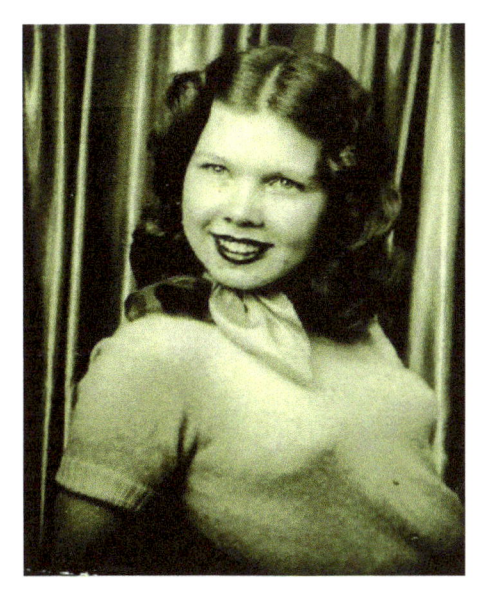

Burt's sweetheart, the comely Connie Campbell.

Burt, still in cap and gown, following his graduation ceremony. The photo was taken on a love seat in Dolly's parent's living room during the graduation party they threw for him and Dolly. (Courtesy of Stephen Schrater.)

Burt getting ready to leave for the army. (Courtesy of Stephen Schrater.)

Burt with his mother Helen, her sister-in-law Betty Schrater, and Betty's son Robert, at Fort Devens, 1953. (Courtesy of Stephen Schrater.)

Vintage postcard of Fort Huachuca.

Burt teaching some kids arts and crafts at Fort Huachuca.

Burt hangs out at Fort Lewis, Washington. The photograph was inscribed to Joan Fox, the younger sister of Richard "Dickie" Fox, a close friend of Burt's, who tragically drowned two years previously. According to Dolly, Burt nicknamed her "Little Phantom" because, "as a kid, she hung around her late brother like a shadow."

Burt enjoying his army leave in Arizona.

Burt's cartoons from the Christmas edition of the *Fort Huachuca Scout*. December 23rd, 1954.

Fagen by Shonberg

A premonition of meeting Cameron? Burt sexually entangled with demonesses, in a drawing dedicated to Ed Fagen. (Courtesy of Ed Fagen.)

Burt's army sketch of Ed Fagen reimagined as an Eastern guru. (Courtesy of Ed Fagen.)

Chapter 2
Frolicking in Flickerville

Beckoned by the lure of Hollywood, whose dream factories breathed cinematic life into the beloved monsters of his youth, Burton crossed the Arizona state line into California, riding shotgun in a car driven by an army buddy he'd grown close to. He was confident that a wealth of opportunities awaited a talented young draftsman like himself, and was armed with the foreknowledge that he could always pick up his art studies again, courtesy of the G.I. Bill, if a dream job wasn't immediately forthcoming. Prompted by this fresh start in Tinseltown, he circumcised his first name, so whenever he introduced himself, it was now simply as Burt.

By that Autumn, he was enrolled at the Art Center, situated on 3rd street near La Brea, a commercial art school with a great reputation and a mission to steer their students on the road to careers once their studies ended. For Burt, this entailed classes in advertising, design, and lessons on earning a livelihood as a commercial artist. Judy Watt was a 17-year-old student when she met Burt on the first day of that Fall semester: "I was the youngest student there, one of only three girls in the entire school, and very cute. I was sitting in class and heard this banging and crashing and this 6-foot tall, handsome guy was beside me. He put out his hand and said, 'I'm Burt, can I be your friend?' and I just melted."

Although Judy felt the college did initially give Burt some direction, it soon became obvious that he really didn't have that much to learn there: "The Art Center was a fine school, but you could tell Burt already had a trained hand. We really didn't know the Art Center was known as an intense commercial art school, which neither of us were interested in. Otis College of Art and Design is where we should've gone or the Chouinard Art Institute – a lot of well-known artists went there. I originally wanted to be a fashion illustrator but that changed once I was there, I wanted to be a painter. Maybe Burt inspired me. I admired and respected him and was in complete awe. I used to sit by him and watch him paint for hours. And Burt had amazing hands; artists' hands, long fingers." One of Burt's first artistic creations was a set of African masks woven from fallen palm tree leaves. Judy chauffeured him around to local galleries in the hope of selling them, but the owners showed zero interest. "I saw him so rejected. People would look at us like we were nuts. 'Give me a canvas and a board!' was their attitude, and I had these *jewels* in the back of the car."

Oftentimes, after school, Judy would drive her carless friend home to the house he was sharing on Stanley Hills Drive, nestled in an Arcadian backwater of Laurel Canyon. Since its heyday in the Roaring Twenties, when it was home to such silent screen sirens as Clara Bow, Louise Brooks and Theda Bara, the Canyon's rustic charm had slipped out of fashion with the current crop of Hollywood celebrities, who favoured dream homes in the highly coveted Platinum Triangle of Beverly Hills, Bel Air and Holmby Hills. As a result, a number of the abandoned dwellings in the Canyon had fallen into disrepair over the years; their once-trimmed foliage and lawns left untended to grow wild, leaving ramshackle reminders of the fading vamps and Photoplay stars of Flickerville's bygone age. More affordable properties, including Case Study housing, were built during the post-war period, so you could rent a fair-sized residence at a reasonable price, especially if you were willing to share, which Burt was, and he was able to cover his costs using the generous stipend his parents sent him each month. He split the rent with housemates Jack and Harry Kramer; brothers from New York's Lower East Side, who'd journeyed West to make a name for themselves, like countless other fortune hunters and fame-thirsty arrivistes.

Jack was trying to break into acting, believing his more than passing resemblance to the movie star Cornel Wilde would increase his prospects. He'd recently played a soldier in an episode of *Crossroads*, a TV series that dramatized the lives of noble clergymen, but he was always on the lookout for other get-rich-quick schemes to invest his time and entrepreneurial spirit. One of these areas of interest was Burt, and once he decided to leave the Art Center in May 1956, after completing two terms, Jack briefly became his ersatz manager.

It was Judy who discovered, to her shock, that the designs Jack had on Burt were personal as well as professional. "Jack was small and beautiful looking, despite his horrible teeth," she attests. "But he was very domineering and he took Burt over. He had a Svengali hold on him. I walked in on them at the house they shared and they were on a couch together. Although I was arty and avant-garde, I was also a sheltered, Beverly Hills girl who didn't know anything about alternative sexuality. And when I walked in I didn't know how to deal with what I saw. It was like being in a foreign land and I didn't know how to compute it. I knew Burt saw me when I walked in, but then I walked straight out, and we never mentioned it to each other."

Although Judy absolutely adored Burt, their relationship was based on a brother-sister kind of love and never approached being romantic. In fact, to her Burt seemed a rather asexual being, whose sexual energy went straight into his artwork. "I was never physically attracted to Burt. There was no sexuality from him at all, never mind it not being directed at me. You feel a sexual energy but it was devoid in him. Perhaps he acted out as part of exploration and questioning. I don't believe Burt ever signed up for anything. He would explore sex if the occasion presented itself, but it was not healthy – the relationship he had with Jack. Burt was so naive; he was an innocent. Jack was going to be doing stuff for him, and he claimed he had all these connections, but it was a dream. He had Burt convinced he would handle his career, but looking back it was crazy."

Hampton Lansden Fancher III was a white, half-Mexican youth, who spent his early childhood skirting the fists of the local street gangs in the tough Boyle Heights district of East LA, under the watchful eyes of his Chicano aunts, who feared for his safety due to his gringo features. From there he moved with his parents into several lower-middle-class neighbourhoods of Southwest LA, where he was bounced from school to school for exhibiting a healthy unruliness. In 1953, aged just 15, he ran away from home and travelled to Spain to pursue his passion for flamenco dancing. He returned to America two years later; a handsome, 6 feet 3-inch Adonis, under his new moniker, Mario Montejo. By the early Summer of 1956, he was living back in Los Angeles, and during a visit to his manager's home on Ridpath Drive in Laurel Canyon, he was introduced to Joann McNabb, a tall, pretty blonde who lived in the guesthouse on the property, and worked as a charge nurse in the psych unit at St. Vincent's hospital. The couple clicked instantly and began courting. "One day, Joann said to me, 'I want to introduce you to a few friends,' Hampton explains, "and we drove to this largish, ramshackle place, that was a typical Laurel Canyon house. It was old and up off the ground, so you could almost walk under it. It had rickety stairs leading up to the front door, and that's where I met Burt, and Jack and Harry Kramer." Hampton was immediately struck by the overpowering sexual vibe of the place. "It was a bachelor dive, and they all immediately liked me. I had tight pants on and they didn't want me to leave. They were fascinated and asked me a lot of questions about living in Spain."

Over the next several months, Hampton got to know all three men very well and observed the curious dynamics of their interpersonal relationships. "Both of the brothers seemed to be bisexual, but they were all after me in a passive, theatrical way – we had a ball. I was a dancer so I was used to queenie people, but these were masculine, macho

Jewish guys from lower middle class, Eastern households, who had all disowned their families. Jack was a crazy guy and a hustler. He was smallish but robust with nice hair and strong bearing, and he would say, 'We'd like to fuck you!' and Burt would grin about it. They talked to me about sex and both hit on me but they were never aggressive about it. There may well have been some hanky panky going on between Burt and Jack, but Burt might have been taking their lead, sexually, to be hip and to act against his conventional upbringing; to break the taboos of the time. He was never ever aggressive sexually. They were all vying for me sexually and as an acolyte also, because women liked me, and they all liked women a lot, too. If there was an attractive wall they'd try to fuck it! They got something from me, some tinhorn glamour, and they'd badmouth each other to me and warn me about each other and it became rancorous between them. Harry and Jack were older and smarter than Burt, more experienced. Harry was a couple of years older than Jack and had a very different personality. He was pragmatic and fun whereas Jack was a hustler with all this energy. They all had dreams but Jack had gas too. However, he could be very manipulative. Jack would be very cruel to his brother and Harry would get hurt by it. West Coast people are cool; they're not into anger or personal pain. They wouldn't say something like, 'You hurt me!' but Harry was a New York Jew and was more transparent, but there was a lot of bullshit and hyperbole. Jack was meant to be a killer with his hands, with his karate, and claimed he fought as an Israeli commando in the 1948 Jewish War. And Harry said he was a war hero in WW2. He would've been a very young soldier, but maybe he lied about his age and got in early. Although he was very thin and sometimes sickly, Harry could roughhouse and was quick, so we all had delinquent, roustabout stories to share, except Burt, he was not like that at all. He was laid back and regarded himself in a certain way; not smug, but something inbuilt and unearned. He felt he knew stuff nobody else knew. He pretended to be superior, which was maybe a defence of feeling the opposite. He didn't wanna be vulnerable. Jack was a man about town; entrepreneurial. He had big plans but they never came to fruition. He would use the term "psychological," and that was the first time I'd ever heard it. He called himself a "Freudian" and used terms like "ego" and "id." Burt used "ego" too, as a derisory term. Jack would say, 'Do you sleep on your side or on your back?' and he'd have these bullshit theories about things."

As if the sexual entanglements in the homoerotic household weren't complicated enough, Joann confessed to Hampton that in the months prior to them getting together, she'd been lovers with Burt, and had undergone an abortion after falling pregnant by his army pal, whom Burt had also slept with. Though Hampton remained smooth on the surface about this news, the underlying facts ate away at him, even after he and Joann wed a couple of years later: "I loved Burt like a brother, but it was hard for me internally, knowing that my wife had fucked him."

In spite of this, the two of them became boon companions and opened up to each other about their earlier lives. "I ran away at an early age and Burt was impressed by that," Hampton recalls. "He would enjoy saying my full name but would also call me Mario. He told me that he was called Bitsy when he was younger, but he said the word contemptuously. I got the feeling his life in Revere was so depressed, with his house and family, and he couldn't get out of there fast enough. He was horrified by his mother, and he joked how he went into the army with ulcers and came out as a paranoid schizophrenic! Schizophrenia often doesn't happen to you until your 18-23 years of age – that's when it usually occurs. You become a different person. Burt described himself that way but not as a liability. It was also to enhance himself; to make him sound more interesting because the culture was different back then." They also shared a boyhood love of Captain Marvel: "Superman was kinda dorky; an eagle scout. Captain Marvel was more boyish, who became this guy, and the colour of his yellow boots – y'know, how kids are into getting a new pair of shoes? Well, I wanted to eat them when I was a kid. It was like we were seven or eight-year-olds again and you're looking through comic books together and you're comfortable and excited to be with each other."

Hampton did not allow a little technical detail like being in a romantic relationship with Joann to impinge on his nocturnal adventures with Burt, and the two young bucks enjoyed a roistering time. "There were so many girls around and we'd have sex with three or four of them a day, but Burt seemed to mime his enthusiasm. He wasn't physical but he was sexual in a lazy, laid back, passive way. He wanted sex and liked to talk about it, and his art brought women into his life." And yet, to Hampton, Burt seemed an unlikely ladies man. "He had bad posture; sloped shoulders, and I was aware he could get plump. He seemed to embody unhealthiness." Furthermore, exercise was an anathema to him. "We hitchhiked a lot back then. It was very common. Burt hated the bus. He would hitchhike two blocks rather than walk. He wasn't comfortable walking. He was very flat footed, which almost kept him out of the army. He had a splayed walk, like a penguin. He chain-smoked, wet-lipped, like Humphrey Bogart, and like a baby who had some issues with his mother's breast, and he drunk a lot of coffee with a ton of sugar in it. He needed to be taken care of. He'd been brought up by this overbearing Jewish mother and he'd get glum if he didn't get his coffee and eggs. I saw him almost naked a lot, due to the heat. He was hairy and wore tighty-whitey underwear. He also jerked off in front of me once. I was staying at a house in Laurel Canyon belonging to a beautiful woman who was a screenwriter and he slept over. He had an adolescent mind, and we were talking about sex – you're always ready to go at that age – and he was on the floor, under the covers, and said: 'Do you ever spit in your hand to lubricate your cock with saliva, like this, man?' and he started jerking off. It was an infantile act."

Amped up on amphetamines like Benzedrine and Obetrol, they stayed up for five days at a time, only crashing on weekends. It felt like they had the run of the town, and they plundered its spoils for anything they needed. "Everything was a new world in L.A., even though I was born there," Hampton explains. "We didn't think of the future and we laughed about the past. It was anything goes. We had no responsibilities. I was a big boozer; Burt wasn't, but we'd take uppers and downers together. One pill would knock you down and you'd be all languid and the other would get your mind racing like a buzz saw."

They invariably started their evening sprees frequenting hangouts along the Sunset Strip, such as the famous drugstore Schwab's. Then, when it closed at 9 pm, they continued their carousing at Googies, next door, where they broke bread with their newfound friends, Vampira actress Maila Nurmi (whose local TV show helped introduce the Universal creature features to a new generation of Los Angelenos), and the actor Jack Simmons, who were both still mourning the death of their recently departed lover James Dean, whose patronage put the all-night diner on the map. [1] As they were prone to keeping vampiric hours, it was only fitting that on more than one occasion they managed to bump into one of Burt's childhood heroes, Count Dracula himself, Bela Lugosi. They would spy him shuffling down the Sunfax supermarket isles, in the wee small hours of the morning, a lonely shadow trailing his long, black cape. Although morphine-ridden and not long for this world, the King of the Undead indulged Burt's impression of him with good humour, and when the two of them ran lines from his most famous film – "Rats! Rats! Rats!"– he responded with an easy-going, "Yeah, okay, boys... okay."

Lack of money proved no obstacle for the artful dodgers, who were not opposed to shoplifting and the old dine and dash: "We lived hand to mouth," Hampton recalls. "Burt didn't give a shit about money, so he'd mooch. There was an immorality about it. We stole food from supermarkets and got away without paying the bill in restaurants. We'd get free stuff at Thrifty's drugstore. There were these old ladies behind the counters who would ask us, 'Have you had enough to eat today, my son?' We were selfish and amoral: stealing, fucking, we never questioned it." Thanks to an understanding cafe owner or a generous fellow patron, Burt was sometimes able to pay for his coffee and pastry by making a drawing on a paper napkin drawn from the dispenser. They also found a couple of stores where it was easy to palm any art supplies that were needed, particularly tubes of casein; Burt's favourite paint to use because it was so quick-drying and enabled him to build up layers fast, as his use of speed only exacerbated his impatience. Hampton loved Burt's artwork, and soon the walls of his shoebox apartment on Olvera Street were plastered with them: "I had so much of his stuff; Indian ink sketches that were stuck together using Vaseline, and Frankensteinian cartoons drawn all over my clothes. Burt had a kid-like mind, like a precocious 12-year-old, and his paintings reflected that."

Hampton's parents, however, were not so keen on their son's latest discovery: "We lived on handouts and were hungry a lot, so one time we went to my parents to eat. They lived in Palos Verdes and weren't too impressed by Burt. He mumbled and was not engaging. He was another kind of creature... out of their realm." Nevertheless, Hampton shared Burt's offbeat outlook and loved the sly vein of humour that ran through his drawings, like his cartoon of the three-eyed intergalactic traffic cop, writing a speeding ticket for a UFO while perched on satellite far out in space, or the one of a barman conceding to the Great Sphinx of Giza, who is propping up his bar: "OK I'll serve you, but you still don't look 21 to me." Both wouldn't have looked out of place in the *New Yorker* magazine, which makes sense when Hampton confirms he owned a book of Saul Steinberg's work, the *New Yorker* cartoonist, which he and Burt enjoyed flicking through.

Hampton was especially impressed with Burt's gift for mimicry, and he began to understand the psychological ramifications behind why his friend began doing impressions of famous people and monsters, starting when he was very young: "It created a safe place, in a world he didn't like, where he could become the hero." Burt was a great quick-change artist, too. "We went to see *The Last Ten Days*, a German film about the end of Hitler, starring Oskar Werner, and Burt was attracted to Werner, who had this godlike profile, and he started talking in that Nazi voice, 'Have you got your papers?' He was fascinated with that. Burt was a great put-on artist, and we'd put-on voices together. I'd be a Scotsman for a week and Burt would talk like Walter Brennan and say 'ain't' all the time in that Maine accent. It was fun to become someone else. It would release him and he was lauded."

Hampton's car often provided the perfect environment for Burt to entertain. "I remember driving and Burt had it in for stoplights, he'd say, 'Why should a red light tell us what to do?' He liked music and sung pop songs. People sang together back then. He had a good voice and he'd sing a love song in the car and I'd harmonize with him. He could impersonate singers like Vaughn Monroe and we'd get into a romantic fantasy, more so than in real life. He liked mellow, slippery, mystical songs and novelty hits, too, like Ghost Riders in the Sky. He'd talk nonstop and imitate things. I knew he was crazy and he performed his madness for me. I'd ask, 'When was the last time a bird talked to you?' and Burt would say, 'Birds talk to me each morning, and they say 'We love you, Burt. We love you, Burt.' We laughed over our shared absurdities and animal commonality." On those occasions when they found themselves sat together in the backseat of their pal Walter Levine's ride, Burt would launch into a word-perfect recitation of Brando's memorable "I coulda been a contendah" monologue from *On the Waterfront*. And although he never spoke in the thick Bostonian brogue of his birthplace, Burt could lapse into it for comic effect: "Where did you pahk the cahr?"

Burt's ability to contort his body and facial features into ghoulish shapes could have an unsettling effect on some people though, including Judy Watt, especially when the goof went on that little bit too long, to the point where it became genuinely disturbing: "Burt was such a natural wit. Words just flowed out of him. And he was such a good actor and impersonator, he had it down to a science," she recollects. "It was the body language. You put yourself into the posture of the person you're trying to impersonate. He'd do Frankenstein's monster and his face would contort and his body would hunch and he'd do the walk and start twitching. He'd turn and have fun scaring me with that and the Wolf Man." Burt didn't reserve his ghoulish antics just for friends either. He'd also creeped-out unsuspecting members of the public with his physical transformations, as Hampton recalls: "We made fun of things and acted out stuff. We'd pretend to use a phone on a wall or in a booth on the street and we'd get on the phone and get the attention of a passerby and Burt would point in the opposite direction and the passerby would look at where he was pointing and when he looked back at Burt he had this ghoulish look on his face, real freaky."

Though known primarily as a dancer, Hampton harboured an ambition to become a writer/poet, and he gave readings at Pandora's Box, a popular hangout on the Sunset Strip, while Burt presented a slide show of his artwork. "We thought we were geniuses," Hampton contends. As well as their forays into mixed media performance, they collaborated on a screenplay together. "We were brothers in that, but we never finished it. We had no concept of structure. We worked on it in a coffee shop called Tops, at the intersection of Kings Road and Sunset. We'd spend the night there, drinking coffee. He'd draw and I'd write and we'd do dialogue about this guy who came to Hollywood to seek his fame and fortune, and we'd work in people we knew. We were night owls so we met washed-up Hollywood types in these late-night dives: music people and actors who'd become drunks, like the guy who sold the newspapers in (the movie) *Laura*. We loved these people. One day, a cement truck ended up crashing into the coffee shop and killed people. We knew it could've been us if we'd been there during the day. I then wrote a short story about three bullfighters who all die on the same day by three different causes of death, and Burt illustrated it, and we sent it to *Playboy* who turned it down but said they were interested in the illustrations, but I don't think anything came of it." Burt's illustrations did pique the interest of *Escapade*, however, a rival men's magazine, and he began receiving a regular remittance from them for his contributions, which ranged from downright saucy cartoons to the highly decorous illustrations, like the one dedicated to Valentine's Day, that featured in their February 1957 issue.

Despite setbacks, the friends continued to encourage each other on what would ultimately become their chosen paths. "Burt was one of the reasons I got into movies. He cut my face out from some of my dancing photos and drew bodies on them, showing me performing different dramatic activities, and we sent a sheet of them to Jerry Wald Productions, who had an advert in the newspaper that said they looking for talent. Well, they sent a telegram saying, 'When can you come into the studio?' So, I went to Fox Studios and met Wald's associate producer, Mike Garrison, who paid me $100 a week to hang around until they figured out what to do with me. Well, after two weeks of doing nothing I threatened to quit, so they put me in *Traffic Court*, a live TV show. Cornel Wilde saw it and called me from Paramount Studios, where he had a production company, and said, 'I wanna talk to you. You need to get an agent etc.'"

Hampton's first film appearance was an uncredited role in *The Brain Eaters*, a low-budget science fiction horror directed by Bruno VeSota, in which creatures from another planet invade Earth to colonize the minds of the citizenry. "VeSota was in his car when he saw me and asked if I wanted to be in a movie and I brought Walter Levine with me and we played monsters in the film. It's a terrible film, a real backyard, playacting endeavour. I'm lying in the street and I put some glob on some guy's neck." Burt was also brought in as a storyboard artist, but despite the 750 sketches he created, there was no money to realize his imaginative ideas, where even the spaceship in the film was nothing more than a cheap, silver cone. Hampton confirms that all in all, his and Burt's first experience of working in the film industry left an unpleasant aftertaste, and there was no love lost between them and their taskmaster: "VeSota held court at Googies but he was hard to take. Although he was in *The Wild One* and would regale us with stories about Brando, who we never ran with, he was a virulent anti-Semite and anti-black, and his acolytes were these deep, nasty losers. Although he didn't care that Burt was Jewish, he tried to boss him around regarding his storyboarding." [2]

As disappointing as working with VeSota had been, things began looking up after Burt and Hampton made the acquaintance of Forrest J Ackerman, a charter member of the Los Angeles Science Fantasy Society, who worked as a writer, editor and literary agent specializing in the genres of horror, fantasy, and sci-fi – an abbreviation he is credited for coining. There had been an uptick in interest in Dracula, Frankenstein and the Wolf Man, in recent years; ever since Universal Studios sold their library of those classic films to television, and Ackerman's home on Sherbourne Drive housed an impressive collection of monster movie memorabilia, that became a magnet for fans of the genre. Burt had previously met "Forry," as his friends called him, through George Clayton Johnson, a talented young fantasy writer, who hung out at the Cafe Galleria in Laurel Canyon, as Johnson explains: "The Cafe Galleria had an outdoor a patio where writers, artists, poets, musicians, and actors congregated, who were becoming interested in expanding their consciousness. At the time people referred to each other as 'The Faces' – 'Have you seen The Faces?' Burt was an extraordinary guy and I immediately recognized his talent. He was a transcendentally interesting fellow who was modest and considered himself a good Jewish boy, who believed, if he was good, he would go to heaven. He was willing to be innocent and play that role, but he had a streak of madness in him. We were attracted to each other because he had a strong belief in himself."

Hampton recalls how: "We'd go to Forry's on Sundays for brunch and through him, I met some Hollywood people. Forry was an avid man; kindly and zealous, with endless enthusiasm and full of interest. He was a hustler of sorts and wanted to be a champion for Burt and for me, too. I met George Clayton Johnson there, who wore sandals and had hammer toes and monstrous fingernails. He was a very unselfconscious guy. George then introduced me to Charles Beaumont, the fantasy author, who Burt already knew. He was an appealing, attractive guy but he died later from an aging disease. He wasn't even 40-years-old, yet he looked like an old man."

Impressed by his portfolio, Ackerman took Burt on as a client, with the promise to introduce him to contacts in the publishing world and other leading lights working in the entertainment industry. To celebrate their partnership, Burt presented Forry with a drawing of Frankenstein, chest deep and half-buried in a meadow, that was plainly inspired by the photographic portraits of Audrey Hepburn and Dame Flora Robson, taken by the surrealist photographer Angus McBean. It was a droll comment that equated the status of the movie star monster with those famous actresses. The top of the drawing was also humorously inscribed:

Mr. Shonberg and large friend (below) are both available thru the Ackerman Agency.

Background: The monster is from the Actors Studio in New York and also trained occasionally at Straman's Gym.

Burt Shonberg is highly influenced by the Martian School and first began painting while living amongst the Abominable Snowmen in Tibet

Ambition: Monster – To be on This is Your Life.

Burt – To return to Jupiter after making a cool million thru the Ackerman Agency.

While at the bottom of the picture, Burt used Frankenstein to deliver a personal ventriloquized plea, that referenced the recent Hammer Film, *Curse of Frankenstein*, starring Christopher Lee as the tragic, stitched-together monstrosity:

> *"Forry, please tell me WHY the film industry refuses to do my true life story as told in Mary Shelley's book??? Karloff did a nice job with a character who had the same name as mine, but unfortunately, the story was not about me. Then came burlesque, and now England did a take-off on one of Hollywood's worst. Oh well, I guess I'll just have to wait till Burt becomes a movie producer.... (and he will)!!"*

The moon – in this instance a crescent one, that hung just behind the nape of Frankenstein's neck in the picture – was becoming a reoccurring motif in Burt's work. For it symbolized the moment when Dracula is stirred from his crypt; the time when the Wolf Man is resurrected; witches flew across it, and it provided a radiant source of pleasure for Frankenstein. Furthermore, on a personal level, it signalled the hours when Burt and Hampton came out to play, as committed night crawlers, in rejection of the normal, daylight, workaday world. One commercial job that appears to come about via this new professional arrangement was the pen drawing that Burt supplied for Ron Goodwin's *Music in Orbit* album, that depicted a fanciful space station, welded together from oil derricks, hi-hat cymbals and high-voltage insulators, that appeared to be powered by pulleys and pistons. [3] Then, when Ackerman launched the inaugural issue of *Monsters of Filmland*, the following year, he used Burt's sketch of Frankenstein's noggin resting on a plinth as the magazine's masthead.

Undaunted by his unpromising start in the film industry, Burt was given a second bite of the cherry when he was hired as an art director by the actor-writer-director Mel Welles for his latest B-movie *Code of Silence* (aka *Killer's Cage*). Welles was an admirer of Burt's talent, having already hired him to decorate his office at the film studio: "Burt had started painting on cork and he did eight or nine pieces for Welles at $100 apiece, and Welles loved it," Hampton confirms. "They were these fantastical cityscapes: surreal versions of the Venice canals with lanterns and gondolas."

The movie – reportedly based on a true story that was serialized in *Life* magazine – centred on an organized crime syndicate in Mexico and, to Burt's excitement, it was going to be filmed on location down there. In stark contrast to VeSota, Welles was a gregarious fellow, who was in tune with the changing times, due in no small part to his love of bebop jazz and his friendship with the wonderfully eccentric entertainer Lord Buckley; known for his surreal monologues and his amusing ability to translate Shakespeare's soliloquies into hipster argot. (It was Welles who penned Buckley's screwy take on The Gettysburg Address.) In a role that was originally created for Buckley, Welles recently portrayed Sir Bop, a slanguage-spewing hepcat in *Rock All Night*, a rock n roll exploitation movie made by rising independent filmmaker Roger Corman. And as a neat tie-in for the film, he'd authored a "hiptionary" of terminology, that was sold in the foyers where the picture was shown.

In early August of 1957, Burt flew down with the cast and crew for a month-long film shoot that took place at Estudios Churubusco in Mexico City and on location in Baja California and Acapulco. Although stills, posters and lobby cards of *Code of Silence* have survived, no actual print of the film is currently available, unfortunately, so it's impossible to garner exactly what Burt brought to the screen (though he may have been responsible for drawing the image of a fist breaking an iron chain that graced the movie poster). When he returned to L.A., Burt showed up with a serious foot injury, due to a tumble. With his noted sedentary lifestyle, Hampton knew it certainly wasn't incurred whilst cliff diving (a popular pastime in Acapulco). "I was excited to have him back," he recalls, "but he was on crutches and couldn't walk and he didn't have any money to get his foot fixed. As it happens, Joann had been out of town visiting her aunt, who gave her an envelope containing $500, which was like $50,000 to us! And when she returned, we went to pick Burt up at LAX, and he was on crutches. So, I just handed the envelope to him to get his foot fixed. He was limping and people had to help him get upstairs and carry his groceries. He was totally inept but he didn't make a peep about the foot. He was stoic. Back in town, Burt would tell people the same story he'd told someone the day before. He'd say, 'I've just come back from shooting a film in Acapulco. It was a vacation and an education.' And he'd repeat that line to people for months afterwards. I realized he did things like that all the time."

Having gotten a taste of what a successful career in the movie business might be like, Burt sunk into a funk when no further work materialized. He was also wearied by the task of having to transport himself around on the damned crutches; so, to raise his spirits, Hampton hit on a brainstorm: "Although I was only 18 or 19, I was pompous, and told Burt, 'You need a famous guy to buy your work.' We'd been up all night and we came across a newspaper ad for a Hitchcock movie and I said to Burt, 'Do something for Hitch and I'll take it to him,' and he did. So, I called Paramount Pictures and asked to talk to Mister Hitchcock, and my name impressed them because they asked what it was about and I said I had a work of fine art to give to him. Soon after, Burt and I drove over there in my 1937 Plymouth convertible. Burt was fun but not outgoing with strangers, he could be taciturn, and we get onto stage 18 where they're shooting *Vertigo*, and there's Jimmy

Stewart, sitting in a highchair with his makeup on and his eyes closed. He's got this orange face and looks asleep. We were taken to Hitch's dressing room, where we met him, and he's about five feet 5 inches, and he looks through Burt's portfolio and there was an ink drawing of Hitchcock's head and each aspect was made up of gory scenes. Hitch is droll and we're hoping he'll buy something and he held up this drawing and said, 'Dali did one of me like this – I'll take this one.' And he just left the dressing room with it."

Jack Kramer in the TV show *Crossroads*.

Burt's choristers graced the Christmas 1956 issue of *Escapade*.

Burt's saucy illustrations for the joke page in *Escapade*.

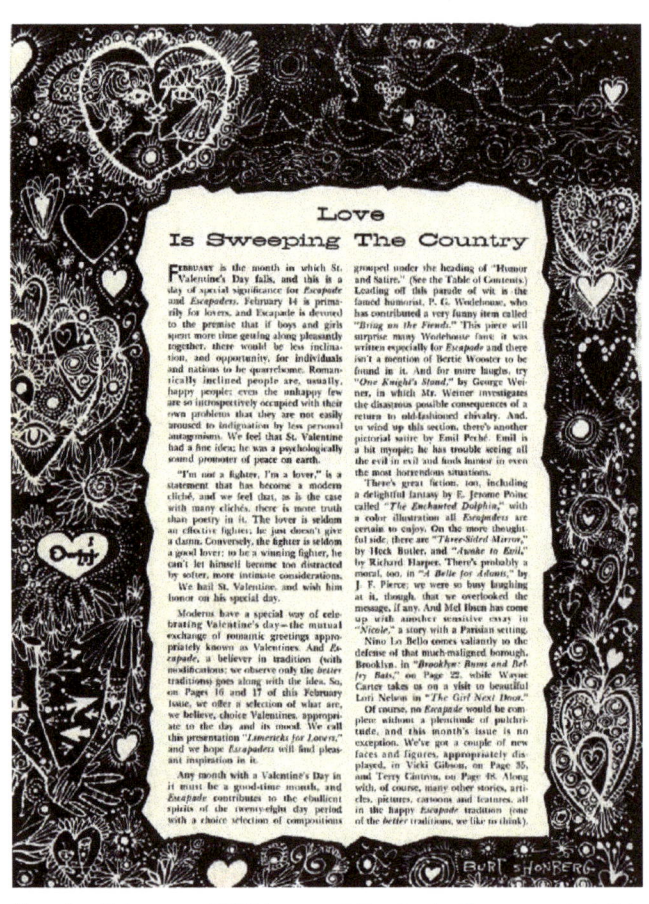

For the February 1957 issue of *Escapade*, Burt created this illustration celebrating Valentines Day.

bring on the fiends!

death adders and hungry cantonese rats add immeasurably to the joys of living

by P. G. WODEHOUSE

HOT DIGGETY DOG, I don't know when I have been more pleased than when I read in the paper the other day that my old friend Sax Rohmer had sold the radio, television and film rights of his famous character Doctor Fu Manchu to a motion picture company for four million dollars. It is not that the price is particularly high—I shall get about that for writing this article—the significant thing is that it shows that Fiends In Human Shape are back in the money again.

I can remember the time when you couldn't open a magazine without flashing half a dozen fiends in human shape. Then they were superseded by Master Criminals and men seeking vengeance for ancient wrongs, and were down in the cellar with no takers. Now the bull market has apparently started once more, and the man cheering and waving his hat in the crowd is me. You can't, in my opinion, have too many of these admirable characters about the place. Come right down to it, they are the only really satisfactory villains—or,
(Continued on next Page)

THE FIENDS *(Continued from Page 11)*

as we say now, heavies—for what used to be called thrillers and today are labelled novels of suspense.

The great problem confronting those who write stories of that type has always been the selection of a convincing louse to handle the dirty work. The detective was easy. You could make him almost anything from a Scotland Yard man to a Private Eye, and the heavy was a different matter and one that called for more thought. Apart from the fiends in human shape there were really only three classes.

(a) Sinister men from China or Assam or India or Tibet (or practically anywhere except Yonkers or the Bronx) who were on the track of the jewel stolen from the temple,

(b) Men with a grudge against someone which had lasted as fresh as ever for thirty years.

(c) Master Criminals.

None of these were really satisfactory. Sinister jewel-trackers reached saturation point around about the beginning of the century, and the age we live in is so practical and matter-of-fact that we are no longer able to believe, as our fathers did, in the man who cherishes a grudge for thirty years. It was all very well in the old days, when there were fewer distractions, but what with golf and tennis and crossword puzzles and following the fortunes of the Dodgers and the Milwaukee Braves and wondering how to get seats for *My Fair Lady*, it seems incredible to us that a man would have the leisure to keep his mind on some unpleasantness which happened in the early Spring of 1926.

Which brings us to the last class, the Master Criminal.

The first M.C. I ever came across was Professor Moriarty, and I remember in those days thinking him as hot as a pistol. As a boy, he thrilled me. (I mean when I was a boy, not when he was a boy.) He curdled my blood on the printed page, and he curdled it again in William Gillette's stage version of the Sherlock Holmes stories. 'Gosh, that protruding face, forever slowly oscillating from side to side in a curiously reptilian fashion!' But more recently, I must confess, keeping a wary eye out for the thunderbolt which Christopher Morley and his fellow Baker Street Irregulars will probably hurl at me, I have come to the conclusion that he was pretty off-Broadway stuff.

Sherlock Holmes, you will recall, comes to visit Doctor Watson and speaks of this Moriarty in high terms. ("He is the Napoleon of Crime, Watson. He is the organizer of half that is evil and of nearly all that is undetected in this great city. He has a brain of the first order."). He then tells how he is on the point of knoving the Professor—("I have woven my net round him until it is now ready to close")—and explains that the Prof, taking umbrage at this, is using all the resources of his vast organization to destroy him.

"Watson," he says solemnly, "on my way here I was attacked by a rough with a bludgeon!"

A rough with a bludgeon, forsooth! Gosh, sir, if I were a Master Criminal with a brain of the first order, I would think up something a little better than roughs with bludgeons.

The psychology of the Master Criminal is a thing I have never been able to understand. I can follow the mental processes of the man who, wishing to put something by for a rainy day, poisons an uncle, shoots a couple of cousins and forges a will. Activities like that are based on sound commercial principles. We all like to salt away a bit of cash, and inserting strychnine into a rich uncle is about the simplest and pleasantest way of doing it. But the Master Criminal does not need money. He already has it in sackfuls. What with the Delaney Emeralds and the Stuyvesant Pearls and the bearer bonds he got from that big bank robbery, he must be a millionaire several times over. So why go on? Why not retire and enjoy himself?

The way I look at it, it's no good stealing jewels and secret treaties—which is where the big profit is these days. No income tax—if you don't get any fun out of it. If I were a Napoleon of Crime and was well ahead of the game, I should call it a day and make a splash. An apartment on Park Avenue up in the Seventies, a house at Southampton, a yacht, a racing stable, a villa on the Riviera, some good cigars and a new razor blade every morning . . . all that sort of thing. But could you make a Master Criminal see that that was what he ought to do? Not in a million years.

In that same issue of *Escapade*, Burt illustrated the P.G. Wodehouse article Bring on the Fiends! The piece was inspired by the recent multimillion payment made by Republic Pictures to the author Sax Rohmer (Wodehouse's chum), for the radio, television and film rights to his Dr. Fu Manchu series, which was used as jumping off to point to examine the role of "Heavies" and Master Criminals in literature.

Detail from the Wodehouse essay.

BURT SHONBERG ➙ *OUT THERE*

Burt's cartoon, *O.K. I'll Serve You... But You Still Don't Look 21 To Me!*

Burt's intergalactic traffic cop cartoon.

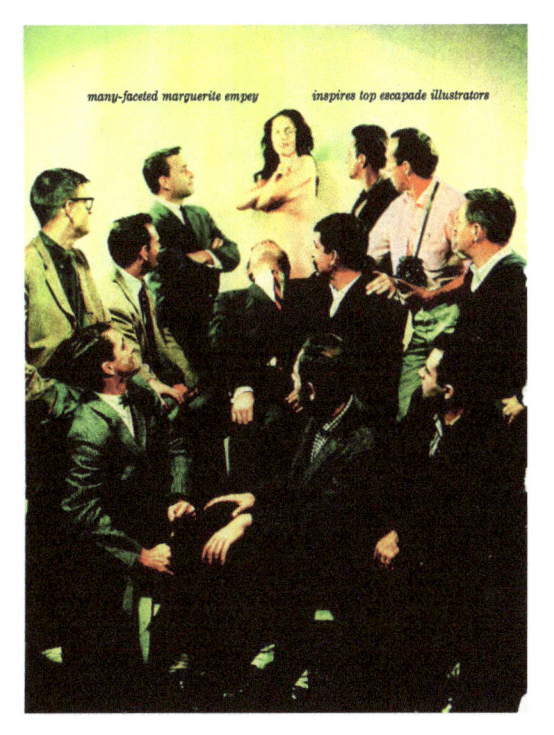

A besuited Burt (front and center) and his fellow illustrators behold the wonder of Marguerite Empey.

Burt's fetching rendering of Marguerite Empey.

49

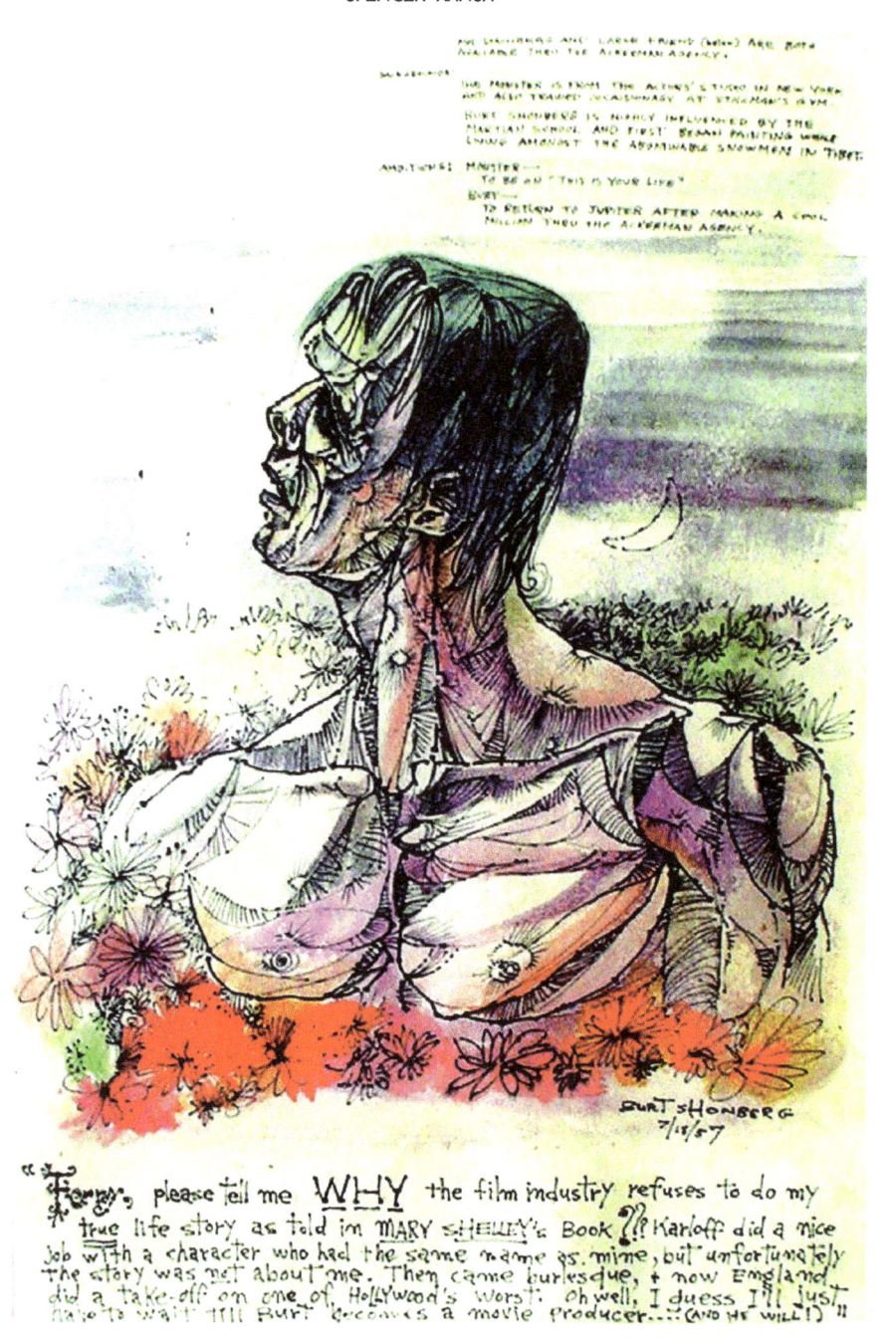

Burt's illustrated missive to Forrest Ackerman.

Chapter 3
Cafe Frankenstein

Spearheaded by its literary insurgents, Jack Kerouac and Allen Ginsberg, the Beat Generation became the catchall term for a subcultural movement that evolved, in part, as a reaction to the prevailing materialistic values and bourgeois conformity, encouraged by the powers that be, to re-establish some societal order in the country, following the sociological chaos of the war years. Having spent most of the 1940s soaking up all the sleaze the Times Square underworld had to offer, and revelling in hedonistic jaunts across America, the two writers transformed their raw experiences into glorious poetry and powerful prose that brought a compelling new candour to American literature. Although their military service during World War II only amounted to brief stints in the Merchant Marines, they nevertheless fought the good fight for individual freedom and cultural liberty via their radical writing.

Published in 1956, Ginsberg's epic poem *Howl* was a (com)passionate exaltation of those marginalized from the mainstream of American society: the blacks, the queers, the junkies, and, above all, those mentally fragile, like his mother Naomi and best friend Carl Solomon – to whom the poem is dedicated – who'd both been institutionalized in psychiatric hospitals in New York, along with the poet himself. In September 1957, Kerouac's roman a clef *On the Road* was published to rapturous reviews that brought him national recognition. The novel romanticized the adventurous road trips he'd made the previous decade, in a breathless, Benzedrine-laced prose that reflected his empathetic search for spiritual connectedness, meaning, and brotherhood.

These and even more outré works, penned by their mentor, William

Burroughs, and their protégé, Gregory Corso, found a willing audience among the more restless members of the post-war generation, who slipped their mostly middle-class moorings to embrace this new bohemianism. And although Burt wasn't exactly a fully paid-up member of the Beat Movement, he certainly benefited from and thrived in the vibrant ecosystem it created. [1]

To cater to this burgeoning Beat audience, as well as fans of the folk music revival, the music impresario Herb Cohen and the actor and folksinger Theodore Bikel opened the Unicorn coffeehouse on the Sunset Strip in 1957, an event that brought a slice of Greenwich Village to Southern California. As well as food and beverages, it provided a paperback bookstore and sold artisanal sandals, pots, and hand-tailored jewellery. It offered live musical performances of jazz and poetry (and even mime) most weeknights, and to enhance its ambiance, Cohen commissioned Burt to decorate its walls and illustrate the menu. Inspired by the success of this hipster hangout, other coffeehouses sprung up all over the city, and Burt became the muralist du jour for many of their proprietors. *Rogue* magazine namechecked him as "one successful pro (that) has already emerged," and for his next big project, the Bastille coffeehouse on 8277 Santa Monica Boulevard, he simply keyed off on its name, painting scenes from inside the infamous Parisian prison, only now it caged his favourite movie monsters. Then, for advert he designed to publicize the place, Burt drew a moonlit Madame la Guillotine; glimpsed through prison bars.

It was against this flourishing bohemian backdrop, that Burt fell under the witchy thrall of Marjorie Cameron, a titian-haired, gimlet-eyed occult artist with a scandalous reputation. At 34, she was ten years older than him, and though not yet middle-aged, her shadow-lit life was riddled with incident and intrigue. Beneath her fierce facade, however, was a woman of immense sensitivity, who'd survived several suicide attempts, and was barely scraping by on the breadline, while raising her toddler, Crystal.

She was born in Belle Plaine, Iowa, in 1923, and, like Burt, her aptitude for art was recognized early on in life, as was the strange air of otherness about her. She was also a fellow veteran, having served as a naval WAVE during World War II, in Washington, DC, where she worked first as an aide to the Joint Chiefs of Staff, then as a cartographer, and then finally as a wardrobe mistress in the photographic laboratory that produced propaganda films. After the war ended, she rejoined her family who had relocated to Southern California, where her father and brothers were gainfully employed at the Jet Propulsion Laboratory in Pasadena. Shortly afterward, she was introduced to the company's co-founder Jack Parsons, a self-taught rocket scientist and acting head of the Agape Lodge: a fraternal order dedicated to the neo-pagan teachings of the Edwardian magician and philosopher Aleister Crowley. Cameron and Parsons embarked on a torrid love affair that led to an open marriage in October 1949, but with Jack embroiled in important research projects across America, there were prolonged periods of living apart. Retaining her independence, Cameron travelled alone to Europe and Mexico, and though she remained an agnostic throughout most of their marriage, towards the end of it, Jack began to initiate her into Crowley's sacred, central text *Liber AL vel Legis* or *The Book of the Law*. By the Summer of 1952, the couple was planning to leave America to start a new life in Israel, but they were robbed of that dream when Jack was killed in a chemical explosion in the laboratory of their Pasadena home. It was while she was rifling through her dead husband's papers that Cameron discovered she'd been an unwitting magickal partner in the Babalon Working, an Enochian ritual Jack conducted in partnership with the science fiction writer, L. Ron Hubbard. Although Jack's writings on the matter were open to interpretation, Cameron came to believe she was the living embodiment of Babalon, the sexually licentious Goddess in

Crowley's cosmology; an agent of change, whose rule on Earth heralded the spiritual toppling of the Abrahamic religions and ushered in Crowley's Neo-pagan era of scared-sexual liberation. In the wake of Jack's death, Cameron orchestrated a series of interracial sex-magick rituals designed to create his magical heir but her messianic plan was thwarted by a series of miscarriages.

Cameron's stature as a sexual outlaw, who did not hide her bisexuality or her illegal, taboo-flaunting penchant for multiracial lovers, brought her notoriety and earned her kudos and scorn in equal measure. She smoked marijuana habitually and risked arrest and imprisonment for smuggling it back in the lining of her clothing when she returned from her trips to Mexico. She'd been experimenting with the hallucinatory peyote button since 1953, intrigued by the personal testimony of the English writers Gerald Heard and Aldous Huxley, who wrote glowingly about its most active ingredient, mescaline, and its capacity to expand consciousness to create a wider spiritual awareness. (The men learned how the hallucinatory drug was used in ritual ceremonies among some American and Mexican Indian tribes, who believed the cactus was inhabited by an ancestral spirit who imparted wisdom to them from the afterlife.)

Like Burt, Cameron was a true believer in the existence of UFOs, but her idiosyncratic belief in the phenomenon was a far cry from the sensationalist accounts splashed across newspapers, or the rash of robots in flying saucer movies, spawned from them. Her first encounter with a UFO dated back to 1946 when she spotted a cigar-shaped craft hovering soundlessly in the sky in the back garden of the Agape Lodge. Though she mentioned the incident to her husband, Jack remained silent on the subject, and it was never raised again. But, sifting through his papers, after his death, Cameron discovered he had indeed marked the momentous sighting, by drawing a symbol of the UFO – a circle with a trine set within it – in the marginalia. To her mind, this was Jack's celestial confirmation that she was the chosen vehicle for Babalon, and she came to believe that UFOs were the "war-machines" prophesied in Crowley's *Book of the Law*. While she attributed another (more famous) UFO sighting – where a group of glowing orbs were photographed hovering above the Capitol Building in Washington, DC, just weeks after Jack's death – as an inter-dimensional tribute to his tragic passing.

Through L.A.'s underground scene, Cameron met the young avant-garde filmmaker Kenneth Anger, who couldn't wait to exploit her cinegenic countenance by casting her in his visually dazzling film, *Inauguration of the Pleasure Dome*, that he spiked with Crowleyean symbolism, once he got to know her. Cameron's own artistry reflected her life as a practicing occultist, and she applied her exquisite touch in an array of styles, ranging from ink drawings redolent of Aubrey Beardsley to expressionistic portraits of Joan of Arc and the Elizabethan magus John Dee. But it was the mind-warping properties of peyote, which she turned Burt onto, that inspired her most daring artwork to date: a carnal line drawing depicting her naked on all fours, being ravished by a fungal-skinned alien. The picture first appeared in *Semina*, an art folio created by her friend and champion, the artist Wallace Berman, and it then found its way into an exhibition of his work held at the Ferus Gallery in L.A. that year. But when a fellow artist brandished it in the faces of a pair of undercover vice cops, Berman was arrested and the show was shut down for obscenity.

Cameron's magickal studies enabled her to self-actualize and unleash her inner genius, and she lost no time turning her impressionable beau on to Crowley's Thelemic creed so that he could do the same. Although it may have been an open relationship, it was evidently an intense, mind-melding enchantment: "Burt was intoxicated with Cameron," Judy Watt recollects. "My impression was that she was like no other person that he or I had met. She didn't fit into any category. Burt held her in very high esteem because she was "connected." Burt would say, 'She represents the mysteries,' – the occult, all the things he was interested in. That was his attraction. Her attraction to him was the same plus his unbelievable talent."

Hampton echoes this: "Burt had an eyebrow lifting response to people he approved of. He and Jack Kramer coined the term 'elite' – people who possessed an elite spirit, and they tried to set themselves apart; be superior, occult." But as a horny, young dude, Hampton failed to see the attraction to this kooky, older woman, especially when there was an abundance of dewy, young starlets to feast upon. "Cameron seemed like someone from Mars, and I thought she was from there. I didn't like her, but she wanted me to like her because of my closeness to Burt, but she kinda horrified me. I walked into his place once, and I saw Cameron naked and it turned me off. She was lying down and I had a brief glance of her pussy; her pubic hair and bone, and it didn't interest me. Then, I was invited out to a sex ritual they had out in the desert, but I didn't go. Burt said, 'Come on, you can fuck her!' but I didn't want to tell him I wasn't attracted to her."

In the wake of meeting Cameron, Burt was struck by a dramatic series of mystical epiphanies, which he claimed were not brought on by drugs or "yogic-type efforts," though it's tempting to view them as a side effect of Cameron's sorcery. He later recorded: "In the year 1957, in Los Angeles, California, I had my first dramatic experiences beyond the limits of so-called ordinary, everyday consciousness. I was hit by a number of widely-separated, momentary blasts of unexpected light. These initial experiences (of being unexpectedly and mysteriously shanghaied out of moving time and into The Eternal now were of such a nature that I saw all the usual, generally accepted notions of what this world is all about as being sheer imagination. Also, the quality of these experiences was such that I knew that what I was seeing, strange and shocking as it was, was unquestionably true. At that time, I had been wholly unprepared for this robbery of my dream state and so my initial reaction to this experience was stark terror. During these first awesome unveilings of where we are and how it is, I witnessed the undeniable truth of our situation in ordinary worldly life and this was so frightfully staggering that I no longer had any choice in my life concerning what to be serious about. I knew I had to experience that Great Light again, somehow, but also, I knew I had to be able to withstand the great shock of full Consciousness. It was at this time that I actively began to search for A Way." [2]

While enjoying their hot cappuccinos in the Unicorn one afternoon, Burt and his folksinger pal, Doug Myres, hatched the idea of opening their own coffeehouse, feeling that many of the others were a little on the tame side. They found a perfect spot: A Tardis-like shack in Laguna Beach, that was surprisingly more capacious that it appeared from the outside. While Burt set to work redecorating the place, Myres took charge of organizing the refreshments and entertainment, and they brought in their mutual buddy, George Clayton Johnson, to act as a silent third partner.

Burt christened the joint Cafe Frankenstein, in tribute to his favourite monster and he plastered his likeness across practically every surface, depicting him as a blithe spirit riding a dinky train; frolicking with a butterfly, and in one portrait fixed to the outside sidewalk, playing chess against a tentacled space alien. Another marvellous mural captured Frankenstein in a heroic pose, reclining in gold plated armour, but for many, the piece de resistance was the eye-catching, faux-stained glass image of the monster that Burt painted on the cafe's bay window. "Burt was enamoured with the monster, like myself. He saw him as a victim," George Clayton Johnson explains. "Everything (the monster) did was intended to be right – it was just that in certain ways he was defective, and he was made up of spare parts. Anybody of my generation who amounted to anything felt like that." [3]

On a wall panel inside the cafe, Frankenstein's head perched on a plinth next to a kneeling Wolf Man playing the violin, as a mushroom cloud exploded in the background between them. Burt also contributed another painting of Frankenstein, swaddled inside a padded spacesuit and helmet, to Designs in Leather, a sandal shop operating just behind the cafe. The steaming coffee machine had an eyeball painted on it and was nicknamed "Monster" in his honour, though the menu stressed how the cafe was actually dedicated to Boris Karloff, who brought so much pathos to the character. On another interior wall, Burt scrawled an ominous cartouche:

Every Once in a while, during our accepted journey through life, we encounter something "STRANGE." Something directed towards ?US ? and we Do Not understand it. But, anyhow, daylight, a familiar sound or somebody will jolt us back to the ABSURD reality of "How Things Are Supposed To Be" and we will be safe again... PERHAPS!

While outside, a sign bore the words: Cafe Frankenstein European Coffee House, spelled out in curlicue script, and its post was speckled with strange snowflake-white glyphs. While some, like the Ankh and the Eye of Horus hieroglyphs, were well-known Ancient Egyptian symbols (and obvious nods to Cameron and the roots of Crowley's creed, not to mention the Egyptological storylines found in Captain Marvel), others resembled magickal runes, alchemical symbols, or sigils from a sidereal civilization. There was a definite tribal quality to some these glyphs, and Hampton wonders whether they may have derived from Burt's Arizona experiences and the Navajo and Hopi cave calligraphy he may have seen there. (There is also a resemblance between them and the Sky Rock petroglyphs, located at the Volcanic Tablelands in Northern California.)

In a photo taken of the artist, posing with his handiwork, there's a noticeable change in his countenance. The young man who was once armed with an ever-ready smile, was now a model of moodiness whenever he was photographed, as smiling was now decidedly uncool (a fact seized upon by the comedian Lenny Bruce in one of his popular riffs).

Burt also designed the cafe's menu, and its back cover substantiated how allied he felt to the Beats, as it showed Frankenstein holding a copy of Ginsberg's *Howl* behind his back, pitying a working Joe, caricatured as an automaton, who was stood at a bus stop carrying a lunch pail, with the numbers 9-2-5 (summing up the working day) emblazoned across his chest.

The cafe opened in March 1958, and though it was meant to close a 4 a.m. it rarely did, and business was brisk. On Sunday and Monday nights, patrons were welcome to bring their favourite LPs to play on the cafe's hi-fi system, and the venue played host to a variety of performers, ranging from the established chanteuse (and reigning "Queen of the Beatniks,") Judy Henske, to game amateurs like Ed House, a Marine Corps major, who enjoyed singing calypso songs. Doug himself made regular appearances, singing his own folk tunes, and even Burt was bitten by the stage bug for a while when he joined a musical group fronted by Harry Kramer, who performed the kind of folk repertoire that was being popularized by Pete Seeger. "It was folk music but with humour," Hampton Fancher explains. "Harry was the leader of the band and he sang and played guitar, and there was a bass player and his wife, who was also a singer, and Burt would do his Frankenstein impression and recite the lyrics to Goodnight Irene as Dracula." The group played sets at Cafe Frankenstein and Pandora's Box and also performed at military installations like Edwards Air Force Base, where they'd receive $15 and a free meal for their efforts.

But while such lively festivities brought joy to many, trouble was brewing for the hotspot. Although Laguna Beach was considered an art colony, it mostly consisted of traditional seascape painters, not monster movie mavens, and it was, in essence, a rather staid community. This was evident when Burt's faux stained-glass painting of Frankenstein inflamed the ire of a local ladies' church league, who deemed it macabre and sacrilegious, and only withdrew their complaint when he threatened to hang a crucified dummy of Frankenstein over the entrance instead. Then, in June, the cafe's acting manager, Sid Soffer, and the waitress, Ruth Adrian (whose husband Allan penned the *Killer's Cage* screenplay), were arrested by the police for the trumped-up charge of serving an espresso flavoured with a brandy extract. The police seized on the fact that the cafe didn't have a liquor license, and argued there was a chance that juveniles could purchase a cup. Although the petty charges were subsequently dismissed, it was clear to Soffer that the authorities were gunning for them. "Laguna Beach was kind of closed, Doug Myres recollects. "They didn't like blacks, they didn't like Jews and they *hated* beatniks." [4]

Even in spite of such setbacks, the cafe began turning over a nice profit, though Burt's presence by then had trailed off, and he only showed up to collect his share of the spoils. The reason for absence was clear to his partners: his infatuation with Cameron. Inspired by her sojourns to the art colony in San Miguel de Allende, Mexico, the couple came up with a quixotic idea to create their own commune for artists, and they scouted several desert outposts for its location. Their first choice was Randsburg (then known as Rand Camp), a former gold mining town located 97 miles north of Los Angeles, until they realized it was far too remote to lure any like-minded visitors, so they settled on a ranch near Pioneertown which they christened ERONBU, a romantic portmanteau, or perhaps more fittingly, frankenword, fused from their names: camERON+BUrt. [5] A photograph taken of the couple there revealed how the alchemy of speed and sunshine had transformed Burt into quite the hunk, complete with a macho moustache, who embraced his paternal role with Crystal, on whom he rests a protective hand.

Courtesy of Doug Myres, Cameron acquired a hearse that she used to shuttle them around, and although it wasn't as flashy as the one Vampira spun about in, Burt remedied this by graffitiing it with glyphs. Despite decorating the ranch with their paintings and mobiles, the art commune failed to get off the ground, but friends did trek out to visit, including Hampton Fancher: "In those days there were raggedy-ass places that you could take over; very cheap rent, like $25 per month." But meeting Burt again, in this new environment, Hampton was struck by just how remote and serious he'd become. His usual playfulness and jocularity were absent, and Hampton held Cameron responsible; a woman he now viewed as a manipulative Lady Macbeth figure, with hooks in Burt that penetrated deep: "He wasn't the good ol' Burt anymore. Cameron took him over – she robbed him. There was a stumblebum aspect to Burt and she could put a string around his neck and he'd follow. He was handcuffed, and we contributed his downfall to her. She was aloof and quiet; influencing Burt but in a quiet way. She was an all-knowing witch, though she didn't proselytize. Her silence passed for wisdom and being esoteric. They were Siamese twins – inseparable. As I've said, Burt had this eyebrow lifting response to people he approved of, so if I said something about her he'd lift his brow and say she was 'initiated' and then add, 'We know stuff nobody else knows.' He was convinced she was beyond our simple, everyday bullshit. They were in a club of their own."

Such sentiments are echoed by Burt's partners at Cafe Frankenstein, who also witnessed the marked change in his manner and personality, which they attributed to the dark object of his desire: "Cameron was a very strong woman and Burt had a respectful attitude towards her," George Clayton Johnson stresses. "She had an earth mother presence about her and she dressed flamboyantly. It looked like her clothes were from Salvation Army counters, which gave her a distinctive, commanding character. Burt was very influenced by her, which surprised me because he had his own reality going on. They recognized something in each other. There was a shared madness."

Doug Myres passes an even more damning verdict on Cameron, viewing her as a malign presence who broke up his friendship with Burt: "Burt was so enamoured with Cameron, and when she got ahold of him everything went to hell. She was heavy into witchcraft and took him away from a lot of stuff, and he lost interest in things. He got into drugs, and she took him to places in his mind, and he changed. He became more aloof and distant. He came down to the cafe one last time for his money, then disappeared, and I never saw him again."

Cafe Frankenstein's mission statement.

BURT SHONBERG ➡ *OUT THERE*

Cafe Frankenstein.
(Photographer unknown.)

Cafe Frankenstein in colour. (Photographer unknown.)

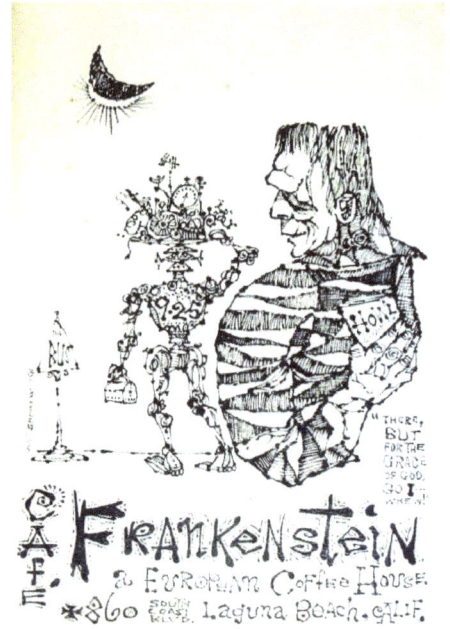

Cafe Frankenstein menu back cover.

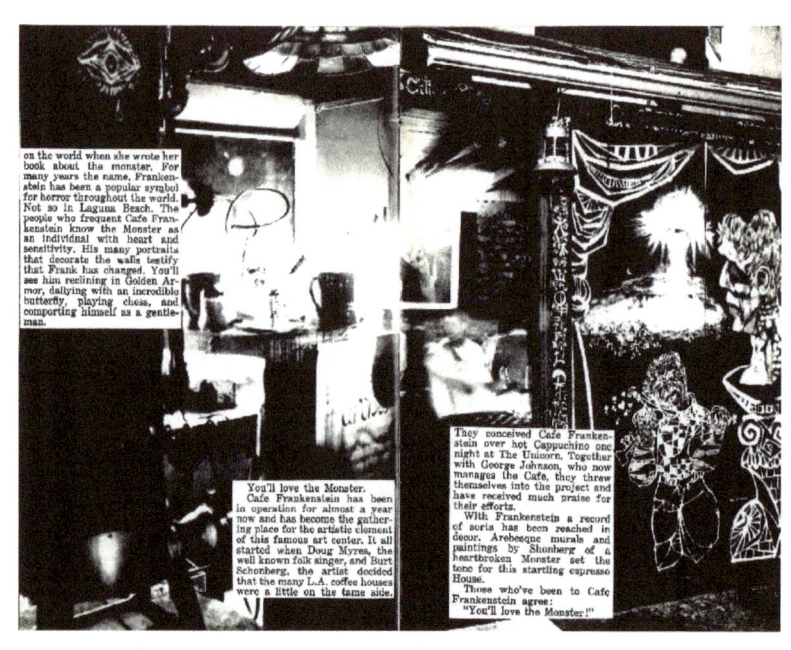

Cafe Frankenstein interior featured in *Le Petit Sphinx*. (Courtesy of the collection of Brian Chidester.)

George Clayton Johnson with Robert Redford on the set of *Nothing in the Dark* episode of the *Twilight Zone*. (Courtesy of George Clayton Johnson.)

Burt and Doug Myres in Cafe Frankenstein.

BURT SHONBERG ➥ *OUT THERE*

Bert Schonberg, producer of C.H. murals and fine paintings with Doug Myres (Cafe Frankenstein).

Burt and Doug Myres in Cafe Frankenstein featured in *Le Petit Sphinx*. This would not be the only occasion in which Burt's surname was misspelled. (Courtesy of the collection of Brian Chidester.)

DOUG MYRES
BURT SHONBERG

CAFÉ FRANKENSTEIN
EUROPEAN COFFEE HOUSE
860 South Coast Boulevard
Laguna Beach, California

Cafe Frankenstein advert.

65

Frankenstein's monster plays chess with an alien.

The *Magnificent Monster*. Casein on Masonite. 4 ft x 8 ft. (Courtesy of the private collection of Suzanne Roach.)

Burt's mural on the walls of the Bastille coffeehouse.
(Courtesy of the collection of Brian Chidester.)

Burt's poster for the Bastille.

More Shonberg decor in the Bastille.

Entrance to the Eronbu ranch.
(Photograph courtesy of Aya.)

Burt, Cameron and Crystal at the Eronbu ranch.
(Courtesy of the Warburg Institute.)

A rare, blurry photo of Cameron and Crystal at Eronbu ranch, with the hearse parked behind them. (Photograph courtesy of Aya.)

Chapter 4
Firestarter

Though they never would've expressed it to him in person, some of Burt's buddies felt quietly vindicated when the spell cast by his sandy Shangri-La with Cameron suddenly wore off, and the couple amicably went their separate ways. As a stopgap, Burt moved back in with Jack Kramer, who, not to be outdone, had grabbed his own piece of the coffeehouse action by opening the International on 1608 Cahuenga Boulevard in a section of Hollywood known as mid-Movietown. The place provided diners with live jazz and flamenco music most weeknights, except Tuesdays, which was theatre night, and Sundays, when a classical music recital was given.

Cafe Frankenstein, the Bastille, and the International were all profiled by *Le Petit Sphinx*, a short-lived review that chronicled the coffeehouse scenes in Los Angeles and San Francisco. Burt and Doug Myres were both photographed in its debut issue, sitting in Cafe Frankenstein, and Burt was invited by its editors to illustrate an excerpt from *Thus Spake Zarathustra* by Friedrich Nietzsche, whose denunciations of Judeo-Christian morality was finding favour among the young beat crowd, for whom existentialist philosophizing was very much in-vogue. (*Le Petit Sphinx* dubbed the Unicorn "the Jean-Paul Sartre of coffeehouses.")

Although he loved being the boss of his own place, Kramer ran the International more like a clubhouse than an ongoing financial concern. His lack of business acumen was evident, considering many of his patrons were friends, like Burt and Hampton, who either ate on the house or insisted on putting their drinks and meals on a tab that never got settled. So, it was not entirely surprising that, in less than a year, the International was shuttered. [1] In fact, there were now so many new coffeehouses in town they oversaturated the market and had an adverse effect on established businesses like Chez Paulette, owned by Max Lewin, who bore an uncanny resemblance to Napoleon Bonaparte. Trade was flagging for the family-run bistro on the Sunset Strip until Marlon Brando caught wind of their troubles and began to patronize the joint, which in turn attracted fellow movie stars, as well as fans hoping to cadge an autograph. Brando, and fellow famous philanderers like Steve McQueen and Warren Beatty, also came to flirt with the virginal waitresses: Sally Kellerman, a young, aspiring actress, and Morgan Ames, a budding jazz singer. [1] It was Brando's seal of approval that first brought Burt and Hampton through the doors, though they were looking for a new eatery now that the International was gone. They became regulars and befriended the waitstaff, including Barry Feinstein, the barista, who had yet to find his niche as a renowned rock n roll photographer. "I met Burt through Sally; she was the hub for a group of people," Morgan Ames recalls. "We were young and guys like Burt were a bit older than us and they all wanted to fuck the girls – the virgins – and we weren't into that. My first guy was Troy Donahue. But Burt was very, very special. It was overwhelming to see his paintings, and he loved to share them with his friends. He would drag you over to his place to see them, and I was there many times. He was manic. He must've worked 24 hours a day. And I got into a comfortable thing with him. I felt safe and happy with him because he was a teddy bear-type guy and would look hangdog and ask, 'I don't suppose you'd like to go out with me, would you?' If we ever went to bed I was unconscious. I don't remember him with a girlfriend, just on his own, and I related to his lost soul-ness. I was a wild child; he was a lonely guy. Plus, he needed a bath, which was another reason to say, 'No thank you.' And his pads were small and dirty and messy with paintings stacked up. Not someplace you'd want to spend (romantic) time in. Also, Burt went to dark places and liked it. Figures like Crowley, and I didn't wanna go to the dark side. I didn't want to follow him there. I remembered one thing he used to say that stayed with me: we smoked a lot of weed back then, I mean a lot, and no one more than Burt, and he loved to be really stoned and spaced-out. He used to speak of two states: reality and real reality. And I often reflect on "real reality." These were stoner reflections. And after such a discussion, Burt would go off on a spaced-out trip and say, 'Now, reverse that!'"

Sally Kellerman also found Burt "lovely and sweet" and was touched when he gifted her a painting for her 21st birthday that June: "Everyone knew I liked green so they all brought me green items, like chlorophyll green toothpaste and green chewing gum, and Burt painted me a picture called *Something Greeen* which featured a space monster." The painting's full title: *Something Greeen for Sally*, actually featured the head of a robot, shooting beams of light from its eye sockets onto the mailbox of Kellerman's home (1334 Havenhurst Drive). Morgan Ames notes with amusement that the purposeful misspelling of the word green, (with three e's) in the title, was... "so Burt to do that. He's being affectionate and silly. Although I found his interest in UFOs boring, his work was so strong and distracting. The more he went that way – into UFOs – the less humanity the work had."

That certainly couldn't be said of the man himself, who always seemed to put a premium on friendship. One shining example was the way he responded to Sally Kellerman after her friend, the promising young actor Tom Pittman, died in car crash on October 31st, 1958, aged just 26. He'd been speeding in his souped-up Porsche Spyder (the same model that James Dean drove to his death) around a sharp bend in Benedict Canyon when he smashed through a guardrail and plummeted 150 feet into a ravine below. His body and wreckage weren't discovered until 19 days later, and his father sued the LAPD for what he considered a lackadaisical search. At the ensuing trial, Kellerman was called to testify on her departed friend's behalf, and Burt accompanied her to the courthouse for moral support. Because marijuana was found in the totalled Porsche, Kellerman was asked whether Pittman was a drug user and she lied under oath that he wasn't. Even though she defended Pittman's character, a malicious rumour – that she ratted out Pittman to the police – was spread by one of her Chez Paulette regulars, and many of her so-called friends deserted her. Burt's friendship, in contrast, remained steadfast.

Along with their shifts Chez Paulette, Kellerman and Ames also waitressed at Club Renaissance, a live music venue and art space located on 8428 Sunset Boulevard. To make some seasonal cash, Burt designed some Christmas cards that were sold in its bookshop, alongside those made by the fellow artist John Altoon, who taught art classes there. The two artists were familiar with each other, having been brought together (with nine other artists/illustrators) for an interesting artistic exercise setup by *Escapade* magazine, to view the varying ways each of them captured one of the choicest pin-up models around, Marguerite Empey. For the accompanying photo shoot, Burt was forced to wear a suit, as were the other artists, a marked change from the casual habiliments he tended to wear that invariably consisted of jeans, white T-shirt, flannel shirt and a pair of fawn-coloured, cork bottomed boots that Hampton gave him. "I think Burt was trying to get into that (Altoon) circle," Morgan Ames asserts, "because John and Billy Al Bengston were already hot and above him."

As well as live gigs and art shows, Club Renaissance also projected Japanese movies and offered classes in pantomime. (Another major draw to the place was that a local character named Art Grady would leave peyote buttons on the tables for patrons to sample.) Following suit, Cafe Frankenstein expanded its range of entertainment to include its own bookshop and theatre nights, while a poet named Jack Phillips (aka Philipo) would quiz young couples and offer them personality profiles, as George Clayton Johnson recollects: "Jack would sidle up to a couple at a table and he'd ask the girl: 'Do you remember your favourite movie?' and he'd start typing the answers on his portable typewriter. He'd fill the page with prose about her and then hand it to her saying, 'Barbara you are a provocative person,' and her guy would give him a couple of bucks. Then he'd go off to another table and do it all over again." These new activities were implemented after killjoy residents began to object to the all-night noise coming from the cafe (including the flamenco dancers stomping on the patio tables outside), so the Laguna Beach Board of Supervisors put the kibosh on live bands performing there, claiming its entertainment license fell outside the requisite zone. This didn't affect acoustic musicians or bongo players, but from then on in, when it came to electrified instrumentation, only solo pianists were allowed to perform. But the local authorities weren't finished with them yet.

On March 10, 1959, Burt's editor at *Escapade* dispatched their staff photographer Ron Vogel and the topless model Freddie Robbins (real name Freda Kellogg), to Cafe Frankenstein to shoot a pictorial spread for the magazine. George Clayton Johnson closed the cafe early that evening to accommodate them, but Ms. Kellogg's pneumatic presence aroused the prurient interest of some local youths, who stole a peek at her through the cracks in the cafe window as she posed for some cheesecake shots inside. Unfortunately, their antics alerted a passing police patrol who investigated and promptly arrested George, Vogel and Kellogg for "lewd and obscene conduct." George generously paid the $500 bail set for each of them, and when interviewed by the *Laguna Beach Post* newspaper, he protested: "The whole thing was artistic; there was nothing smutty, lewd or indecent at all. This is supposed to be an art colony, and models pose in the nude here for artists in everything from attics to basements."

When the case came to trial at L.A.'s City Hall, all three defendants plead not guilty and were summarily acquitted by Judge C. C. Cravath, who surmised: "I see a wilful act but don't see anything lewd involved." The negatives that had been seized and confiscated by the police were then returned to Vogel and *Escapade* ran the photographs in their December issue of that year. Not long after, Burt, Doug, and George sold their interest in Cafe Frankenstein to Michael Schley, husband of Constance Vining who owned the Designs in Leather store. Together they reopened the cafe as the 860 Club, which remained in business for a further two years. "We lasted for a little while," Schley laments, but once Shonberg was gone, everything that made the place unique went with it." [3] The 860 Club eventually closed in 1962, and though Vining's Designs in Leather continued operating until 1964, both buildings were subsequently demolished by local officialdom, who, in their infinite wisdom, really did pave paradise to put up a parking lot.

On July 10th, 1959, a brush fire swept through Laurel Canyon, destroying 36 residences, including the upper two floors of the Houdini House, a mansion on 2435 Laurel Canyon Boulevard, where, in 1919, the famous escapologist stayed briefly with his wife, while he was in town making movies. The conflagration was a big local news story, and several nights later, Burt and Hampton spent the night in the fire-damaged Houdini House, hoping to make contact with any ghostly inhabitants. "We spent the night camped out and scared ourselves in a giddy way," Hampton recollects. "I went along for the ride in terms of mysticism. I came from an atheist, humanist background, from my father, so Burt's machinations were just fun for me. I'd had a couple of supernatural experiences in my travels that couldn't be explained, and the place was so haunted, we confabulated certain things. Poltergeist was a big word for us. I didn't believe in it and still don't, but they happened in my mind. We're limited by our senses and psychic awareness; the more we know about the brain the bigger it becomes."

Though many of Burt's ideas came via popular media rather art galleries, Hampton does recollect a visit the two of them made to the Los Angeles Museum of History, Science and Art to view an exposition of Henri Matisse, and though he was enthused by the offerings on show, the experience seemed to haunt Burt, and sparked within him a sense of competitiveness – not just in relation to the quality of Matisse's draftsmanship, but his prolificacy as well. In response – as a way of measuring himself artistically against such modern and Renaissance masters, Burt began reimagining classic and iconic portraits. His playful take on the *Mona Lisa*, for instance, transported Leonardo da Vinci's Florentine maiden through time – from 16th century Italy to present day Cafe Frankenstein – its ambiance softening her pursed expression as she sat perched at the bar with an aperitif in front of her. While his tribute to Picasso's *The Kiss* – in which he shifted the amorphously-shaped lovers devouring each other to a four-poster bed, decked with pennants and bunting – graced the front cover of the fifth edition of *Le Petit Sphinx*.

With Cameron's magickal incantations still reverberating in his psyche, Burt happened upon a new mentor in metaphysical matters. Ray Shevin was an adherent of George Ivanovitch Gurdjieff, the Russian-born, Sufi-inspired mystic, who believed much of humanity was simply sleepwalking through life. To remedy this, he developed the Fourth Way System that awoke aspirants out of their slumber and taught them how to become fully conscious of every unfolding moment. By maintaining this state of total self-awareness, they could then attain a higher state of consciousness. Shevin introduced Burt to the Fourth Way System via *In Search of the Miraculous*, the explicatory work written by Gurdjieff's student and compatriot, P.D. Ouspensky. Having read the book, Shevin wrote to the publisher, who put him in touch with a local Gurdjieff group, with whom he was now an active member. Though Burt was not interested in joining them, he took on board many Fourth Way precepts, and axioms relating to its study wound up on several of his canvases. Shevin was intrigued by Burt and admired his talent and, as he was between places, he invited him to stay at his bungalow on N. Orange Grove, near Fairfax High. By day, Shevin worked in the distribution department at Pacific Jazz Records – home to such elegantly wasted cool jazzers as Chet Baker and Gerry Mulligan – so he was used to dealing with dissolute artists, but living with Burt was something else entirely. Considering the use of hallucinogens did not contravene any Fourth Way principles that he was aware of, Shevin threw some wild peyote parties, and whenever Burt was present, they took on a supernatural dimension. Darryl Copeland was pals with Shevin and became fast friends with Burt through him: "Burt was a walking mystical experience. I remember taking peyote at Ray's house and it was just too weird. Suddenly this fire started and it was definitely a vortex of some kind of psychic energy – and Burt was the magnet." Friends wondered whether this might have been caused by the infernal forces Burt was exposed to by Cameron, as a sense of ritual immolation seemed to vibrate from her being. Intimates were well aware of her Joan of Arc complex; she was convinced she'd been burnt as a witch in a previous lifetime, and now believed her first husband secretly wanted to burn her alive too. She would also, on occasion, incinerate her own paintings, believing they already existed on the astral plane for those who could reach them. So, when a number of Burt's canvases met the same fiery fate, suspicion grew that it was the result of a curse thrown on him by Cameron.

In the Fall of 1959, Burt was hired to create some interior tableaus for the 7 Chefs restaurant on Sunset Boulevard. The gig entailed months of hard graft, so to be closer to the job, he moved into an apartment above the Sea Witch nightclub, where his artwork already adorned the walls. George Clayton Johnson visited him there: "One-half of the room was his drawing space and the other half was taken up by his bed. The 7 Chefs was an old building that had a stairway running down to the bar. Burt painted lagoons on these Masonite panels, with exotic birds and junk ships. They paid his food bill across the street where he ate and gave him a few dollars."

At the beginning of January 1960, while he was still working on the project, Burt was approached by the filmmaker Roger Corman, who was himself hard at work, bringing to the screen his movie adaptation of Edgar Allan Poe's classic short story, *The Fall of the House of Usher*. The film – Corman's first in colour, was shot in Cinemascope and starred Vincent Price as the surviving patriarch of the accursed Usher family, who entombs his sister to extinguish the romance between her and her visiting suitor, to finally eradicate the family's blighted bloodline. Corman was already familiar with Burt's artwork having seen marvellous examples of it in the coffeehouses on the Strip, so he hired him to create the ancestral portraits that hang in the Usher mansion, confident he could convey the evil inherent in the faces depicted. "When I came to do Usher, I needed portraits of Usher's disreputable ancestors and Burt's work had a mystical, mysterious quality," the director explains. "It was almost surrealist. I felt that quality in his paintings. So, I gave him each of the characters' histories and left it to him to interpret that, and he captured their tormented spirits and the spirit of the film perfectly." Burt was given only three weeks to complete the task, and to keep abreast of his progress, Corman asked his art director Daniel Haller to liaise with him: "I would go over to his place and see how the paintings were coming along. I had no input into his style and I never critiqued his work, but I encouraged him and he wanted to do the best he could. We just turned him loose. I only knew him while he was doing those paintings, and sometimes it was hard for me to talk to him. He spoke about traveling out on the astral plane, but he was unique and produced such great work for us."

It was clear from the spookiness he ably imbued in each of the resulting works that Burt had been successful in fulfilling his brief, especially in the standout piece: a portrait of the witchy ancestor Vivian Usher (described as a "blackmailer, harlot, murderess" who died in the madhouse) whose blacked-out eyes were eerily similar to a self-portrait created by Cameron entitled *The Black Egg*. Amusingly, Burt appears to have snuck himself and Ray Shevin into the deranged dynasty, as his depiction of Bernard Usher, ("swindler, forger, jewel thief, drug addict"), looks remarkably like his friend, while the painting of Francis Usher (a "professional assassin") is a total self-portrait. Vincent Price, a connoisseur of fine art, was enamoured with the portraitures and expressed an interest in meeting their maker: "When we hung them on the film set, Vincent was very complimentary," Haller recollects. "He said how good they were, so I invited Burt to the set and they had a great discussion together. Vincent was a champion of struggling artists." In the fiery climax to the film, Usher's mansion is set ablaze, and although the family portraits appear to perish in the flames, Burt's pieces were undamaged, having been sprayed with a flame retardant beforehand. Once the film wrapped, Vincent Price helped himself to Burt's portrait of David Usher, the sea captain, with the red molten eyes, and Corman bagged two others, including one of the Usher mansion itself that also featured in the film. Regretfully, both were stolen from his office at Amco Studios, shortly afterward, a theft that still irks him to this day. (These and the whereabouts of all the other *House of Usher* artworks are currently unknown.) [4]

The dry ice used to create the fog that wreathed the crumbling Usher mansion in Corman's movie permeated Burt's next set of paintings: a magnificent series of classical subjects and mythological beasts inspired by the Greco-Roman murals and frescoes found in pictorial books that Hampton shared with him. The approval of Corman and imprimatur from Price was a real shot in the arm for Burt's confidence, and even by his own obsessive standards, he became absorbed in a white heat of creativity. The quality of his craftsmanship now shifted up a gear, and he created some of his finest works. It was now evident that he possessed a proficiency and technique that enabled him to move into any aesthetic style that piqued his curiosity, including his most recent foray into the realm of Romanticism. *Mars* was an outstanding departure from what had gone before. The composition – clearly sparked by Goya's *The Colossus* – portrayed the Roman God of war as a gigantic Trojan gazing down on a peaceful, hillside hamlet. While the accompanying *Mars, God of War*, captured the valorous warrior in profile, his eyes shaded beneath his Galea helmet. According to Hampton: "That kind of reality appealed to Burt. He fancied himself along those lines – heroic. In fact, he gave those figures his nose." *Atlantis* was reimagined, not as a sunken water-world, but as a mist-blanketed, empyrean citadel ruled by griffins. And for the series based on the painting *Lord and Lady of the Flame*, Burt stole a leaf from Cameron's sketchbook and honoured his relationship with her and Crystal by depicting them, lovingly, as a family of sphinxes, suffused in soft-focus. The symbolism of the Sphinx as a guardian of hermetic secrets and mysteries was seized upon for a related canvas, that captured the beguiling profile of another shadow-eyed Sphinx, wearing a Nemes headdress and caressing the Star of David, with the ghostly presence of her child resting on her shoulder. The creatures were enveloped in a swirling, ethereal haze creating such a ravishing effect it was reminiscent of the white-out seascapes of that other Romantic master, J. M. W. Turner. But the most impressive canvas of all was *Magic Landscape*, a resplendently realized portrait of Lucifer, relaxing against a tree while stroking a sphinx-like pet on his lap. The golden horns and wings of God's most beloved angel illuminated by a yellow moon, that cast its light over moss-covered rocks in a demi-paradise. This magnum opus became the prized possession of George Clayton Johnson, as did several other Shonberg "treasures," as part of his payoff from the selling of Cafe Frankenstein. Regrettably, the photographs George mentioned, that were taken of Burt's workmanship inside the 7 Chefs went missing after the magazine (possibly *Le Petit Sphinx)* ceased publication and never published them. This turned out to be a double blow when it came to the posterity of Burt's artwork because on June 22nd, 1960, the eatery was gutted by a fire. When Burt and Hampton visited the site, they searched through the charred remains but only found one surviving fragment of his laborious handiwork: "There was a feeling of residue, of what was left, and it stayed there like that for a while. Burt was philosophical about it." Although the restaurant was most probably set alight for insurance money, which was not an unknown practice for failing businesses or mob-affiliated establishments, coming so soon after Burt's portraits were supposedly extinguished by flames in the *House of Usher*, and with tales of fires breaking out in his presence still fresh in people's minds, George Clayton Johnson – who recounts how even a frame store burned down after Burt left some of his canvases there to be fitted – playfully wondered whether his friend might be a secret pyromaniac.

BURT SHONBERG ➡ *OUT THERE*

Burt's beatnik *Mona Lisa.* 1957.
(Courtesy of the George & Marzia Greif
Family Trust.)

Freddie Robbins poses at the counter and next to the coffee machine in Cafe Frankenstein.

Pinup model Freddie Robbins poses in front of Burt's Frankenstein painting.

Burt's wonderful birthday gift to Sally Kellerman *Something Greeen For Sally*. 1958. Casein on Masonite. (Courtesy of Sally Kellerman.)

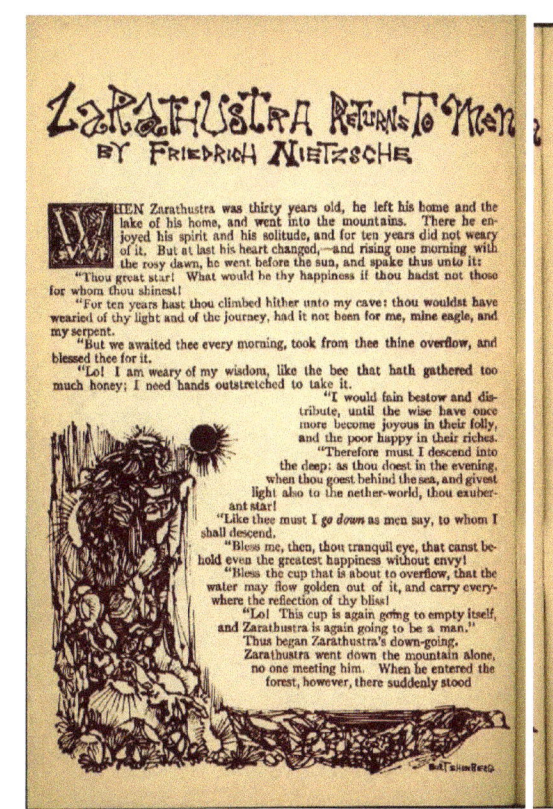

Burt's illustrates an excerpt from Thus Spake Zarathustra by Friedrich Nietzsche for the Le Pettit Sphinx. According to Hampton Fancher: "The Burt I knew wouldn't have read Nietzsche. His was more of a Vegas thing, a quicker fix. He wanted it NOW! He had no patience."

Jack Kramer sat in the window of his club the International.
(Courtesy of the collection of Brian Chidester.)

Burt's Picasso-inspired cover for issue 5 of *Le Petit Sphinx*. (Courtesy of the collection of Brian Chidester.)

Burt's advert for the Sandalsville store.

BURT SHONBERG ➡ *OUT THERE*

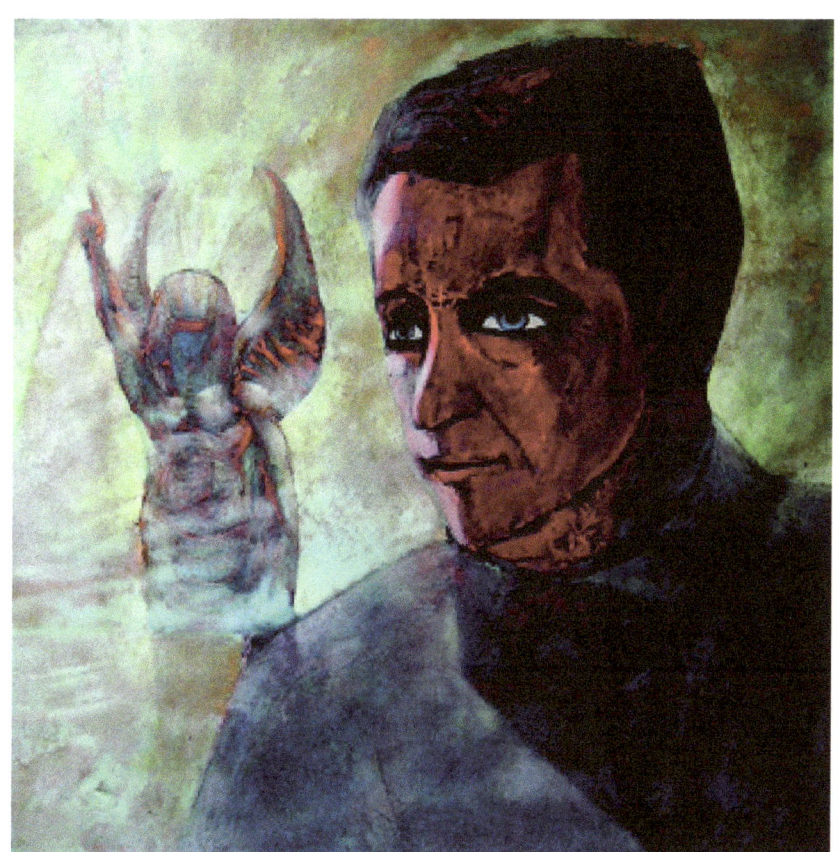

Burt's portrait of Ray Shevin. (1961) Casein on Masonite.
(From the private collection of Judith Shevin.)

Burt hard at work. It's believed he's painting the facade of the Sandalsville store. The woman on the ladder appears to be Valerie Porter. (Photographer unknown.)

85

Magic Landscape. The catalyst for the painting appears to have been a photograph taken by Baron Adolf de Meyer of Vaslav Nijinsky, in 1912, for The Afternoon of a Faun ballet, based on Claude Debussy's symphonic poem, *L'Après-midi d'un Faune.* In it, the famed dancer reclines, dressed in a full-length, particolored unitard, wearing pixie ears and blowing a pan flute. (Photographed by Brian Sawin.)

BURT SHONBERG ➡ OUT THERE

Atlantis. 1960. Casein on Masonite. 4 ft x 3 ft.
(From the private collection of Richard Christian Matheson.)

Burt's portraits of the Sea Captain and Vivian Usher. The latter was inspired by a Cameron self-portrait entitled *The Black Egg*. In the film, the family portraits are presented as the work of Vincent Price's character, Roderick Usher. Roger Corman praised Burt's portraiture for not only capturing the evil in the faces of the Usher ancestors but also successfully suggesting how their evil poisoned the mind of the person who painted them. Vincent Price was similarly impressed with how Burt's artworks echoed Poe's sense of agony.

Ray Shevin was used as inspiration for Burt's portrait of Bernard Usher.

Burt's portrait of Francis Usher is actually a self-portrait.

Burt presents his paintings to Vincent Price as Roger Corman looks on.

Vincent Price appraises another one of Burt's paintings in the *House of Usher*.

Mars. (Courtesy of Marshall Berle and LaughDome Records LLC.)

The Lord and Lady of the Flame. Casein on Masonite 4 ft x 3 ft. (From the private collection of Clara Jean Peterson and Sunny Liberty Berle.)

Mars The God of War. 1960. Casein on Masonite. (From the private collection of Judith Shevin.)

Burt's glorious *Sphinx with Star of David*. 1960. Painted in oil.
(Photographed by Mercy Baron.)

Shonberg *Sphinxes* inspired by Cameron and Crystal. (From the private collection of Rick Anderson.)

Chapter 5
The Experience

In June 1960, Burt was buoyed up when *Fantastic* magazine used one of his space-age illustrations for their latest front cover. The striking and darkly humorous image depicted an astronaut, wearing a space helmet decorated with Burt's signature glyphs and a spacesuit consisting of soft, imbricated plating, on a volcanic planet, glancing at a fellow crewman who was languishing neck-deep in magma, seemingly resigned to his fate.

The summer also marked Burt's return to Laurel Canyon, when he found a funky new crib on 2222 Laurel Canyon Boulevard. The living quarters were spartan: a bed, an easel, and a cubbyhole for his books and food, but it suited his purposes. Hampton remembers visiting him there: "It was so small; you could walk across his room in five steps. He just had a single cot and the place smelled of cigarettes and casein. His door was open if it wasn't cold, and the radio was always on, which gave him a sense of community. He was autonomous and a lonely guy, well, maybe not lonely because people could "fall by" – that was the term we used back then – no one called first, even if someone was asleep in bed. So, he had an audience, and he was open for business all night long. The door was always open and he'd be working. He liked having people around while he painted. I loved watching him work. When you're engrossed in what you do, it's endless and a gift. "

Three years had elapsed since Judy Watt last saw her Art Center crony; they'd lost touch when she got married, ("for the wrong reason – to get out of my parent's house"), but they renewed their friendship after she spotted him standing on a corner in the canyon, in a peculiar state: "Burt was looking up at the sky and talking to whoever. Still, we were so glad to see each other again." To celebrate, they made a date to take some peyote together, which didn't sit well with Judy's friend Ira Odessky, who had a crush on her, and was a greenhorn when it came to hallucinogens. "I told Ira what a wonderful fellow Burt was and how we were really good friends at art school. But when I told him I was gonna take peyote with him, he said, 'How can you do that? Who is this guy? What are you doing?' After we took it, I laid down on Burt's bed, while he painted, and waited for it to come on. As I waited, unbeknownst to me, Ira had found out where Burt lived and was peeking through the window, like a Kilroy Was Here cartoon, to make sure I was alright. He had good intent. So, I invited Ira in to meet Burt and he quickly appreciated who he was but, at the time, they were from different zip codes. Burt said let's go down to the beach and I drove, which was unbelievable. Laying on the beach, I looked up at the cloud formations in the sky and found that I could make them do whatever I wanted them to do: form them into a Da Vinci and then a Matisse. It was an external feeling the first time."

While they were getting reacquainted with each other, Burt shared with Judy some of the Gurdjieff and Ouspensky material he'd inherited from Ray Shevin, an initiation that she freely admits "changed her life." He then introduced her to Shevin himself, a man who would soon become her second husband. "I met Ray at Burt's and I knew he was the one within moments. We were married in Mexico within a few months of meeting each other, once my divorce was final." Sadly, for all concerned, Burt did not take their union well, for, amongst other worries, he feared he was losing them to each other. "When we got married Burt felt hurt and betrayed and became distant. He was not happy. He was disappointed because he felt that marriage was too ordinary, something that mortals did. He was disappointed to see we were so conventional. It was hard for him to understand. He felt abandoned and didn't respond in an ordinary way because he was an extraordinary person. He came over several times to our little house on Walnut Drive, but I left them alone. Ray was very fond of Burt, and once we got married, I became very close to him on a certain level; it was like family. And Burt was so attracted to Ray. He considered him so otherworldly, but my husband was very much part of the world. Burt held Ray in very high esteem, even in unrealistic ways, because he had a fantastic imagination. He was convinced Ray was an evolved being and he had a lot of fantasies about him; that he was not just human. Ray was his mentor and defender and he felt my husband was in touch with things that he also aspired to, like Gurdjieff and other metaphysical ideas. My husband had that quality, like a teacher. He was smart and spoke beautifully and had information no others had. He was a magnet for people who had questions, and he didn't come from a negative place like others. He took care of Burt when he lived with him. He showed him how to live, how to keep his paints and brushes neat, how to organize his life. He was very good for Burt because Burt was a mess." In tribute to Shevin, Burt painted his portrait; emphasizing his cerulean blue eyes and a spectre in the background representing his consciousness ascending. "It came from Burt's love and admiration of Ray."

Considering that both men were so utterly unconventional, it was only a matter of time before Burt struck up a friendship with Vito Paulekas, a sculptor who taught lessons to a diverse mix of paying customers, in the basement studio of a two-story building at 303 North Laurel Avenue. Vito was an immensely charismatic individual, with a storied past, and a Mephistophelean mien that magnified his well-earned reputation as a satyr.

Born in 1913, Vitautus Alphonsus Paulekas grew up not that far from Burt, in Lawrence, Massachusetts, one of five children whose Lithuanian immigrant parents toiled in the town's linen mills. They moved to Cambridge, Massachusetts, when their father acquired a more lucrative sausage-making job there, which meant he could invest in his children's education, including music lessons for Vito, who become an accomplished violinist. He also excelled as a school debater and storyteller and, like a Boston Brahmin, he prided himself on his perfectly enunciated command of the King's English.

During the severe Depression-era, Vito scrapped a living schlepping around ballrooms as a successful marathon dancer and was even called to testify in front of Congress about the legitimacy of these endurance contests. (Coincidently, a year before Burt was born, Vito actually won a competition at the Oceanview Ballroom on Revere Beach.) At the time, the dance marathons were vying with movie theatres for much-needed audience revenue, and in a reckless act of self-interest, Vito disguised his face with greasepaint one night and robbed a movie theatre. Needless to say, it was an amateurish attempt and he was soon apprehended and sent up the river, where he became the leader of the prison's orchestra band. His sentence was then commuted on the understanding that he would enlist in the Merchant Marines, which he did, successfully participating in the Murmansk run in the final year of World War II. After the war ended, he sailed around the Pacific, working as a mess man in the kitchen. He returned to America and married his girlfriend after she fell pregnant. In 1949, he moved to Los Angeles where he sired another child with his wife, but the marriage crumbled due to her unwillingness to engage in her husband's extracurricular sexual activities. This freed Vito and cast him out into the world of Bohemia. For a while he laboured as a housepainter, then, in 1954, he won a whopping $5000 guessing the magic word on Groucho Marx's popular quiz show *You Bet Your Life*. With the winnings, he travelled through Europe with a girlfriend and enrolled at the prestigious Accademia di Belle Arti di Roma, where he studied sculpture. He returned to Los Angeles a year later, and put what he learned to commercial use by creating long, flowing lamp bases for a lamp manufacturing business. He then set up his own clay studio to teach his artisanship. Sueanne Shaffer was only 17 when she answered an advert looking for a coffee maker at the studio and, once hired, found herself irresistibly attracted to her boss's animal magnetism. The 30-year age difference didn't matter one jot to her either, as she was used to dating older men, such as the actor Cameron Mitchell; and her parents were happy that she was earning while learning sculpture, whilst still maintaining her good grades at Franklin High school. They were, however, shocked when Vito asked her to marry him a year later, but by then they powerless to stop the ceremony at City Hall, because by then their daughter was of legal age. Now calling herself Szou, the newly-wed transformed Vito's bachelor pad on the mezzanine floor of the building into a proper love nest and drew up plans to convert the ground floor area into her own boutique. Before they tied the knot, Vito made it abundantly clear to his prospective bride that their forthcoming nuptials would not infringe upon his free love lifestyle, when he arranged a mini-orgy at the Hollywood home of his friend Mary Mancini, who taught art and English at the all-girl Immaculate Heart High School on Franklin Avenue. "Mary had style about her," Szou recollects. "She was short, always wore high heels, and taught all day and hung with us all night. The nuns at the school wanted her to follow suit because they were concerned about the effect she seemed to be having on her female students, and the sexual ardour directed back at her by them. She was a closeted lesbian who enjoyed affairs with men, including one with Joe Maini, the married alto sax player in the Gerald Wilson jazz band. She got so hung up on Joe, she stalked him until he begged Vito to get her off his back."

Burt was also invited to the sex party and partnered up with Vito's nubile bride-to-be. "Burt approached me at the orgy and I was flattered because I really appreciated his art. Having sex with him; knowing who he was and admiring his work so much, it stood out in my mind. It was captivating for me and it was available to me because my partner made it available to me. Vito and I were never swingers but we were close to it. But that was the end of my intimacy with Burt because I became a full-time student and got married to Vito. Burt didn't get that I was attracted to Vito. He thought he would capture me but my heart was already invested in Vito, even though he was having a secret affair with my friend Nancy Friedman, who was Jewish and also my age, but I didn't know it at the time because they never glanced at each other. Another girl, Arlene Posner, was also there at the sex party, and she'd already had an affair with Burt. She was a Jewess from Chicago who was beautiful, like a femme fatale, so I was the most goy looking one."

As Hampton Fancher has already confirmed, a great deal of matchmaking and sharing of lovers going on at this time, and one prime example of this was Valerie Porter, a vivacious, free-spirited woman, who he and Burt knew intimately. For even though she was married, she revelled in her promiscuous reputation. Born in 1927, Valerie came into the world with the non-Anglicised name Velinka Lubitsa Miloskovich, one of two daughters of expatriate Serbian parents. She grew up in the impoverished Eastside of Detroit, whose demographics were roughly 50 percent black and 50 percent, Eastern European immigrants. Growing up, "Luby," as she was known, exhibited a contagious verve for life and an irrepressible ambition that would elevate her far beyond her humble beginnings. By her early twenties, she was honing her sexual prowess as a dancer, as well as a chanteuse fronting the Don Tosti band. She performed in the city's Black and Tan nightclubs; racially mixed joints catering to GE executives and other well-heeled businessmen, who were drawn by the club's hotsy-totsy hostesses and the sophisticated jazz of artistes such as Nat King Cole. One night, her sensual shimmying caught the eye of Louis A. Porter, a wealthy copper baron who'd made an absolute fortune from military contracts during World War II.

Despite being a married man, the industrialist was so captivated with Valerie he wooed her away from her agent/boyfriend, showering her with expensive gifts. He then walked out on his wife and family one day – supposedly "for cigarettes" – and never came back. Once his divorce was finalized, the couple wed and started a brand-new family in 1954 when Valerie gave birth to a son, Louis Jr. Then, 18 months later, having relocated to a palatial residence in the Los Feliz section of Los Angles, she bore another boy, Julian. Valerie only agreed to motherhood on the promise that her husband would provide all the necessary nursemaids to take care of the offspring, for she had no intention of turning into another rich, jaded, Hollywood hausfrau.

She began frequenting actor hangouts like Schwab's and Googies, and her wealth enabled her to live a life dedicated to doing exactly as she pleased, unencumbered by financial concerns. Using her Hollywood connections, she won a role playing one of the platinum bombshells in the B-movie murder mystery *Three Blondes in His Life*. Though her movie career subsequently stalled, she became a bona fide libertine; notorious for throwing herself lustily into the bohemian swing of things in Laurel Canyon, which is how she became romantically entwined with Burt and Hampton.

"I spent a couple of months with her," Hampton recollects. "Even though she was married, she was delinquent. She worked at being an actor and was excited to get that film, and used it to get out of the house. Her husband seemed downcast by it; passive. He didn't know how to handle her. Filming meant she and I could stay together in a hotel and I remember the first night well – the intimacies. In the morning, she got up for the shoot; we hadn't slept much and she was frantic. She was on and off: either full of fun and sexual or desperate, scared and nerve-wracked. She was like that that morning: 'You gotta go! I've got to have a shower!' Hygiene was iffy back then; people had STDs. Valerie had a great body but also an odour that meant a bacterial infection. I cant actually imagine her bathing when she awoke for work that morning, yet she was yummy. We were staying at the Roosevelt Hotel and as I left the lobby for the sidewalk her husband was walking in and he gave me a look. She was a stunning and a compelling and fascinating person. She had electricity. She played the wifely role, but she was also fucking other people. My friend, the actor Michael Greene, originally introduced us, and she'd already fucked him and Burt before me. Still, I was totally in love with her but she was crazier than all of us; certifiably crazy. I was 21; she was 35, and she was leaving me and I said, 'No, you can't leave me!' and I thought art might be the way to win her back, so I said, 'Let's go to the LA Museum in Exposition Park, and we were walking around, hand in hand, when all of a sudden she starts screaming at the top of her lungs and I tried to hold her to calm her down but she ran out and took a cab back to her place. So, I take her car, an MG convertible, and we meet back at her place and the cat was out of the bag because the husband found out we were fucking and I said to her, 'Fuck him! Be with me. Give up your million-dollar lifestyle.' And as I'm pounding on the door, he comes out and says, 'She doesn't want to see you anymore!' She'd hired me to paint these faux stained-glass windows in the tower room of her house in Los Feliz, by the Griffith Observatory. It was octangular and had windows for each section. She said we could do a 'pre-Renaissance thing there' and I thought Burt could do it. It was Burt, of course, who taught me how to do faux stained glass. Each glass panel had one disciple but it was not as colourful as Burt's stuff. It was more in the style of (Georges) Rouault, who we both loved at the time. More Byzantine or in the style of (Andrei) Rublev. I don't think Valerie's husband liked them, but she sure did."

It was thanks to a referral from Valerie, that Burt was accepted as a volunteer for the LSD-25 research being conducted by Dr. Oscar Janiger, a research professor at the University of California-Irvine, with his own private psychiatric practice. Inspired by Aldous Huxley's *The*

Doors of Perception, which documented the author's visionary experiences under the influence of mescaline, Janiger inaugurated a research study into the clinical effects of Lysergic Acid Diethylamide (LSD-25), which he'd heard about and tried while teaching a class at the California College of Medicine in the early 1950s. The powerful compound biochemically stimulated the receptors and neurotransmitters in the brain, that control the visual and auditory facilities, and manipulated the prefrontal cortex region of the mind, which orchestrates thoughts and impulses and perception. Test subjects reported how they felt their consciousness (or soul if you're that way inclined) being transported out into an uncharted, transpersonal realm, beyond the veil of material reality – a state that many ancient Eastern religions deemed illusionary – where the natural laws of space and time were suspended. Many subjects found the experience genuinely blissful and oftentimes described it as a spiritual awakening. But for others, the profound rearrangement of the senses engendered nightmarish hallucinations and triggered a terrifying descent into (temporary) madness, that left them traumatized.

For Janiger, however, the drug was a revelation and, in concert with fellow radical researchers in the U.S. and Great Britain, he purchased a sizable quantity directly from the Sandoz Corporation in Switzerland, where it was discovered serendipitously by the research scientist Albert Hoffman, who'd been experimenting with the compound while trying to synthesize a new pharmaceutical drug. Janiger (who happened to be Allen Ginsberg's cousin) had been trialling the drug since 1954, studying its effectiveness in the treatment of personality disorders, as well as its viability as an anaesthetic. But his current purview focused on the impact it exerted on the creative process, and being in the heart of the American entertainment industry, he had some quality subjects to choose from. Hollywood's biggest movie star, Cary Grant, found that the drug enabled him to psychologically work through and conquer the painful memories of his impoverished and neglectful childhood, while Lord Buckley credited the drug for sharpening his improvisational skills and loosening him up on a stage. In fact, he felt so indebted to the doctor, he bestowed on him the affectionate pet name, The Great Oz. Janiger eventually purchased a residence on Wilton Place (that was previously owned by Clara Bow), where he decorated several rooms to create the most relaxing environment for his test subjects. An adjacent garden was also used as a setting for sessions, but when it came to monitoring the effect of the drug on professional painters, he created an atelier with a blank canvas and an easel ready for use.

Janiger screened his volunteers for any mental health issues (Burt, it appears, was obviously economical with the truth; keeping shtumm about his army discharge) and he rejected those suffering from any serious physical debilitations, such as heart and liver disease. With a nurse on hand in case anything untoward occurred, volunteers were asked to sign consent forms, confirming they understood the possible dangers and consequences involved and accepted the responsibility for any difficulties that arose during or following the session; thus, absolving the doctor of any legal liability. Sessions generally began midmorning, with volunteers urged to only take a light breakfast. The LSD was administered orally, a moderate dose of two micrograms per kilograms of body weight, and subjects were monitored throughout the session; free to halt the experiment anytime they wanted to. The effects of the drug generally lasted between four and five hours and volunteers were required to stay on until the end of the day, having prearranged with a family member or friend to accompany them home. They were then asked to keep in contact with the doctor for several days afterwards, to make sure there were no adverse side effects. Valerie had already participated in the study herself, so Burt kind of knew what it all entailed, and when asked on a preliminary questionnaire what he would like out of the experience, he replied, "An experience of different states of consciousness." Then, asked if he'd ever had a comparable experience, he quipped, "Much peyote."

Burt's session took place on December 6, 1960, starting at 10:30 am, when he was asked to capture the likeness of the Hopi Deer Kachina doll that Janiger liked to have artists paint; once before the LSD was administered, and again an hour later, once the drug had taken hold, to see the difference. Like all the other test subjects before him, Burt was then asked to write up his LSD-25 experience at the end of the session, or as soon as possible afterwards, and his testimony could not have been more laudatory. It is reproduced here for the first time (all emphasis his):

"The speeding up of the centers. Somehow slows everything else down. So one may get a good look at how "Things" really are. The phenomena of so call "Passing Time" does not exist. Now is always here!!!! Eternity is on the scene – and is constant. Humanity is literally hypnotized in the "Dream Reality" of momentum caused by life (meaning external influences). There is an illusion of movement in life which is not the truth. This all relates to so-called time. Time is motion – is evolution. One might say that the Big Criminal in all this is "identification." To be apart from the form is the answer to real vision – consciousness. To be awake is to be really alive – to really exist. It's the "I Am" and indeed, the real "I" is invisible. You are not your physical body or anything else (ex, – your name – work – etc..) The Real "I" is an invisible entity that occupies and/or possesses a physical form to utilize as a vehicle to ride around in and do things through – like flesh and bone and blood etc...is the clothes or costume (or form) that the Real True Self wears. "Consciousness" is apart from the form – !

Now, about the painting – after I was "on." the Cochina {sic} Doll itself is like – a dead wooden thing, a bent hollow dead figure with decorations and no meaning. Like – nothing. I sort of painted a creature that was perhaps this Dolls "God." Alive – fiery – pagan – evil – and very dumb. All evil is literally dumb ... dead, in motion, but somehow mechanical and going by itself for the purposes of its own subjective desires ... fulfilling its own greedy needs... no love, anyhow, to hold a brush while on LSD was something else ... like it was a magic wand and I could create any kind of image I wanted. Each stroke was an experience that added up to the total painting, but to me, it was not the finished painting that was important (like I could've painted it over flat black) but much more important was the joy in painting – itself."

Thank you, Oscar. Burt Shonberg

Janiger was clearly impressed with Burt's contribution because he arranged a further session the following Spring, that took place on March 6th, 1961, only this time he increased Burt's dosage from 100 to 125 micrograms. During the session, Burt completed an abstract painting, but what happened next remains unclear. According to one account, Burt told friends the (increased dose of) LSD had no effect on him, so he physically left Janiger's studio, with the doctor's permission, seemingly unaffected by it, only for the drug to kick in belatedly, while he was walking the streets outside. Though such a scenario illustrates the sheer unpredictability of the drug, it seems unlikely considering all of Janiger's safeguards, and Burt's own written account suggests he only left the studio mentally, to embark on an adventure that was recorded in highly descriptive detail:

"I sat quietly but with joyous anticipation as The Experience began to come on. A kind of noise inside of myself (closely resembling the frantic sounds of a hundred different radio and TV sets being played at a low volume) was suddenly shut off. Only when all that noise stopped did I know there was any noise. The mechanical monster left me. I was Free.

Off in the distance, I could hear the coming of a great quiet. A large ring of flickering ember colored fire-light revolved continuously about the ceiling as animated ancient hieroglyphs flashed off and on across the floor. The onrushing sea of quiet got thicker, louder, closer. The room demanded my attention. The floor came forth and dramatically announced itself by making me fully conscious of my relationship to it. The walls made themselves known and I became conscious of that which was outside of the room in every direction. The ceiling could not stop the sky from coming in and the ground rose up through the floor. The walls, struck by a silent blast of light, became incapable of protecting the room from the outside. There was no such thing as inside anymore. Now, I was outside . . .

Outside the day of the week, the year. Outside of moving time, I was not in "The City." There was no city. I was not in "The World." There was no world. I was right where I was, at that location, on the outer surface of the earth. I knew exactly where I was. I could see it. I was Here In Existence, And fully Conscious of it.

Los Angeles, California. Outdoors. Walking along the main boulevard. The wall-to-wall asphalt and cement carpeting and the tall stone and iron buildings did not prevent my being conscious of the planetary aspect of this setting. The illusion of the all-pervading city was shattered and I saw not only the city but also where it was located on the earth. I experienced seeing these two major features of my environment simultaneously. Another thrilling visual treat had to do with the afternoon light reflecting on buildings nearby. The daylight on the buildings became visually more important or outstanding than the buildings themselves. I saw the object and the light shining on the object as two separate things, and I experienced seeing these two things existing simultaneously.

The result: The experience of whatever I looked at became new, unfamiliar, and it was as if I was being reintroduced to the scene I was in. Also, I experienced completely new conscious recognition of the individual existence of the various structures.

Another remarkable aspect of the light on objects had to do with being simultaneously conscious of the light upon things and the source of the light. I was completely aware of where the light was originating from without having to look in that particular direction.

In the hills overlooking the San Fernando Valley, I saw a vision in the clear sky above the clouds. The image was that of a colossal oriental warlord wearing ancient armour and a head-piece. There was a slow-motion-like up and down movement of the figure which gave me the impression that he was on horseback although I did not see whatever it was that may have been riding. He was smiling as the vision faded.

Kaleidoscopic Aztec-like imagery, continually revolving and changing within itself, came rolling out of the sky. As this was occurring, winds of coloured light were sweeping across the landscape. As I watched the manifestation of this fantastic imagery, it became increasingly move vivid. After several minutes, I happened to look down from this, at the environment I was in, and a surprise golden sea of light was present everywhere. It was as if I and my surroundings were suspended in this visual ocean of crystalline energy. A moment later, a great white light suddenly splashed down from up above, and the appearance of the-world-in-time was dramatically transformed and I was on a field in Eternity.

The musical soundtrack from the motion picture Mondo Cane was being played in stereo. With eyes closed, I listened in silence and began seeing fantastically varied visions in full color. With each individual vignette of the music there came a different visionary story. (The visions I saw had nothing whatever to do with the film.) One story went like this. Above the earth appeared a giant, sensuous beautiful female dancer. As she performed her magnificent, wild, provocative dance, activity was visible on the Earth. Historical-like occurrences were being depicted at a greatly sped-up rate of movement. She was moving at normal speed. All kinds of things were happening on the Earth. Civilizations rising, falling, war, peace, hordes on horseback, children playing, people running – the world in actions of every conceivable type. All the while, no matter what kind of life event or action is seen taking place on the Earth, this colossal epitome of sensuosity and physical beauty swung through her dance completely unaffected by the ever-changing panorama of motion down below." [1]

Burt subsequently concluded: *"I came to realize that the significance of art resulting from 'the psychedelic experience; could possibly reach to actual magic and beyond. There are, of course, certain things that one experiences in the transcendental state that are not possible to communicate in the usual way, so new types of parables would have to be created to get the message through. These discoveries*

I refer to could be insights or revelations into various aspects of the world we live in, nature, the mind itself, time, the universe, reality, and God." (2)

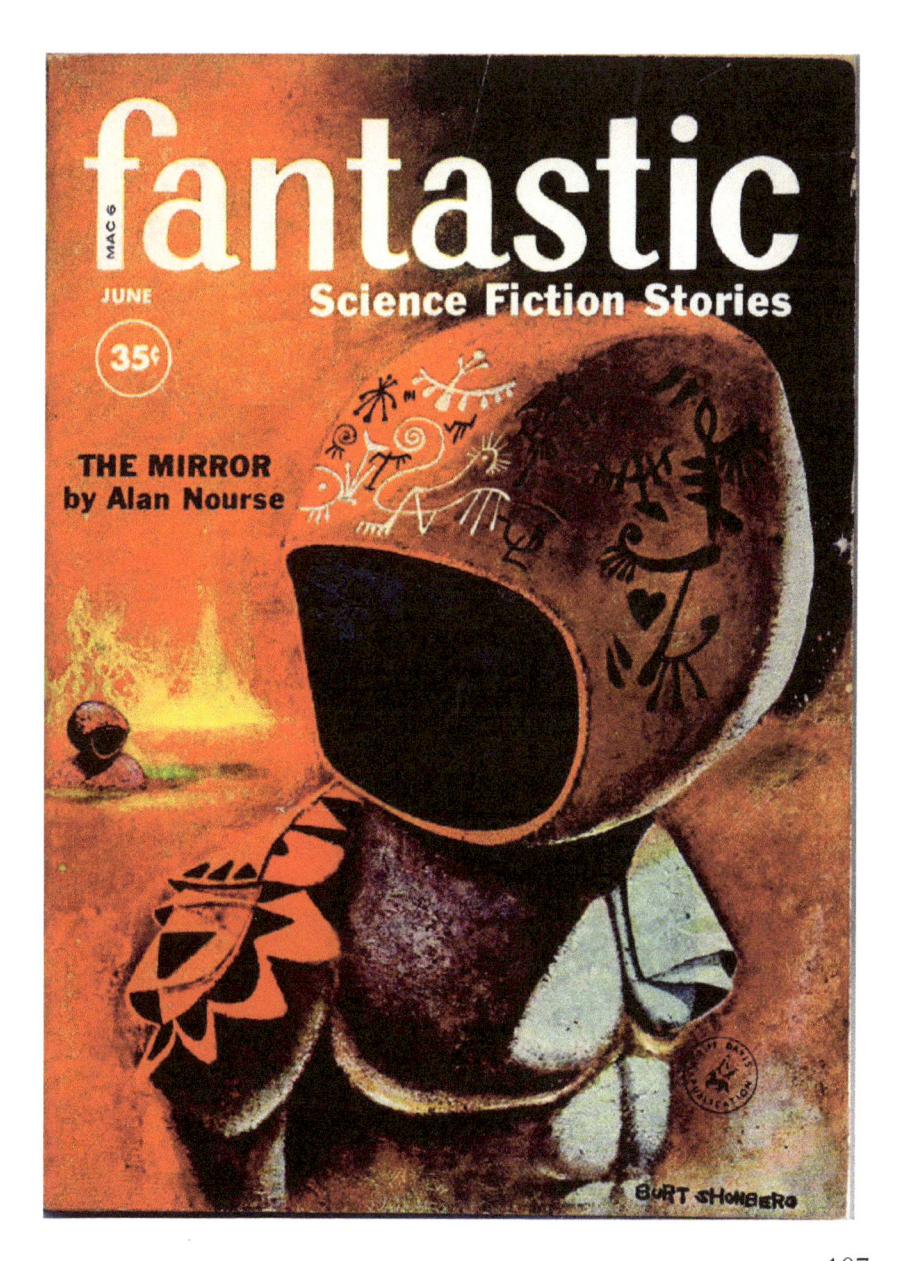

Burt's stunning front cover for *Fantastic* magazine. One of the glyphs looks very much like the alchemical symbol for reverberation.

A young Valerie singing with the Don Tosti band. (Courtesy of Julian and Louis Porter.)

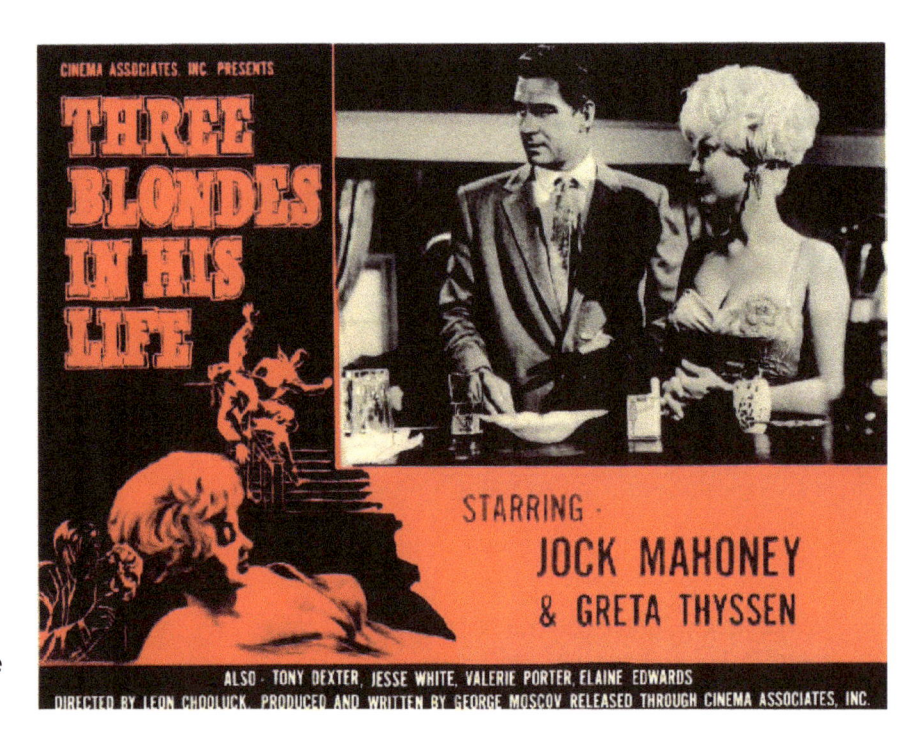

Valerie Porter featured on the *Tree Blondes in his Life* movie poster.

Earth Child. Casein on Masonite 2 ft x 3 ft. 1961. (From the private collection of Sheldon Jaman.)

> Burt Shonberg — LSD — Dec. 6, 1960
>
> The speeding up of the centers somehow slows everything else down so one may get a good look at how "things" really are. The phenomena of so called "passing time" does not exist. NOW IS ALWAYS HERE!!! Eternity is on the scene —— and is constant. Humanity is literally hypnotized in the "dream reality" of momentum caused by life (meaning external influences). There is an illusion of movement in life which is NOT the truth. This all relates to so-called time. Time is motion — is evolution. One might say that the BIG criminal in all of this is "identification". To be apart from the form is the answer to real vision — consciousness. To be awake is to be really alive — to really exist. It is the "I AM." And indeed, the real "I" is invisible, you are NOT your physical body or any thing else (ex. — your name — work — etc.…) The real "I" is an invisible energy that occupies and/or possesses a physical form to utilize as a vehicle to ride around in and do things through --- like flesh & bone & blood etc… is the clothes or costume (or form) that the real true self wears. "Consciousness" is APART from the form ———)
>
> Now, about the painting — After I was "on". The Cochina doll itself is like --- a dead wooden thing, a bent hollow dead figure with decorations and NO MEANING. Like --- nothing.
>
> I sort of painted a creature that was perhaps this doll's "GOD." Alive — fiery --- pagan --- evil --- and very dumb. All evil is LITTERLY dumb… dead, in motion, but somehow mechanical and going by itself for the purposes of it's own subjective desires… fullfilling it's own greedy needs --- no love.
>
> Anyhow, to hold a brush while on LSD was something else --- like it was a magic wand & I could create any kind of image I wanted. Each stroke was an experience which added up to the total painting, but to me it was NOT the finished painting that was important (like I could've painted it over flat black) but MUCH MORE IMPORTANT was the joy in painting --- itself.
>
> Thank you, Oscar
>
> Burt Shonberg

Burt's handwritten notes from his first LSD-25 session with Dr. Oscar Janiger on December 6th, 1960. (Courtesy of the Estate of Oscar Janiger.)

BURT SHONBERG ➡ *OUT THERE*

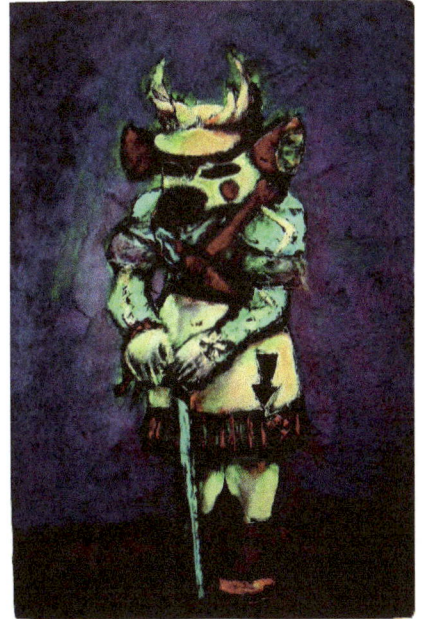

The abstract Burt painted while on LSD under Dr. Oscar Janiger's supervision. (Courtesy of the Estate of Oscar Janiger.)

Burt faithful rendition of Dr. Janiger's Hopi Deer Kachina doll, clearly completed in the period before the LSD was taken. (Courtesy of the Estate of Oscar Janiger.)

Burt's decorated window in his pad on 2222 Laurel Canyon Boulevard.
(Courtesy of Darryl Copeland.)

BURT SHONBERG ➡ OUT THERE

Burt's vision of the "Oriental" warlord in the sky, while on LSD.

Burt's vision of the gigantic, writhing woman, while on LSD.

Chapter 6
Baphomet

At first, Burt's exposure to LSD-25 proved an immensely positive experience, especially in the development of his artistry. It intensified the colour mixing of pigments on his palette and it inspired him to dive deeper into abstraction. Several self-portraits depicted featureless faces, denoting the disintegration of identity and ego, or his skull bathed in an effulgent glow, symbolizing his transcendent state of being. Burt also captured the common visual effect of "trailing," where a user is able to perceive each stage of movement whenever their hand, for example, passes across their field of vision, and new sketches revealed intricate worlds within worlds.

In 1962 the U.S. Congress passed a law handing control of investigational drugs, such as LSD-25, over to the Food and Drug Administration, and in reaction, Sandoz Pharmaceuticals began limiting its supply of the drug to only government-designated agencies, curtailing its usage among independent psychiatrists like Dr. Janiger. Despite these efforts, the drug was now available to buy on the black market and Burt tripped-out whenever he could get his hands on it. Concerns grew, however, that he was sacrificing his sanity on the altar of acid, and after viewing several of Burt's abstract pieces from this period, Hampton Fancher can discern the deranged and diabolical forces burbling beneath the impasto: "Those abstracts are Dantesque phantasms of drift and swirl, taking their cue from anatomy. They're more torture chamber than sky. Burt was disappearing into his vortex." This was confirmed when he began to tell friends he was being possessed by the preternatural entity Baphomet. The image of Baphomet, also known as The Goat of

Mendez, was originally conjured by the 19th-century occultist Eliphas Levi and featured in his seminal work *Dogmas and Rituals of High Magick* (a book Burt owned). In the occult world, Baphomet was revered as a divine androgyne, a unification of light and darkness, male and female and the macro and microcosm, yet alternative theories have abounded down the centuries concerning its genesis. Some Templar historians, for instance, believe the name was a corruption of the Muslim prophet Mohamed, created by turncoat Templars, who were allegedly seduced by Saracens and converted to Islam. While a competing notion maintains that Baphomet was the name given to a severed head the Templars worshiped, in veneration of John the Baptist, having discovered, during their travels through the Holy Land, that he was the true Christ figure – not the Nazarene. Regardless of where the truth lies, the final judgment of the Inquisition meant these renegade crusaders were condemned as Antichrists and executed. The belief that Baphomet is a pagan or Gnostic, pre-Christian deity, was one shared by Aleister Crowley, who adopted the name as an alias. In popular culture, however, the visage of Baphomet was often employed as a cinematic shorthand to denote the Devil in all his bestial majesty; and it was in this guise that Burt first visually deployed him, in one of the several new canvases commissioned by Roger Corman for his latest Poe-inspired movie, *The Premature Burial*. The painting in question is actually unveiled by the film's leading man, Ray Milland, whose character suffers from taphephobia, the fear of being buried alive. Titled *Sin Consummations Devoutly to Be Wished* (an epithet paraphrased from Hamlet's "To be, or not to be" monologue, in which the Prince of Denmark meditates on death), Baphomet looms large as a satanic overseer, perched on a mountain of skulls in a grisly hell-scape, where condemned souls are nailed to crosses; beheaded by guillotines; burnt at the stake, and over flaming cauldrons. While in the background, volcanoes belch smoke and brimstone into the atmosphere, as new arrivals rain down from a leaden sky.

For Hampton, Burt's embracing of Baphomet was a dismaying development. It was as if the mask of madness he once wore, during their merry days of pantomiming, had fastened and fused to his physiology, to become a very real part of his mental makeup. "Burt was flirting with his own insanity and he fell. He didn't have the discipline and intelligence to see what he was doing. It was like he was playing cowboys and Indians and then he becomes a cowboy, or in his case, Baphomet. He'd say, 'I am Baphomet and I know what you're thinking!'"

Burt could also use Baphomet to his advantage. According to Shep Sanders, another aspiring actor and chum, who'd also been a test patient of Dr. Janiger, when Burt was busted by the cops for drugs "he went into his insane act," and due to his maladjusted state, he was given the choice of either going to jail or the psych ward at the VA hospital. Burt chose the latter and was kept under observation until the headshrinkers were satisfied he was sane enough to leave. His pal George Clayton Johnson signed him out of the facility and took him back to his home in Pacoima to recuperate. "Burt was into being present, which he got from Gurdjieff and Ouspensky, and he had a certain level of awareness and this remarkable ability to stare. I'd seen the way he would fix his eyes on something, like leaves on a tree, and stare at it to see how he was going to paint it, but this was different. He would gaze at himself in the bathroom mirror for hours, and then he started drawing in there, he did a profile of a demonic face." (Quite possibly Baphomet's) "I ended up covering it but it's still there. He had gone through the LSD stuff with Janiger, and he'd sit in a quiet room and one of the walls would take a breath and it doubled his awareness of reality. Burt was at the forefront of this. But he was also fearful of going mad."

Hampton was kept abreast of Burt's condition through mutual friends, and believes he may have institutionalized himself "because he was scared or needed to be taken care of, or because Baphomet told him to." When the two met up again, following Burt's convalescence, Hampton introduced him to an anthropologist named Bill Smith, who was curious to meet Burt, having been told so many crazy stories about him. "Bill was a big influence on us and he was interested in making a record of Burt's madness," Hampton explains. At the next available opportunity, Hampton drove Burt over to Los Feliz, where Smith lived in a guesthouse on Cockerham Drive." It was there that Smith made a 45-minute tape recording of Burt, who imitated the voices inside his head and animated his transcendent experiences. "Burt was very theatrical," Hampton recollects. "He had no reluctance to show his stuff." For Bill Smith, Burt was as rare a specimen as anything he'd found while exploring through the Amazon, and he made a great scientific subject. But regrettably, the tape recording that was made was lost within the year.

Hampton was treated to another dose of Burt's delusionary state of mind after he handed him a battered copy of Alfred Bester's science fiction novel *The Stars My Destination*, which he'd read after finding it lying in a gutter one day.[1] The revenge fantasy, set in outer space in the 25th century, featured a lead character who had unlocked the secret of teleportation, known as "Jaunting." Hampton knew his friend would dig the intergalactic drama, and the next time they met, Burt was boasting how he'd already mastered the ability to "Jaunte" through space and time himself. "Burt had to be bigger than anything around him," Hampton explains. "He was looking for power in a way. He wanted to be God."

Clearly perturbed by his recent turn towards the satanic, biblical themes began to emerge in Burt's artwork, encompassing portraits of Jesus, and the Magi, and the Holy Cross of the Crucifixion. For Judy Shevin, this was all perfectly understandable: "Many people of Jewish origin, like Burt and myself, hold Jesus Christ in very high esteem. It's not to do with being Jewish or Christian, and it's not even to do with religion. We consider him as being one of the living prophets – the man!"

Another popular prophet in Southern California at the time was Jiddu Krishnamurti, and Burt sometimes accompanied the Shevins on the many trips they made out to his ashram in Ojai to listen to his meditations. For anyone working in the Fourth Way, Krishnamurti is highly respected," Judy explains. "He was a world teacher, and it was an amazing experience for us to hear him talk." Despite such peaceful interludes, the Shevins were painfully aware that Burt was in psychological trouble, and they were particularly unsettled when he claimed he'd been struck by lightning, which paralyzed his arm. "It just hung there, limp," Judy recollects. "Ray told me how, when Burt was living with him, he felt he was being bombarded with lightning and fires kept breaking out. This is why Burt couldn't truly be accepted by the Gurdjieff group because in The Work you have to be psychologically balanced and stable of mind, otherwise, it can tip you over and cause problems. The group felt it would be dangerous for Burt to partake in the inner exercises, meditation, and dances, despite his interest. It's a very demanding system. And though he embraced the ideas and studied the books, Burt lived in another realm. And his use of psychedelics was instrumental in pushing him over the edge. You can go into so many rooms inside yourself. Ray had gone on a mescaline trip with Gurdjieff people and when he came back we had a meeting with the head of The Work, Lord John Pentland, who was in town from London, to sit in with us. Ray was so excited to discuss his experiences on mescaline and he spoke about it and asked if there were any questions, and Lord Pentland said, 'Excuse me a moment, Mr. Shevin, there's something I want to discuss: it is possible to have a higher experience through the use of drugs but the continued use causes permanent scar tissue, so I discourage you from damaging your evolution.' Ray felt so exposed. Pentland said you can have one experience, but Burt had so many trips that it became very dangerous. I feel his psychedelic experimentation and his mental state wasn't anything rooted in reality – he'd become schizophrenic. He might have always been there, but it brought it out of him."

Not everyone associated with the Gurdjieff group was opposed to Burt's inclusion, however. Rosemary Vail entered into a casual but meaningful romance with him, a time she remembers with nothing but fondness: "Burt didn't talk much, but he was a spiritual master, and we were connected spiritually and psychically. He was attracted to the Fourth Way because it was about increasing and expanding consciousness – you see things differently, and he was a very visual guy. Inside, though, he was a bundle of nerves and there was a confusion about life and what it's all about. I could see it in his eyes. There was a knot inside him. We were lovers and he was a wonderful lover, very compassionate. He was easy to love; such a warm, magnetic person."

Burt was affectionate with Rosemary's young children, too, Bonnie and Edward, and during a trip to Venice Beach, where they attended a 'No More War Toys' sandcastle building event, he whisked up sketches for them, including one of a Romani Gypsy caravan. Rosemary was well aware of Burt's drug intake but she took a nuanced view: "He took too much LSD and got very out there, so there was some damage. But for someone on that level, the damage was an interesting thing."

Naturally, for those who were newly acquainted with him, Burt's spaced-out persona was a defining aspect of his identity and a major part of his allure. Sheldon Jaman was part of a growing gang of good-time guys and gals who had coalesced around Szou and Vito: "Our main attraction with Burt was his mind – he was far-out! He would see stuff we couldn't see, and we all looked up to him. I really respected him as one of the greatest artists. I had a hip apartment and thought his art would work with it. I also felt I was helping him by buying his work."

Sheldon was especially enamoured with a new series of Burt's paintings known as the "Stone People," that took their cue from Henry Moore's life-sized sculptures, particularly his 1938-piece *Recumbent Figure*. These portraits featured a race of hairless humanoids, with doleful expressions on their faces, who looked like they'd been chiselled from limestone. "Most of his paintings I bought for $300. My favourite is a piece called *Earth Child* – that one just gets to me."

At Schwab's drugstore – a place Burt now dubbed "Checkpoint Charlie in the *Twilight Zone*" (inspired by the popular TV series that George Clayton Johnson was now writing for), Burt hooked up with a new clique of chums, like the actor Stanley Dyrector, whose credits included the teensploitation flick *Dragstrip Girl*. "Burt was a unique figure there. He'd have his breakfast; he loved Worcestershire sauce on his eggs, and I would spring for the food. Food and money meant nothing to him. He would say, 'Food is just food' and 'bread will come when it will come,' like an existentialist. He was not extravagant with anything, and I was greatly influenced by him. He was an abstract kinda guy, with this other form of consciousness. Whereas I was on the straight and narrow; an ambitious actor. I had a purpose – to be a movie star – and when I met Burt I was going to showcase myself in a play, but he put my mind in another direction, in an esoteric way. I took it all very seriously. You had to be successful, and his idea, that success was not important, created a clash of worlds that affected me greatly. I thought more superficially, and Burt was the antithesis of that. Here's somebody who's contradicting everything I'd been brought up to believe in and it was a traumatic positive awakening. He pulled the rug from under my feet. For him, it was all about NOW. THE MOMENT. TO BE. This was not the life I had been brought up in, which was the standard capitalist ideal. He was proselyting Gurdjieff, but in a very subtle way, and he gave me a copy of Ouspensky's *In Search of the Miraculous*. I would do my acting thing for him, and he would be silent and then say,

"You have to be real!" I was still insecure, despite being in *M Squad* opposite Lee Marvin and Burt Reynolds. I asked Burt a lot of questions. I was very inquisitive, but he would say to me, 'I am not your guru!'"

Despite this admonition, there were lessons to be learned for Stanley, even when it came to taking drugs: "I'd had experiences with grass and peyote years before, when I'd gotten out of the navy, but Burt's thing was, if you were gonna smoke grass, you were to say, 'Who am I?' and let your higher being come through – and not be mechanical." Stanley subsequently bought two enigmatic, Fourth Way-inspired canvases from Burt; with their titles written on them. *To Be Is the Answer* was a split image of a medieval knight, his face riveted on like armour, standing outside a fortified encampment, juxtaposed against a serene skyscape. While *Who Am I? No Thing. Here. Now.* depicted a musclebound man with a pearlescent face, in a barren sandscape, dotted with drab abodes. Stanley spent hours in Schwab's with his friend, watching him nursing coffees and chain smoking Pall Malls, and there were many lighter moments between them. Stanley found some of Burt's vocabulary highly amusing, though other humour was deemed off-limits: "One of Burt's favourite words to put down someone's rhetoric was 'poppycock!' That kind of anachronistic word was something that Charles Coburn could've said in a 1930s movie. Yet, I remember a joke I told him about Jesus riding a mule on his way to the cross and then Jesus went the other way, and Burt took umbrage at that. There was a moralistic vein within him."

Because of his mercurial personality, Burt could often appear supremely self-assured and unfazed by anything. Robert Storr was a sound technician in the film industry, who first met Burt at his Laurel Canyon Boulevard pad, after being driven there by their mutual friends, Boyce Mosco and Johnny Ramos. It didn't take him long to understand why they treated him with such reverence: "I found Burt more than interesting," Storr recollects. "He had a lot of knowledge, and I was a

Fourth Way novice, so I listened more than I spoke. I was more of a disciple. He'd gone through stuff psychedelically, and the expansion of the mind is a spiritual experience. Burt spoke of Dr. Janiger often and he called LSD a 'field-trip upfront,' where you see some of the destination. You can get there, but you need training to live there. He said he felt it could be achieved 'on the natch,' but I felt you had to earn it."

Burt related one particularly interesting acid trip where he could hear the inner condition of a friend talking to him: "This guy came up to him and said, 'Man, I really need a woman!' But to Burt, the voice sounded really ghastly because he could hear the need and greed in him. I didn't turn onto LSD; I ate peyote and had a psychedelic experience that way, more natural, but I could relate. Burt was a psychic magnet – you were either attracted or repelled by him. He was too far out for most people, but I felt it was imperative that we met. He had a way of talking; an argot. He made a repetition of many things that, if you knew him, you'd hear day after day. Burt's dark side was light but people didn't understand because he'd cast his dialogue in Fourth Way oration. He would throw an imaginary tennis ball in the air and whack it with an imaginary racket and then put his fingers in his ears as if a bomb had gone off. People would say to me, 'Bob, you're a squirrel – you're always collecting nuts!'"

As with Hampton, the two men shared a youthful fandom for Captain Marvel: "It was the fact that Captain Marvel was vulnerable to attacks; his mortal vulnerability made him more human, I guess. The Fawcett Comics version was about Nazis and Egypt and the Crocodile Men, and Burt was very much into Egyptology." They shared a similar sense of humour too, and Storr enjoyed Burt's shaggy-dog stories. In one of them, he gave a glimpse of what life was like on the Eronbu ranch with Cameron: "Burt told me one day he found a tarantula arrogantly walking up the path towards him, and his reaction was, 'They're a mistake!'" Storr also dug the irony in Burt's cartoons, like the one of a monk sitting on a bus stop bench as a nabob drives by in a limo, but they both have the same thought bubble above their heads: "How can someone be so happy with so little?" And he still treasures the Christmas card Burt sent him: a sketch of a shrunken head on top of a Christmas tree with the inscription "A little head for Christmas."

Oftentimes Storr would meet up with Burt purely to go cruising; they'd get loaded and drive around the city together in his 1950 Plymouth: "Burt loved these excursions and would describe the car as 'an exploratory vehicle traversing the surface of the planet,' in his authoritative, stentorian tone. Some of his artworks are based on what we'd see in the hills we drove through. He'd speak about the dark area of architecture. He'd see a building without any windows and say, 'I wonder what's going on in there!'"

One architectural aspect Burt could never resist was a blank wall and, when the offer arose, he seized the chance to continue illuminating the town with his eye-catching visuals. For his next mural, he amalgamated the faux stained-glass look he deployed to such dramatic effect on the Cafe Frankenstein window with the mosaics found in those pictorial books on Classical Antiquity in a glorious fusion that became his trademark. Burt first applied this tessellated technique to the facade of the Purple Onion nightclub, which was currently being run by his old employer at the Unicorn, Herb Cohen. Painted on three 6-foot by 8-foot panels, and built up with brick and tile-shaped areas of colour, in a crazy paving style, it depicted a row of tapering brownstones, rendered in the Romanesque Revival style, facing onto a woodland. The streetscape was viewed from beneath an awning-covered portico, supported by a baroque column etched with petalled mandalas and, once finished, its patchwork pattern elicited a mesmerized response from those who gazed upon it, especially if they were stoned. Barry Feinstein, Burt's pal from Chez Paulette, was so impressed he used it as a backdrop;

posing members of The Modern Folk Quartet (who Herb Cohen was now managing) in front of it for the cover of their debut LP. And even amid the busy billboards and distracting marquees, Burt's masterwork stuck out as the main cynosure on the Sunset Strip. [2]

It was thanks to their mutual friendship with Hampton (not to mention their shared sexcapades with Valerie Porter), that Burt became buddies with Michael Greene, an imposing, six-foot-six-inch grifter, who'd gravitated to Southern California from San Francisco, where his gun-toting gangster father ran a mob-affiliated bar. Greene made his bankroll as a card shark, working the gambling tables in Gardena, in Los Angeles County, the poker capital of the country. Greene worked in partnership with his mentor, a "mechanic," who manipulated the cards, while he played the role of the "take off" man, the guy who made away with all the ill-gotten gains. Although he was caught in the act on occasion (and physically roughed up as a result), Greene was usually flush with money, and would generously treat Hampton and Burt to slap-up dinners, entertaining them with tales from his picaresque lifestyle. One story he related centred on how he would dress up in the uniform of an army sergeant and sneak into military bases, where he would hustle the soldiers out of their pay packets. Burt didn't always approve of what he heard and suggested Greene use his skills for roleplaying and subterfuge more legitimately by becoming an actor. Heeding his newfound friend's advice, Greene obtained an agent and, 18-months later, he made his acting debut playing a deputy U.S. Marshall in the TV Western series *The Dakotas*.

It was at this juncture that Cameron floated back into Burt's life. In the intervening years since they lived together at Eronbu, she'd entered into an ill-fated marriage that imploded not long after the honeymoon. She'd also relocated to Venice Beach, where she shot scenes for the mystery film *Night Tide*, in which she was memorably (type)cast as a water witch, dressed in widow's weeds, who was pursued by a matlow played by Dennis Hopper, who, incidentally, knew Burt and rated his artwork highly.

Like Hampton before him, Greene was not exactly impressed when he met Cameron: "She was very individualistic but I didn't like looking at her. I thought she was a witch! She was like Burt's spiritual mom. Burt was a crystal cruncher too, and he was crazy, but she was worse. When it was suggested that she or Burt undergo therapy, Cameron would say, 'Therapists!? There are no answers, just questions!' Burt might say that he didn't always take her seriously, but he would consent to her nevertheless."

Cameron's sensibility harkened back to the simpler Romantic period that was born partly in reaction to the advent of the Early-Industrial Revolution; a legacy of technological advancement that reached its apex with the satellites and manned spacecraft that now orbited the earth, but also its nadir with the almighty horror of the atomic bomb. Throughout the month of October 1962, the news cycle was dominated by America's tense military standoff with the Soviet Union, after it was discovered the Russians had surreptitiously installed ballistic missiles on the island of Cuba, at the behest of its communist dictator Fidel Castro. This geopolitical confrontation very nearly brought the planet to the brink of nuclear annihilation, but even before the drama of the Cuban Missile Crisis developed, the state of Mississippi was already on high alert at the start of that month, due to a smaller, though historically significant, conflict on the domestic front, when President Kennedy was forced to deploy 5,000 federal troops to the University of Mississippi to uell the violent protests led by segregationists opposed to the enrolment of James Meredith, the first black student to be accepted there. The following May, television cameras relayed appalling footage of civil rights protesters being lashed by water cannon and set upon by police dogs in Birmingham, Alabama, the same city where Martin Luther

King wrote his (now famous) Letter from Birmingham Jail, the previous month.

For Cameron – an avowed liberal (when that word really meant something) with a penchant for black lovers, such scenes were only a harbinger of an even more dire cataclysm to come and to evade the escalating chaos, she and Burt visualized their own interplanetary escape. "Cameron felt the culture was so fucked up and so out of control," Michael Greene explains. "For her, everything started to go wrong with the invention of the cotton gin, and living out in the desert was her way of protesting, rather than protesting in the street. She'd say, 'We've got to get off this planet! I wanna get away!' She wanted to escape the culture and for good reasons: it was so out of control that nobody knew what was going on, so it was better to be picked up by a flying saucer."

Burt was in lockstep with Cameron's concerns, and he travelled out to the Mojave Desert with her to wait for the saucers to take them away. "Burt was telling Ray the end of the world was coming," Judy confirms. And Hampton chimes: "Although I never saw him angry, except in an abstract way, this world was too much for Burt; too ugly and horrible. He wanted another world." This attitude was made manifest in his most recently published work; a truly out of this world portfolio he contributed to the November 1963 issue of *Gamma*, a digest for new, cutting edge fiction. There was almost a proto-steampunk element to these illustrations, which included a spaceman wearing riveted-together armour and a helmet visor that reflected the image of UFOs hovering over a desert-scape. A praying mantis-headed alien, wearing similar protective plating, gazing out of the window of its spacecraft upon an Earth-bound megalopolis below. A helmeted humanoid piloting the controls of another spaceship, whose viewport reveals a split-screen image of an Antarctic Research Station on legs and the pyramids at Giza. And, best of all, Baphomet, recast as a clairvoyant, holding a crystal ball in a curtained booth, while in a seemingly unrelated scene above, smokestacks billowed from a factory bearing a monstrous monkfish mouth.

Though Hampton accompanied Burt and Cameron on their UFO trip, he admits his heart wasn't really in it: "I kinda knew I was pretending. I'd grown out of it by then. It was no fun anymore, but Burt remained a total believer – and Cameron was avid." When the Martians failed to materialize; to beam them up and whisk them away to the Red Planet, a place Cameron considered her real home, Burt fled the country in a far more traditional fashion, embarking on his own unique version of The Grand Tour.

Burt's Purple Onion mural. Casein on Masonite. Painted on three 8 ft x 6 ft panels.

Burt's *Sin Consummations Devoutly To Be Wished* painting from *The Premature Burial*. (Courtesy of David DelValle.)

BURT SHONBERG ➡ OUT THERE

Ray Milland with Burt's *Sin Consummations Devoutly To Be Wished* painting in a still from *The Premature Burial*.

Another ghoulish Shonberg painting from *The Premature Burial*.

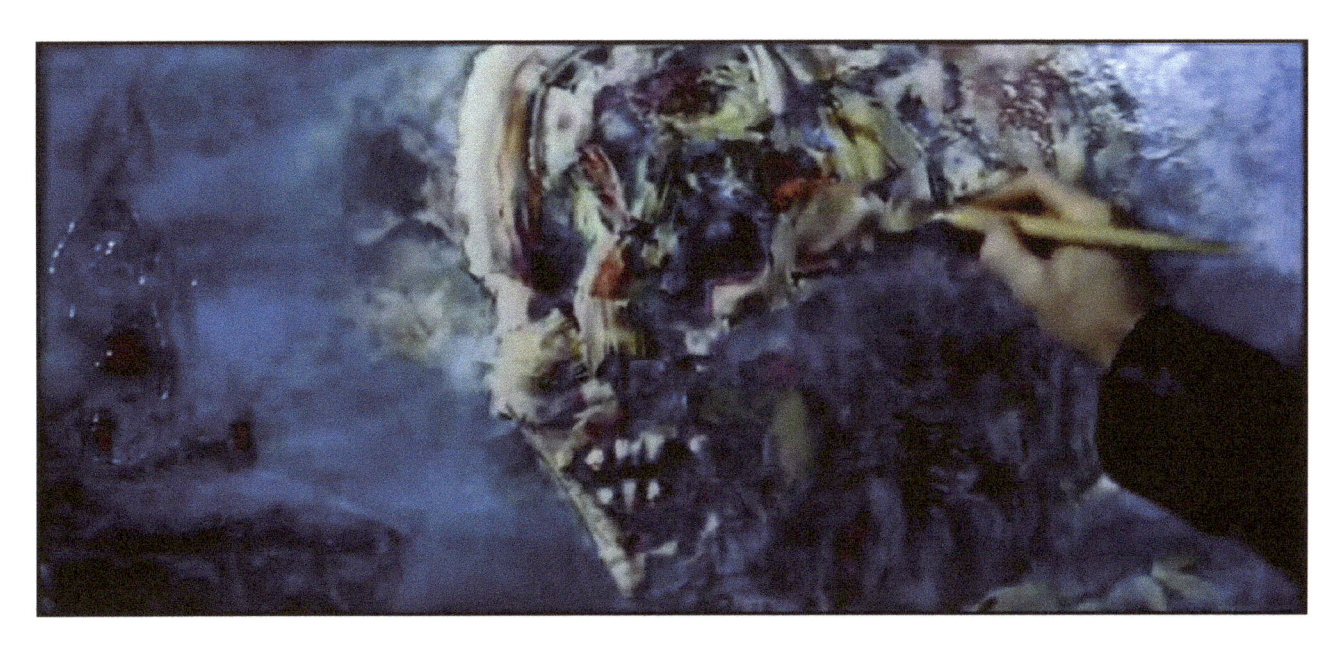

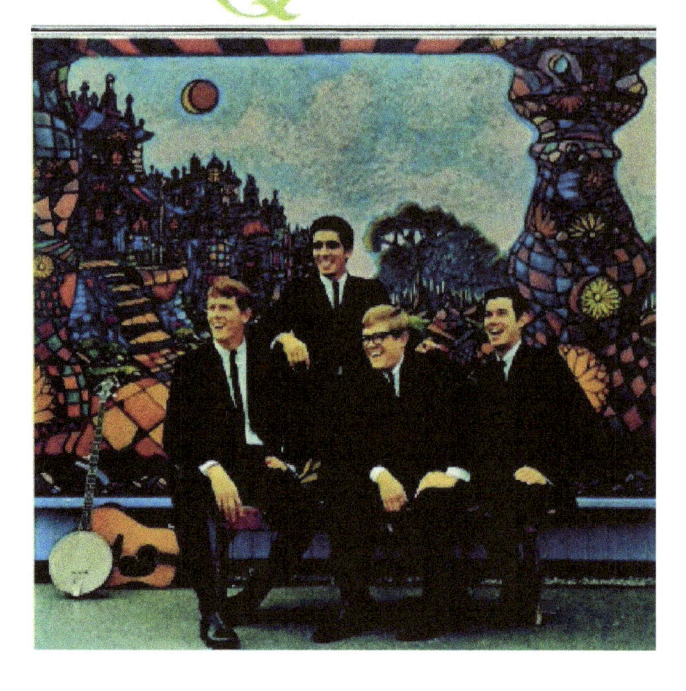

The Purple Onion mural used as a backdrop for The Modern Folk Quartet's debut album cover

A publicity still of Hampton Fancher for the film *Rome Adventure*. It was taken in 1963 just after he and Burt went their separate ways. Fancher's acting career was reaching new heights and he was about to enter into a much-publicized marriage to *Lolita* actress Sue Lyon. (Courtesy of Hampton Fancher.)

BURT SHONBERG ➡ OUT THERE

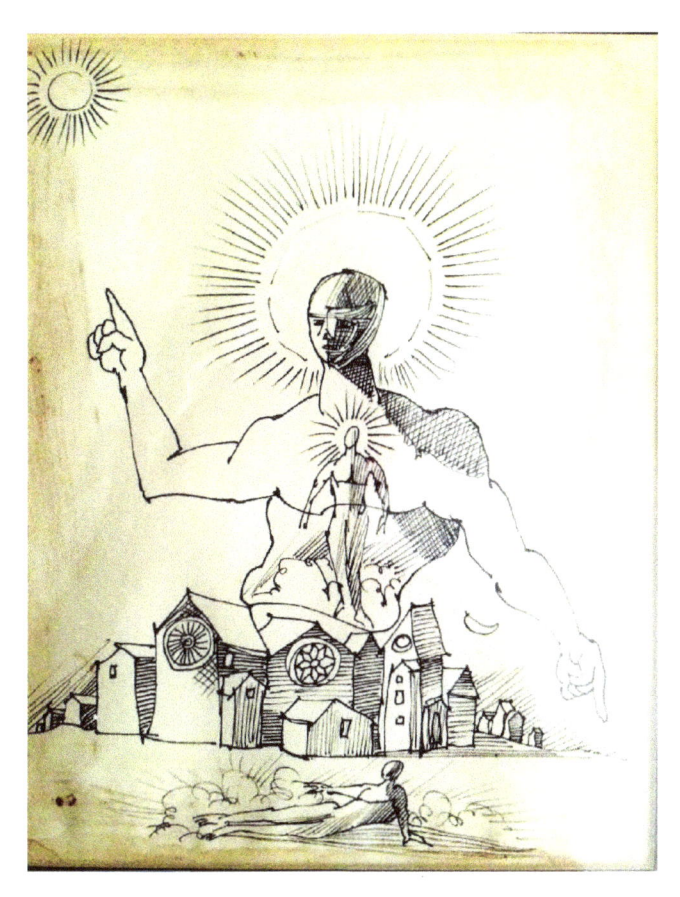

Burt's Baphomet-inspired drawing *As Above So Below*. (Courtesy of Marshall Berle.)

Cameron hanging on the telephone at Burt's pad on 2222 Laurel Canyon Boulevard. One of Burt's abstracts hangs on the wall behind her. (Courtesy of Darryl Copeland.)

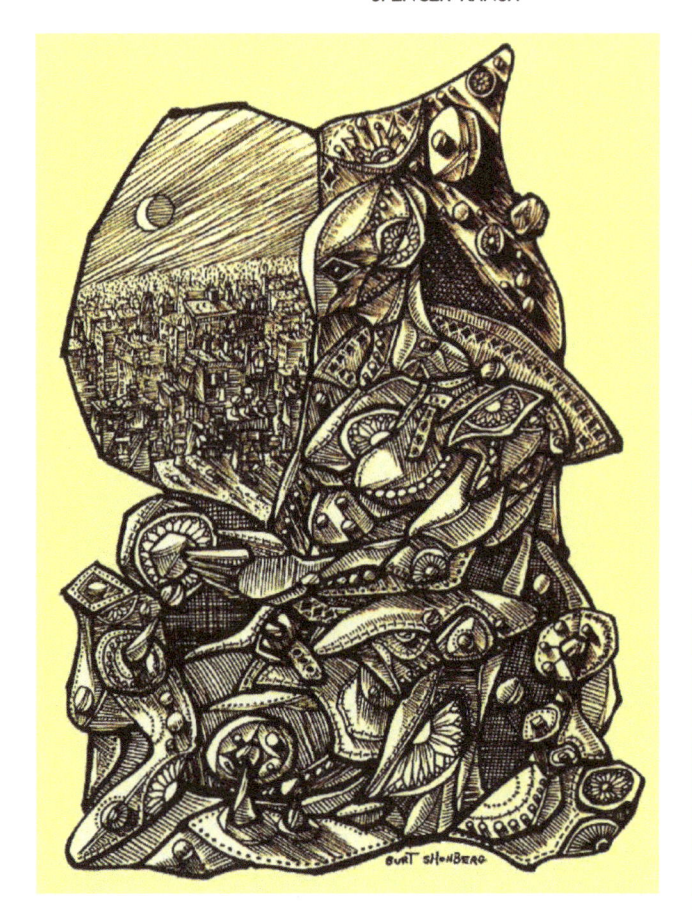

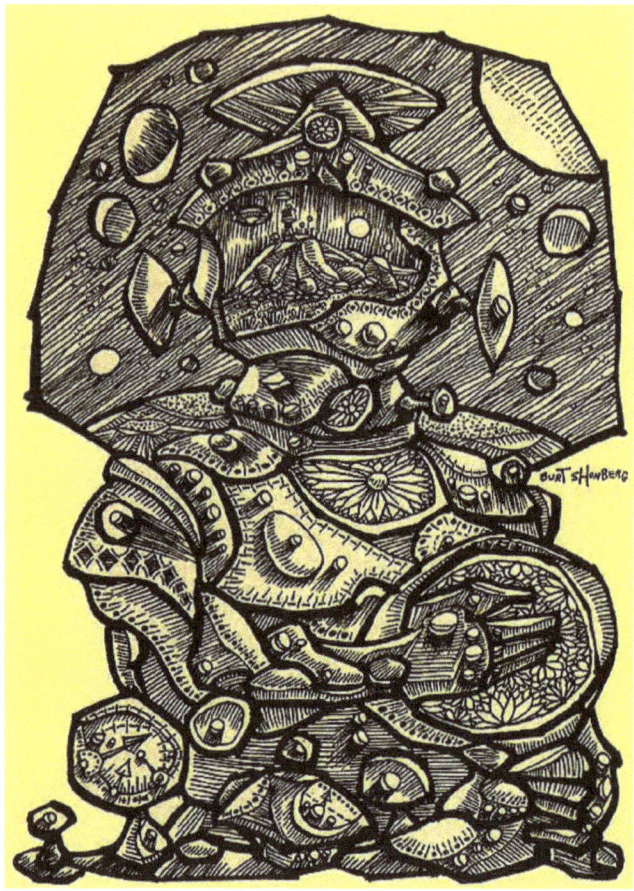

Burt's out of this world portfolio for *Gamma 2: New Frontiers in Fiction* 1963.

BURT SHONBERG ➡ *OUT THERE*

133

With his LSD-sharpened sensitivity, Burt felt riding shotgun in a car was like being in "an exploratory vehicle traversing the surface of the planet." (Courtesy of Szou Paulekas.)

Burt's gypsy caravan drawing for Rosemary Vail's children, Bonny and Eddie. (Courtesy of Bonnie Sussman.)

Chapter 7
Out (of) Here

As his reputation as a master muralist spread, Burt was offered further work, like decorating the bottom of swimming pools for several admiring homeowners. Ira Odessky swears that Burt made it appear as though his images were actually moving underwater, perhaps by cleverly distorting the perspective. There were also commissions requested by starlets, such as Joan Huntington, who used their portrait sitting as a way to buy themselves into the hip scene that Burt personified and they sorely wanted to feel a part of. Reportedly, it was a handsome payment from one such commission that enabled Burt to finance his first trip abroad. The greenbacks came courtesy of the music producer Lou Adler, who hired him to paint a portrait of his soon-to-be wife, the actress/singer Shelley Fabares. [1]

By the time they were married, in June 1964, Burt was already in transit. His first port of call was the Balearic island of Ibiza, an archipelago of Spain, that was fast becoming *the* Mediterranean destination for wayfaring bohemians and gadabouts. The location was popularized by a *Village Voice* article, two years earlier, which trumpeted the island as a new "Beatnik Paradise," where you could live the good life for not much scratch at all. In the proceeding decade, the White Island had been beggared by a famine that left native Ibencencos even more willing to roll out the welcome mat to tourists, even if they didn't quite know what to make of the funny-looking ones. For many first-time visitors, the experience of seeing the island's Old Town quarter emerge through the sea mist, as their ferry cruised into the harbour, was a sight to behold and, like them, Burt was knocked out by the picturesque vista of whitewashed villas stacked up on the hillside, crowned by the island's 16th-century castle. As passengers descended the gangplank, they were greeted by locals throwing toilet roll streamers and offering them places to stay. For Burt, this meant a charming villa in Casta Baratas (cheap housing) located two miles outside of town, which, despite its name, at a thousand pesetas a month, was a far pricier place to stay than if he'd chosen a nearby pensione in town.

During the 1930s and '40s, Ibiza provided sanctuary for left-wing artists and Jewish intellectuals fleeing Nazi Germany, and these aesthetes-in-exile laid the foundations for the art colony it was to become. In more recent times, the avant-garde collective Grupo Ibiza 59 was inaugurated there, and it was home to an already established circle of mostly European abstractionists associated with the El Corsario gallery. The artist and gallerist Ivan Spence was another dominant figure on that scene, and the island's artistic reputation was bolstered further that year when it held its first ever Biennale. Although none of Burt's pictures were exhibited, a couple of his latest canvases, *The Seventh Ray in the Ray of Creation* and *The Unveiling*, were imbued with the blazing spectra of light that lured so many painters to the island in the first place. In fact, with no friends to distract him from his work, and speed tablets available to buy over the counter, his time in Ibiza proved immensely productive. A couple of simple ink wash drawings of haunted faces gazing up at the sky, as though they were about to be raptured up into an alien spacecraft, underlined how making contact with an extraterrestrial intelligence remained uppermost in his thoughts. But his most widely admired work during his time on the island was the monochromatic mural he painted on the interior walls of the Domino, a basement bar on the waterfront, that became his main hangout during his stay. The place was owned by British businessman Clive Crocker but run by an ex-patriot Englishwoman Sally Enright and her partner Luis, a local Ibizan, whose friends took turns making unsuccessful passes at her. The bar – originally a storage shed where local fisherman kept their nets and net mending equipment – was situated below sea level and only 100 yards from the edge of the harbour where the ferries would tie-up, so when the weather was bad or there was a particularly strong incoming tide, seawater flooded the toilet and floor. The Domino possessed a first-rate jazz collection (Billie Holiday, Miles Davis, John Coltrane, Jimmy Smith and Ornette Coleman) and boasted a colourful clientele including British thespians such as Denholm Elliot, the gap-toothed comedy cad Terry-Thomas, and Jon Pertwee (six years prior to becoming the third incarnation of Doctor Who), as well as other far more roguish regulars, like the notorious art forger Elmyr de Hory and his pal, the novelist Clifford Irving, who brought him worldwide attention via his biography *Fake*. "Elmyr was part of an old-fashioned gay crowd who wore white linen suits and Panama hats," Sally Enright explains. "The young model Nico was also around before she met Warhol. She was sweet but dim, and her mother was with her all the time, acting as her chaperone." Though it's hard for her to say if Burt had any interaction with these celebrity customers, Enright confirms: "There was no division socially of who you talked to and didn't, or who you sat down with and talked to and got drunk with. When Ursula Andress came in they all wanted to letch."

With money tight, Burt was once again reduced to selling napkin art to tourists to pay for his breakfast, until he approached Enright with an offer: "Burt must have fallen into a temporary cash-flow problem," she recollects, "most of us did from time to time, but he laid out a deal whereby he would paint murals on our plain whitewashed walls in return for an open-ended credit at the bar. At that time, we were pretty much the only nightlife hangout for the foreign community, so any and all social life depended on being there. Anyway, what the hell, he was a sweet, quiet kind of guy and we liked him." To help fuel his creative firepower for the job, Burt popped amphetamines: "They were these little tubes with tiny pills and everyone I knew had a tube of them," Enright explains. "I was working 17 hours a day so they kept me going." Outside the bar, he anointed the entrance with a sunrise motif and wrote out the name of the bar beneath it. Inside, using only bold, black brushstrokes he recaptured some of the scenes he'd witnessed during his stay: local fishermen catching and bringing home their daily haul; windmills, watchtowers and farmhouses with sloped roofs glimpsed in the outlying countryside; farmers tending their fields, and women picking the harvest from the olive groves. "Burt did the whole thing completely freehand," Enright confirms, "and while he was doing it we would chat and laugh. He was a sweet guy. I liked his style; his quiet positivity. He made me laugh and he had a good aura. I thought the mural was witty and decorative and some of the clientele would while away an hour or so seeing their own stories. It was all black and white and yet it brought a lot of life into the place. And, much to my delight, the punters liked it, with almost no exception. People who got drunk or came in stoned had great fun staring at the pictures and making up stories. Part of our clientele were local fishermen, who were quite a rough lot, but they loved the paintings, and they would point things out in it, which was intriguing to me because they weren't art aficionados." [2]

An even more perfect solution to Burt's money woes showed up when Valerie Porter breezed into town. She'd been holidaying in Italy, celebrating the breakup of her dysfunctional marriage, which reached rock-bottom when her long-suffering husband committed her to the Camarillo State Hospital. There she was administered electroconvulsive therapy, in the hope that it might correct her (nympho)mania and curb her adulterous ways. In reality, the treatment only served to exacerbate her hypersexuality and make her even more of an exhibitionist, and seething over the year she lost in the snake pit, she initiated a divorce. When Valerie got word that Burt was hanging out in Ibiza, she made a beeline for him. On the boat journey en route to Spain, she seduced a

Catholic priest, who for her embodied the ultimate sexual challenge. Reportedly, Valerie fucked him on deck, in full view of her fellow passengers, who were so outraged by their display, they pelted the brazen couple with rocks and stones once they disembarked.

For Rod Salmons, a 20-year-old American ex-serviceman, who'd recently arrived on the island straight from his military base in Germany, Burt's cache was considerably enhanced with Valerie now on his arm. The budding beatnik met the couple several times on the terrace of Cafe Montesol, on the main drag, where hipsters gathered for their morning coffee: "Interesting people would just walk up to each other," he recollects, "there wasn't a tourist scene at that time. People were just passing through. Burt wasn't outstanding looking, but I never forgot his face. He was very laid back, totally unpretentious and unassuming. He seemed a cool guy and was happy to be there. He didn't look cool – he was dressed in off-white shirt and shorts and flip flops – but he was cool on the inside. He seemed completely sane and healthy; not spaced-out. Then Valerie showed up, a lovely looking woman, who seemed to have a touch of class to her, and she gave Burt a kiss on the cheek. And I thought Wow! The life of an artist. {laughs} For me, this was how life should be."

With Valerie's deep pockets, the couple enjoyed a series of trips together. In August, they travelled to Barcelona where they took in such cultural delights as the *Three Nude Statues with Fountain* at Placa De Lesseps and Park Güell, a public space designed by the city's beloved architect Antoni Gaudi, showcasing his beautiful baroque follies and technicoloured mosaics. Stimulated by the spectacle, Burt based a painting on the portal of the Gaudi tower in the park, and another on the Nativity Façade of Gaudi's stunning *La Sagrada Familia*, although Burt's cathedral came complete with flags and turrets.

Then, while they were cruising up the Spanish coastline, they were invited, as part of a group of lucky tourists, to have an audience with

Salvador Dali at his chateau in Port Lligat. When Dali discovered Burt was an artist, he presented him with a blank canvas to use and, thereafter, Burt began referring to himself as a "living surrealist."

Throughout October and November, they explored Morocco, traveling down from Tangier to Marrakesh; both popular pickup points to score and smuggle back kif (Moroccan hashish). They then spent a romantic Christmas and New Years in Paris, staying at the shabby Hotel du Mont Blanc in the Latin Quarter. It was a raucous area, especially at night, but it was close to everything. From there, Burt wrote postcards home, including one to Sheldon Jaman that read: "Hi Shelly, the reality of Paris is sheer fantasy – a magical city. Unhip impressionists depict the place. Walk the streets till dawn. All night cafes. Say hello to the gang." While in a postcard to the Shevins, Burt related how he'd met a New York book publisher in town, who expressed an interest in producing a monograph of his artwork, as it related to the expansion of consciousness. On a separate postcard, he depicted the physiological experience "of a point in (the) back of (the) head opening" as his higher consciousness was jettisoned, using three, small comic strip panels. He then ended his other postcard with the strange words: BORIC IL FUD. A greeting in an extraterrestrial tongue he'd recently invented. By the time these postcards were sent, the end of January 1965, the lovebirds were back in Ibiza, where they resided for a further six months. During that time, Burt completed his first *Magic Ship* composition, an ongoing series of paintings in which the viewer looked out, often from a villa supported by the same baroque columns that graced the Purple Onion mural, onto a moonlit harbour where a Magic Ship was moored. In this instance, however, the ship was viewed from a riverbank by an olive tree, whose trunk was embroidered with one of Burt's patented flower mandalas. While in the background, Burt captured the twinkling lights of Ibiza town, as seen from the other side of the harbour. Although the sails of the ships in subsequent paintings were heavily decorated, this first one featured only one harlequin-patterned sail and another emblazoned with the plasma bubbling surface of the Sun. Inspiration for the series may have derived from the poetic lyricism of Bob Dylan, who spoke of "swirling magic ships" on Mr. Tambourine Man, a recent hit single for The Byrds, and sung of "ships with tattooed sails" on Gates of Eden, one of the many mini-masterpieces on his current album, *Bringing It All Back Home*. Ensconced back at his villa in Casta Baratas, Burt befriended Patrick Burnham, a clean-cut American neighbour, who lived two doors down. Burnham had studied sculpture at Bordeaux University and was earning his keep by painting portraits, working on boats, and picking grapes. "I had a terrace and Burt would come around for drinks. I was never into drugs, but he was into marijuana and speed, and people were crawling around with amyl nitrate. You wouldn't see him in the morning because he was always working and he painted a lot of his pictures when he was high. Valerie was very good looking and ACDC, and she chased, unsuccessfully, after my girlfriend, a Dutch girl called Jo-Anka. Other than the Domino, there were hardly any other bars around, so I thought I'd open one in a very nice property and call it Babylon Square." To advertise the joint, Burnham asked Burt to create a poster, which he did, of a wailing saxophonist silhouetted by a giant, blazing sun. The idea was to print flyers using Burt's design and drop them from an airplane over the town, but, unfortunately, that's as far as the venture went.

Although Burt never developed a taste for alcohol, he was keen to sample absinthe, which was available to buy in bars and local bodegas. The green aniseed-flavoured drink – beloved by masters like Picasso, Van Gogh and Toulouse-Lautrec, as well the decadent poets Baudelaire, Verlaine, and Rimbaud – was said to possess hallucinatory properties, due to its wormwood ingredient, and when Burt tried it, the Green Fairy knocked him flat on his back. "There were two groups at that time: the potheads and the lushes," Burnham explains, "and they usually went to different bars. Burt frequented the Estrella bar sometimes but he was more likely to be seen at Arlene's La Tierra bar. The Estrella was mainly for writers, with the novelist Steve Seley being the leader. I'm sure I drank absinthe with Burt, but I tried to leave the stuff alone as it was extremely strong." Sally Enright corroborates how a division existed between those who smoked and those that drank and adds that even in the rowdy Domino bar: "You had to pick your culture. I couldn't let anyone smoke marijuana inside the bar because the cops would drop by to have a drink, but we had a terrace outside for smoking."

Paradoxically, given the islands proud history of offering sanctuary to Jewish refugees during the Second World War, in more recent times, Spain and its attendant islands – which were still ruled by the military dictatorship of Generalissimo Franco – became an appealing destination for German holidaymakers of a particular vintage, who felt nostalgic for a time when their own country was governed by an authoritarian tyrant. [3]

In fact, during his own initial voyage to the island, on the Trasmediterranea ferry from Barcelona, Burt had struck lucky with a gorgeous German girl, who referred to him affectionately as "my hairy snowflake." When they retired to her cabin for the evening, Burt's passion was chilled, momentarily, when he gulped at the photograph on the nightstand, revealing the young woman's father decked out in his SS uniform. Burt's bar-hopping and brief flirtation with booze occasionally brought him in contact with some inebriated Aryans who were not averse to letting slip some nasty, anti-Semitic comments. Sally believes these bigots Burt mistook for Germans were actually Swedes: "We had a bunch of Swedish guys – who were not blameless during the war either – and they looked like Hitler youth and were drunk at all times, day and night. And I can well imagine one of them saying something. But I'd have thrown them out if I'd heard them. I was extremely anti-German because the buggers had dropped bombs on us. The novelist Stephen Seley was a very good friend of mine. He knew everybody and they knew him, and he would say the most outrageous things. One night a German left the door open and he bellowed, 'Shut that fucking door! Haven't you had enough practice with oven doors?!'"

Though Burt had intended to return home to Los Angeles with Valerie that summer, his plan changed when he heard (perhaps from the book publisher he met in Paris or via the bulletin boards in the back pages of the *Village Voice*) about a forthcoming exhibition being held in New York. The event was billed as the first ever "show of psychological and psychedelic paintings, drawings, and assemblages," and it was organized by the artist Isaac Abrams and his wife Rachel at their Coda Gallery on East 10th Street. Abrams can't quite remember how, but Burt got in touch with him, offering his wares, and he accepted, adding him to their roster of artists that currently included Robert Yasuda, Arlene Sklar-Weinstein, and Allen Atwell.

Because he'd been so prolific during his European sojourn, Burt had accumulated a lot of work, and though some of the larger pictures were shipped back to the States, he couldn't afford to send them all. After sorting out what ones he would take with him to New York, he generously donated the rest, including two to Patrick Burnham: "Burt was not a very good businessman. He'd just give pieces away." A small drawing, titled *In the Walls of Things*, appears to have been prompted by the military pillboxes and lookout towers Burt spotted on the island, and Burnham was overjoyed when his friend left him the *Magic Ship*: "It was painted on the rough side of the hardboard, giving it an interesting texture. And for the sea and sky, he used a palette for layering the paint, giving it an unusual effect."

Days before the June 5th opening, Burt arrived in Manhattan, found a crash pad in Greenwich Village, and pitched up at the gallery to confab with the owners over what he could show. "There was some contention over whether Burt's work was psychedelic or abstract – I thought it was both," Abrams recalls. "But it was good and strong." At the gallery, Burt met Jeri Elam, daughter of western movie actor Jack Elam, whose work was also being exhibited. The two had met years previously in L.A. when she waitressed at the Unicorn. "My father always discouraged me from entering show business, as it's so unpredictable and up and down, so I ended up going in another direction: I became an artist, started doing drugs and dropping out. Burt and I were both into psychedelics, but he was the most famous artist in the exhibit. I was lesser known."

Although the show sounded exciting, the two of them were anxious nobody would show up, as there were no signs in the gallery to indicate anything was going on. So, to help advertise it, Burt designed a poster. "He made it in an hour, that's why there's misspelled words because he was doing it so quickly. And we put it inside the door of the gallery." The poster was quartered into four separate cartoon panels, with each one externalizing how the inner sensation of dropping LSD felt, over four progressive stages. The first image depicted a man's head in normal repose, but by the second and third drawings his features were rattled and his skull warped until the final panel revealed the man's visage completely ablaze as the LSD hit home. (This image predates R. Crumb's famous Stoned Agin! comic strip turned poster by six years. And Crumb's similarly-themed cartoon – a wordless sequence of six frames in which a hippie's head melts into gloop from the effects of dope – is executed in a far more vulgar fashion.) Ultimately, the poster proved surplus to requirement, as the gallery was besieged by so many visitors cops were deployed to keep control of them outside.

As part of the proceedings, each painter was asked to explain their artistic vision and, according to Jeri Elam, "Burt was the most eloquent and verbal." Attendees on opening night included such countercultural bellwethers as Allen Ginsberg and Andy Warhol, who cut through the crowds flanked by his black-clad entourage. But arguably the biggest draw was Timothy Leary, who had risen to national prominence, alongside his fellow former Harvard professor Richard Alpert, as one of the principal proselytizers of LSD, with public pronouncements that praised the drug's ability to "turn you off from the outside world and put you in tune with the divinity within." Leary was one of a group of speakers who'd been invited to lecture at a seminar held in conjunction with the show, and he'd descended from his Millbrook mansion in Upstate New York with several communards in tow, including Michael Hollingshead, LSD's éminence grise, who read some LSD-inspired poetry and dispensed sugar cubes laced with acid to the artists and some members of the audience. (Shortly after the show, Hollingshead decamped to Swinging London, with a mayonnaise jar full of 5,000 trips, that he used to turn on some of the capital's cultural luminaries, including members of The Beatles and the Stones. Their experiences with the drug profoundly altered the song structure of popular music and heralded the advent of acid rock.)

Although Drug Enforcement Agents showed up at the gallery that evening, flashing their IDs, they found they were powerless to do anything as the LSD being consumed were not (yet) illegal. After the show, Burt, Jeri and others celebrated at a club, but despite all the big wheels and hoopla, the exhibition's three-week run ended without any of the artworks being sold.

Nevertheless, inspired by his conversation with the book publisher in Paris, Burt set down on paper a lucid record of his transcendental excursions that he entitled *Out Here*. It began with the daily blasts of cosmic consciousness that first assailed him in 1957, to his exposure to LSD-25 under the watchful eye of Dr. Janiger. He evoked scenes using straightforward felt pen sketches, with an eye to turning his efforts into a published book, but no takers were forthcoming and the project was shelved.

Before returning home to L.A., Burt paid a rare visit to Revere to look in on his folks, and for his 11-year-old cousin, Stephen Schrater, his unexpected homecoming felt like a visitation from Elvis: "Burt was a handsome guy, and though we didn't have a one-on-one, we kept in touch because he would send me tubes containing pictures for my birthday and bar mitzvah, with these strange designs." The jubilant mood fizzled out, however, when the adult members of the family observed Burt's bizarro behaviour, triggered by the LSD he'd been given in New York. Dolly's heart sank when she realized how mentally unsound her cousin was: "Burt was crazy when he came here – his brains were scrambled. He was not the same person. He'd point at a table in the room and say, 'Y'know, that table can talk!' and he really believed it. He told us about living in Ibiza and taking LSD and meeting Timothy Leary, who was a big personality at that time, but I was a young mother from a small town and didn't know about that life. Only in later years have I broadened out into who I am now, but back then it was a whole different world. The man Burt had become was not the man I knew. It seemed the LSD was destroying him mentally. I cared about him, so I wanted to take him to the state institution here in Massachusetts to get help, but you can't sign a person in without their consent – they have rights! And then Burt left."

Burt standing on the pier with Ibiza old town in the background.
(Courtesy of Julian and Louis Porter.)

Burt outside the Domino Bar in Ibiza, with Valerie, Sally Enright, and her twin boys, Niall and Shane. You can see a glimpse of the mural he painted in the bar behind them. Although he was responsible for the sunrise motif and lettering above the entrance, the actual dominoes on the wall were a holdover from when the bar first opened.

In *The Unveiling* Burt captured divine emanations present in the sunbeams blazing over the local Ibizan hilltops. Casein on Masonite.
(Courtesy of Marshall Berle.)

Haunted faces about to be beamed up. *Who Goes There?* Ink wash on Bristol board. Ibiza. (Courtesy of Marshall Berle.)

Magic Ship. Ibiza (Courtesy of Patrick Burnham.)

Burt's poster/flyer for the Babylon Square bar that never was.

Valerie, Ibiza bound, at the prow of a ship. (Courtesy of Julian and Louis Porter.)

Burt in Morocco.
(Courtesy of Julian and Louis Porter.)

Burt with friends in Europe. Sally Enright believes it might have been taken at the Plaça Reial, just off the Ramblas, in Barcelona.
(Courtesy of Julian and Louis Porter.)

BURT SHONBERG ➡ OUT THERE

Burt with a pair of Moroccan *El aguadors*;
water bearers/sellers.
(Courtesy of Darryl Copeland.)

Burt and Valerie: Lovers in Europe.
(Courtesy of Julian and Louis Porter.)

Burt and Valerie: A kiss among the bollards.
(Courtesy of Julian and Louis Porter.)

BURT SHONBERG ➡ *OUT THERE*

Painting of a cathedral inspired by Burt's visit to Park Güell: a public space in Barcelona, dedicated to the city's beloved architect Antoni Gaudi. 1963. Casein on Masonite. 3 ft x 4 ft. (From the private collection of Sheldon Jaman.)

Burt's poster advertising the psychedelic exhibition in New York. Thankfully, Jeri Elam had the presence of mind to ask Burt if she could keep it as a memento.

Chapter 8
Super Chief

Back in L.A., Burt moved into a new pad in Laurel Canyon, a studio apartment on stilts at 8309 Kirkwood Drive. While catching up with pals like Bob Storr, he related tales of his time abroad, including his uncomfortable encounters with those Aryan anti-Semites: "Burt told me there were lots of Germans there – *über stärkers* – great, strong ones, and he was startled to see how many of them looked as if they were products of a eugenics program. They would call loudly down the length of the bar their deprecatory comments if, for instance, someone mentioned Jews in a favourable light, '*Alles für der Juden, ja?*' (Everything for the Jews, yes?) All I can say is it's a good thing for them that Lenny Bruce wasn't there."

Burt would walk or hitchhike down the hill from his crib to chow down at Schwab's drugstore, where he reconnected with Stanley Dyrector: "Burt gave me a big hug. He was so joyful to see me." Stanley, it turned out, was now living just across from Burt on Kirkwood, and being neighbours, they hung out at all hours: "Laurel Canyon had a mystique back then. It was an idyllic era. Burt would paint at night with just a reddish light on, and it was a very surreal experience. He'd created a space. I'm an average Joe, but it was like being in a different land there. He had this unique, eclectic style, a certain rhythm when he looked at a painting. He'd step back for a moment, then go back in with his brush held like a spear in his hand. He had a certain posture and a way of gesturing. Burt would talk about Gurdjieff's "magnetic center" and it affected his hand movements and gait. He was a universe unto himself."

It just so happened that Rosemary Vail was also living nearby on

Kirkwood, and they readily rekindled their relationship. She too watched him as he painted, this time on a 2 by 4-foot *Magic Ship*, its three sails emblazoned with an Easter Island head, a lotus flower, and a sandstone ksar that Burt would've seen during his travels in Morocco. Burt gifted her the finished work, but despite this loving gesture, their love affair ended acrimoniously soon after: "The last time I saw Burt we went to the beach – he loved beaches, they calmed and warmed him – but we had a fight." Rosemary was concerned that Burt's brilliance was being taken advantage of: "A lot of people exploited him but he wasn't interested in money at all. He seemed oblivious to all that. He wanted to be free of the accoutrements of daily living. So, we went home and he was silent. He didn't involve himself in warfare and I was a biddy complaining that he never defended himself, even if he was angry. He just radiated negativity."

On Sunday, September 19th, 1965, several of Burt's artworks were shown at the newly opened American Freedoms Gallery in Topanga Canyon, as part of a group show entitled *The Psychedelic Viewpoint*. The gallery was the brainchild of Edward Lewis, a 23-year-old black cat from the wrong side of the tracks, whose crime-ridden youth resulted in a string of prison sentences. He finally sought some order to his wayward life by joining the Muslim Brotherhood, but when that didn't work out he became a short-lived member of the Communist Party, before finally chancing his arm in the boxing ring. But his life truly changed after he experienced an LSD-induced epiphany that turned his mind away from dogma-driven institutions and the brutality of the fight game to the creative and redemptive properties of art. And the inaugural exhibition he organized featured some of Lewis' primitivistic work, as well as paintings by Burt's pal Michael Greene, and the artists' Fred Adams and Richard Klix.

As a curtain-raiser to the event, Richard Alpert delivered an outdoor lecture in which he sang the praises of LSD to an audience of several hundred people (that most likely included Burt) in Topanga Canyon Park. At the end of his speech, Vito was invited to give a counterargument in which he outlined the political reasons why he was against the drug, warning how its usage would only fog the minds of those protesting the Vietnam War. He also accused Alpert of condoning the use of drugs by American soldiers in Vietnam, as he contended it only alleviated their guilt over slaughtering innocent civilians. Furthermore, he denounced the virtues of LSD as an aid to creativity: "Vito made the point that you needed to have your wits about you when you created art, in order that everything went right," Szou stresses. "You couldn't do it with a different consciousness that was promoted by drugs." [1]

One of the interesting paradoxes about Burt was that although he struck many as a solitary guy deep down, he remained, at the same time, a social butterfly who flitted easily from one group to another. As a result, he'd accrued a wide array of friends, from all different stations in life, and was rarely stuck for company. This was particularly true for the memorable year he shared his cramped quarters with Joe Steck, a successful lawyer in the straight world, who prided himself on never having lost a case. Yet despite his worldly achievements, he'd become disenchanted with his profession and, feeling unfulfilled, he abandoned it to a pursue a more creative life as a writer. Steck was also going through the breakup of his marriage at the time, and instead of buying a new home, he moved in with Burt to soak up some true bohemian atmosphere. "I was very fond of Burt – he was a unique human, as well as a personal joy, and we never had a cross word. We had a rapport. We would discuss his paintings and talk about art but always in an immediate way. Burt was more of an intellectual than people gave him credit for. He knew about general movements of art, like the impressionists, and how they were influenced by Japanese calligraphy. And he knew about primitive art and Buddhist sand paintings. Greco-Roman art was an obvious influence on his work at the time. There's a symbiotic relationship between poets and painters. Often a poet can give an artist the words he cannot find himself – it's one of the reasons why they paint." Steck couldn't have picked a better place to drop out either. "Laurel Canyon was the centre of a lot of things: artists, writers, people down on their luck, but it was rich in character." In no time at all, Steck found success on his new chosen career path when a screenplay he'd written was optioned and subsequently turned into the comedy-Western *Waterhole#3*, starring his close friend James Coburn in the lead role. Coburn was one of the celebrity clients who'd been administered LSD-25 by Dr. Janiger, so Steck was not at all surprised when the hip movie star took a shine to Burt's artwork after he made an introduction between the two men. "Burt's paintings were fashionable and struck a chord within the psychedelic community. Burt was one of the purveyors of that psychedelic vision, which appealed to power people like James and his wife Beverly, who was an art connoisseur. They saw him in that light rather than an artistic one. You could see the influence of psychedelics in his work, theorematically and in terms of colour, it's perceptible and clear. Burt was not lyrical like Jackson Pollock; he was crystal clear like he'd taken a photo of another world. Beverly was as bright a human being who ever existed, and she had a deep understanding and historical knowledge of art; from ethnic art, be it Asian art or Egyptian glass or Native American art. She helped broker the sale of the Dalai Lama's artwork so he could support his community. So, she had an extraordinary eye, and she would've known my feelings about Burt's work and James would've been enthusiastic enough to buy one, though they were seldom available. Burt would sell something if he needed money but no one paid more than $400. Most of the time it seemed the buyer was inferring that three-quarters of the price was doing Burt a favour, somewhat out of pity, but Burt wouldn't react to that. He was a gentle, good man; very tolerant."

Burt's humanity was movingly displayed when Steck, a former naval aviator, became temporarily crippled from an old flying injury that left him doubled over in pain. Although he wanted to retreat from the outside world until he recovered, but Burt would have none of it: "I was bent over like Quasimodo and I wanted to just hide away, but Burt would say, 'Time for us to go for a walk,' and he would take me by the wrist and walk me down Sunset for something to eat. And it would be such an effort just to step off and on a curb, and I needed help. I felt an onus on me, and it was an interesting condition to be in because people would look at this humpback, and I would look up at Burt and he would look down at me with a beaming smile. Burt had no sociological callowness. He was free of bigotry and prejudice. He was as natural with me as with anybody. I remained that way for three months until my back resolved."

Burt also welcomed the fact that Steck was already a devotee of the Fourth Way system, prior to him moving in: "*In Search of the Miraculous* was a revelation for me. It was a common-sense approach to spiritual questions and I expressed that to Burt. But even though the two men shared a metaphysical framework and reference points, actually living with the artist on a day-to-day basis was still an eye-opening experience for Steck, who came to regard his roommate as a latter-day hierophant. "Burt had a different mind-set to most people, and in his wandering around Hollywood there was an array of people who interacted with him: bartenders, waitresses, cab drivers, and many of these people related to him. You wanted to know more about him. He was a mover and a shaker, constantly collating data that was not perceptible to people unless it was pointed out to them. It was not incoherent ramblings, but the words of a bard, a minstrel, a singer with outré songs and themes. He was able to make logical constructs out of disparate pieces of information given to him by the environment. He tuned in on things behind the veil of reality.

The surface of things held no interest to him. He felt there were things going on unseen." One of the things Burt saw right through was the charade of advertising: "He had a preternatural ability to see a pattern in the information around him. He would point out an advertisement on a billboard and say, 'See how the artist has made that whiskey bottle look as though it is about to drop out of that hand and fall on you? Well, the advertising people have done that on purpose, because they want to instil fear, to force us to have a drink to calm down.' Or he'd cite a pipe advertisement, where the pipe was being thrust at you like a swordsman's épée, and say the advertisers were purposely trying to induce an uncomfortable feeling that could only be cured by the very thing that was causing the anxiety in the first place. To him, the forces behind those advertisements bore a spirit that was anti-humanitarian. He saw it as an indicator of who those people were, and he pointed it out with an artist's perception."

Steck confirms that during the many months they lived together, Burt was constantly painting and drawing and yearning to return to the yacht basin in the South of France, which he visited with Valerie, so he could decorate every sail, turning them all into real life Magic Ships. "Burt didn't sleep that much, and if he was awake, he'd have a pencil and paintbrush in his hand. He had a stack of paintings, facing the wall beneath the window, and he'd pull them out and work on them and then put them away and then go back to them again. His work was a novel composed of many chapters, and he was thematically connected to it. He was wide open to any influences, from modern graphics to sacred texts, and that was his style, his fusion. A focus point for many rays of light coming together. Even his easel was a work of art. He painted on it while he mused about what he was going to do next on the canvas. He was an aficionado of classical music – he liked Mozart more than Bach – so we had the classical music station playing on the radio while he painted, often 16 hours a day. Even when we went to Ben Franks for cheeseburgers, he'd be doodling on napkins, which he'd give to the waitresses. It was like Toulouse-Lautrec's relationship with the girls of the Moulin Rouge."

Steck, however, dismisses any notion that speed played a part in his friend's fevered creativity: "I never saw amphetamine use. never saw Burt take a pill or upper and I lived with him for a year or so and was tight with him. Uppers wouldn't do anything for him – he was already there. Burt would go to sleep just so he would be fresh to start painting again. As soon as he woke, he had a coffee and a paintbrush in his hand. In his mind, and mine, he didn't use drugs to escape anything, but to enhance his colour senses or cosmic harmony: the drugs served him. He'd trip and pick up a pebble or a leaf and look at it, but he didn't do drugs every day and to excess. But people would come over and hand him a joint. Guys like Al Gordon, a carny from Mississippi, who was now a successful pot dealer, or Don Rice, this interesting Hollywood street character. A few years earlier, Gordon found a local youngster who had size 22 feet, so he set up a carnival stall and charged people 25 cents to view the dilatory effects of what happens when someone takes LSD. Whereas Rice was truly an adept on the street; a stand-up guy. He was small but dangerous and very protective of Burt. If anyone had hurt Burt, they'd have had trouble with Rice. He would have sacrificed his life and taken a deathblow for Burt. He had no education but he appreciated the artist in Burt and had a reverence for a talent that was out of his reach. And he kept a lot of Burt's napkins. Burt would say to him, 'I've saved these for you!' He was a good person and saw it in Burt. He felt Burt was semi-divine. Rice loved us and tried to do things for us. He procured things and always had something to give Burt – usually it was something to smoke. He could've been his connection, but the last thing Burt was was a user. I believe he was showing the qualities of monomania, which brought him deeper problems later."

Steck was present as Burt worked on and completed *Seated Figure with a Cosmic Train*, a self-portrait, rendered in his mosaic style, that is now regarded as one of his masterpieces. The painting captured the artist shirtless, sitting on a chair in his studio next to an open window, in the midst of an LSD trip. His face is bathed in the dappled beam of light shone from the front of a passenger train, breaking the crest of a mountain, while the disembodied head of a Native American warrior, wearing a feathered warbonnet, hangs suspended in the sky. Steck asserts that the painting was originally called *Spirit Train* or *Spiritual Train*: "Burt believed a machine could have a ghost, and "cosmic" was not a word he used." But to several of his close friends, it was also known by the simpler title: *Super Chief*, in reference to both the Native American brave and the model of locomotive featured. Regardless of its title, the work itself exerted a profound effect on those who came into contact with it, and friends like Darryl Copeland and Ira Odessky swear that when they first viewed it (most likely during an altered state) they could actually *see* particles of energy come to life in each tile of the painted light beam. Beguiled by the painting, Ira asked Burt if he could photograph him with it, and he was so pleased with the result, he took it upon himself to photographically document as much of his friends' prolific output as he could. [2]

"I thought *Seated Figure* was very successful," Steck asserts. "It took Burt three months to paint and he put a great deal of work into it." Steck was equally impressed by one particular abstract that Burt presented to him as a gift: "I gave it back to him and told him: 'Burt, this is the only successful abstract! It belongs to your collection of themes.' It was a bright red and yellow abstract, with a dash of purple, with no graphic content, two and a half feet by two feet in size. It was definitely done in oil, and there were little pieces of stained glass in it that created an abstract pattern. The structure and colour and form had integrity. It was beautiful, but not like pieces by (Robert) Motherwell or (Jackson) Pollock. Burt's craft was formal rather than free flowing. He didn't paint many abstracts then, and he painted it quickly and then put it away. But with that piece, he conquered abstract!"

Steck also witnessed Burt experimenting without his brushes in favour of his palette knife: "He switched over when I was there. It became a tool, and it had an intense effect on the canvas. He used it for months and months and became very skilled in it. He used different sized knives and laid the paint on thin because he had such control over it."

Though infrequent, there were some romantic interludes that gave Burt a break from his hothouse studio: "Burt liked woman as people, maybe because of their intuitive side, and he liked them physically, episodically, and he'd occasionally go on escapades. He'd put down the brush and pick up the phone and hook it up for the weekend. In one instance, he had two ladies at once."

There were also excursions out of the city: "Burt and I visited Krishnamurti's retreat in Ojai a couple of times. Burt would listen and relate to him, as he was an interesting figure. But after talking lucidly for four or five hours, Krishnamurti would then take questions and it became apparent that few understood what he'd said, and I saw the resignation on his face." They also attended the 'Spacecraft Convention' at Giant Rock, in Joshua Tree, though neither men had much time for its organizer, George Van Tassel, who claimed he was in contact with Venusian "Space Bothers," whose technical know-how helped create his Integratron, a structure built on pseudoscientific principles to facilitate time travel and cell rejuvenation. "I knew George and would stop and chat with him, but I thought he was a commercializing fraud. His contact with "Space Brothers" was obvious nonsense. He once described how the UFOs performed a close order march drill aerial display just for him. This was all frivolous to Burt. George was not a nasty person but he was a benign fraud; a poseur, who was duping people. He used UFOs as a way of schmoozing people into buying real estate or to sell hamburgers. He took it all too lightly. I flew jets but never had a sighting of a UFO until I visited Joshua Tree. When I mentioned it to George he reacted as though I'd seen something very mundane."

One of Steck's former clients was Harrison (Harry) Cohn Jr, youngest son of the now deceased movie mogul Harry Cohn, a man who once memorably underlined his hardnosed reputation by boasting, "I don't get ulcers; I give them." Though he enjoyed a privileged upbringing, Cohn's teenage years were marred by the maltreatment meted out to him by his mother's lover, the movie star Laurence Harvey, a sadistic drunk, and he used drugs, in part, as a salve to ameliorate those stinging, psychic wounds. With Steck's encouragement, Harry befriended Burt and found a soulful guy with a sympathetic ear. And it was a mutually beneficial: "Harry just loved Burt," Steck confirms, "and he ended up buying eight or nine Shonberg pieces." Through his fellowship with Steck, as well as Burt and the Shevins, Cohn became active in the Fourth Way, and though he wasn't necessarily a full-on Gurdjieff acolyte, according to Judy Shevin: "Harry sat at Ray's feet. Harry was an amazing guy and so beautiful to look at. He looked like Michelangelo's David. He drove a little Mini Cooper, which was illegal at the time because they were so small, and he'd speed around Mulholland Drive. It was very frightening but fun and exciting." Judy was subsequently hired to redecorate Cohn's plush Laurel Canyon abode, where his Shonberg canvases enlivened the walls, though Steck suspects Cohn was merely collecting Burt's work for the monetary benefits it could prospectively bring him, rather than any genuine appreciation for the art.

It was though his camaraderie with Steck and Cohn, that Burt first made the acquaintance of Semu, a Native American shaman, who conducted peyote parties in the hogan erected on Cohn's 240-acre ranch out in Joshua Tree. I knew Semu well, as I lived at Harry Cohn's ranch for two years," Steck recollects. "He was our Native American shaman but he was a mixed bag. He was in his early 30s then, and a member of the Chumash tribe, who were original settlers in California – they're seashore people. I believe he used his background to make contact with wealthy patrons like Harry, who regarded him as an authentic shaman, but I believe he was an opportunist, too. I'd been connected with the Native American Church and Navajos and gone on prayer meetings. Those were strong experiences and Burt was on the periphery of that and we connected across whole areas of interests and disciplines."

It was while he hanging out in this Joshua Tree scene, that Burt became buddies with George Nazarian, an Armenian writer, and his wife-to-be Eve, who'd travelled to LA from Chicago to become an actress. "Burt and I hit it off instantly," she recollects. "He was very fond of me and I of him. We had a relationship where you don't have to speak. It was a connecting through the heart – not words. It was a magic feeling. He'd sit and stare at me while I did something. He probably did want it to become romantic but he knew I was with George and he was really a gentleman. We were really very close for three years and I thought he was very, very special. I met Valerie too, but I was uncomfortable with her. She was taken by me, and I think it was because Burt was so fond of me, but she was very pushy about it and I wasn't interested. Valerie told stories about Burt being a madman and howling at the moon, but I never experienced it. She was very conniving whereas Burt wasn't. He was so revered by people in LA who admired him and his work, but it never seemed to expand. He was socially a little odd, but his oddity made him the genius he was. We had some great laughs, but Burt tried to catch himself for being too lively and fun-loving. He didn't want to make it a habit." For a while Eve functioned as Burt's new muse: "He made hundreds of sketches of me with ink or felt pen, but with heavier strokes. He'd scribble on a piece of paper, and if he was up all night on speed it would be so black you couldn't see it because he kept reworking it. I could do speed until three or four o'clock in the morning but then I would have to go to bed or take a blanket into the closet. Whereas George and Burt would drive down to the coffee shop and come back at noon and start all over again." One special, lovingly rendered portrait of Eve was executed in her bungalow in Hollywood. "Burt told me, 'Eve, this painting is gonna make you famous!' And I said, 'No Burt, this painting is gonna make *you* famous!'"

Steck confirms that Burt was incredibly stoical when it came to the preservation of his work and its legacy: "There always seemed to be this high statistical chance that his work would end in destruction. His pieces were lost, stolen, mishandled or they just disappeared." And Burt was downright fatalistic when it came to the fate of his mural work: "He was always aware they would be destroyed or disappear. He had a feeling about that, a premonition, and said to me, 'I don't expect any of them to survive!' Burt felt there were dark forces who were antithetical to his thrust, and he was being pushed by these forces. He knew people thought he was crazy – it's why we had a special rapport. I recognised a similar poetic sensibility. We talked about the towers of Xanadu as if they were real. He feared that his friends would have him taken away by the men in white suits, but to us, he was different, not mental. Most people thought of him as "touched," "illuminated," "special." He was focused, in his aberrant way, on his intuitive side. When he was operating on instincts he was invaluable, and he was protective of me. Burt would walk across Sunset Boulevard without paying attention to the traffic, and point people out in the street and say, 'That man over there, don't look at him! He's not a good man!' He knew people better than they thought he did. He had these periods of talking to the sky but then he'd recover and retreat from that. It was more episodic. I'd listen to him as though he were reporting not inventing. It was part of his gigantic cosmic battle between dark and light, and it involved the whole cosmos. These were serious forces capable of reeking cataclysmic destruction, and Burt's psychosis was this projection of his psychological state into an artist's schema. It's like a poet's way of dealing with psychological problems and it's there in his paintings. He saw himself as the protagonist, the hero, the demigod, the fighter on the side of light, and light itself meant a good intelligence. He was sensitive to geography and ambiance, and thunderbolts were very much a part of his fantasizing, but he had not yet been hit. But when he'd see dark, shadowy thunderclouds gathering, he'd say, 'Pull over to the left, they're gonna come down!' It's like he had a foreknowledge of their weaponry. He saw them coming down and knew where they would hit him; their designated target. He even moved me out of the way of one of them. It was all intrinsically connected to the structure of his fantasies. His hallucinations made it work for his art."

When asked how Burt protected himself from such attacks, Steck opines: "He did cabbalistic rituals. I'd hear him mumbling as if he was saying his rosary beads. Part of it was biblical; he identified with creationist teachings of Christianity, and Zen concepts and Native American stories. He once said: 'I found meaning in the Gospels! I was being plagued by the devil and I said "Get thee behind me" and he lost his power over me.' And he was amazed – 'Joe, it worked!' – he banished them. But they were minions and elemental forces in the control of and put into play by a superior, dark intelligence in a complicated universe. There was a mix, primarily legends: Zeus, Thor and a hierarchy of forces and entities, mythic rather than alien, though Burt was aware of an alien influence on Earth. And always hailing from the sky and encompassing the whole galaxy."

Burt alluded to this phenomenon in one of his most recent drawings, published on the inside back cover of the latest (and final) issue of *Gamma* magazine. It showed a windswept woman, brandishing a bouquet of thistles, being surveilled by a disembodied humanoid in the sky. Steck continues: "Burt had such a strong mind that when he was actually hit by a thunderbolt, he took it in and neutralized it by putting it in his paintings. He digested them and transmuted them, rather than transmitted them. Burt had mythic powers that weren't being displayed by mankind – who were asleep to it and unaware of the threat. He understood Gurdjieff's sleeping man principle that proclaims man's potential consciousness is embedded in time immemorial, throughout history, and it submerges and resurfaces. And he had a sense of the sacred. He was not profane or promiscuous. He did not overindulge or drink to excess. He was a moral person. He did not proselytize or preach, but he was a prophet – here to tell us of these dangers: wrong conduct; being manipulated; being under hypnosis. So, he was a danger to the dark side. He was the target of minions who were out to stop his mission, and was plagued by imps and demons and the devil incarnate – whatever form he was taking."

Burt's *Magic Ship* painting for Rosemary Vail. (Courtesy of Edward Vail.

Burt's sketch of *Semu*, made the morning after a peyote trip.

The Dawning of the Clear Light of Reality. 1965.
Casein on Masonite.
(Photographed by Ira Odessky. Courtesy of Judith Shevin.)

Peyote Ritual. 1965. Felt Pen on Paper.
(Courtesy of the George & Marzia Greif Family Trust.)

Burt holding *Seated Figure and a Cosmic Train* 1965. (Photographed by Ira Odessky. Courtesy of Judith Shavin.)

Burt's drawing for the last issue of *Gamma* magazine. September 1965.

Chapter 9
Rimbaud of the West Coast

During Burt's absence abroad, Vito and Szou became cult personalities in town, thanks to their memorable appearances on the popular *Steve Allen Show*, where Szou showcased her boho fashion outfits and Vito spent a week creating a bust of the savvy TV host. Allen had a taste for the offbeat and a proud track record of providing a mainstream platform to a host of countercultural touchstones, such as Jack Kerouac, Lenny Bruce and Bob Dylan. As a result of their TV exposure, the Paulekas' found themselves being invited to Hollywood soirees by the likes of Mickey Rooney and Jill St. John, where they were expected to lend a little colour and kookiness to the occasion. They were asked to dance at Jane Fonda's 27th birthday celebration in Malibu, where they were accompanied by the town's then-hottest musical group, The Byrds, who were indebted to Vito, for helping secure their first ever gig.

Another neighbouring rock band, with whom Vito had ties, was The Mothers of Invention, whose frontman, Frank Zappa, lived nearby in a log cabin formerly owned by the silent film cowboy Tom Mix. The group was now being managed by Burt's former patron Herb Cohen, and Vito and his sidekick Carl Franzoni not only provided backing vocals on their debut album *Freak Out*, they also inspired its opening track Hungry Freaks. Spurred on by his studio experience, Vito even tried to have a bash at being a rock star himself, recording the raucous, organ-heavy 7-inch single Where It's At (reportedly backed by members of The Mothers), that was produced by rock sleaze-meister Kim Fowley.

A cultural and demographic shift had taken place on the Sunset Strip while Burt was away, and he couldn't help but notice how several coffeehouses had been replaced by newly opened rock and roll clubs catering to a teenage audience, a result of the youthquake ignited by The Beatles and the British Invasion. The corner building that stood right next door to the Unicorn, for instance, was now a music venue called the Whiskey a Go Go. It was run by a former Chicago cop named Elmer Valentine, who also took control of the jazz joint the Crescendo; gave it a rock n roll makeover and renamed it The Trip. This teenybopper takeover brought a much-needed injection of energy and excitement to a town whose motion picture industry was struggling to keep its grip on the goggle-eyed attention of the general public, who were increasingly turning to television for their entertainment. However, for some stalwarts of the Strip, like Sally Kellerman, this changing of the guard left a lot to be desired. She was aghast at all the chewing gum that now littered the once-pristine sidewalks, and the noise made by the nightly throngs loitering outside these venues was upsetting the quality of life for some of the older, wealthier homeowners in the area. In what was seen as a heavy-handed response, local officials ordered a curfew, and matters came to a head when Pandora's Box, which had housed a collection of Burt's artworks over the years, was threatened with demolition. On the evening of November 12th, 1966, youngsters rallied outside the popular hangout to demonstrate against these plans. Even celebrities like Jack Nicholson, Peter Fonda, and Sonny and Cher showed up to express their solidarity, but the actual confrontation between protesters and the police, which was later hyped as a "riot," was, in truth, a pathetically one-sided affair, for the soft skulls of the demonstrators were no match for the billy club-wielding centurions of the LAPD, who handcuffed and frogmarched any troublemakers into their paddy wagons and dispersed the rest of the crowd in about 15 minutes.

Szou Paulekas was also now a mother, having given birth to a son, a blonde, blue-eyed angel-child named Godot, and for his second birthday that December, Burt presented the family with a dreamy portrait of the boy, floating on a barge down the Mississippi River with a giant snail as his travelling companion. Vito's workshop now doubled as a dance studio where he taught an eclectic style of choreography, borrowed from Martha Graham, Isadora Duncan, Afro-dance and deep plies from ballet, to an ever-growing troupe. Once rehearsed, they performed their wild routines on the dance floors of the new rock venues, and the spectacle of them using dance to reach an ecstatic state of consciousness (not unlike the whirling dervishes who helped inspired the sacred Gurdjieff Movements), while dressed in their proto-hippie garb, was what initially drew spectators to the clubs, rather than the rock bands themselves. Vito's studio was also used to present theatrical psychodramas, and invariably it was Valerie who stole the show. During one jaw-dropping dramatization for the group, she demonstrated how she'd once been sexually seduced by a gang of sadistic nuns in Catholic school, and as she reached her sexual apogee, she inserted a crucifix in her ass. Valerie took perverse pleasure in screwing guys while she still had the cum of a previous partner inside her, and her lack of emotional connectedness to her lovers led many to believe that, when it came to sex, she was sociopathic. Vito enjoyed officiating fake marriages among his flock, and Valerie entered into a couple them; one with Sheldon Jaman and one with George Hopkins, a hapless stand-up comedian who mitigated audience boos by falling over onstage to raise a laugh. The union with Hopkins soured quickly, though, when Valerie, who owned a collection of Nazi daggers, pulled a knife on him due to a paranoid delusion that he was going to stab her, and it was incidents like these that led Szou to remark: "Someone with empathy and emotions could not live like Valerie."

Since the closure of Googies, and other after hour hangouts, the all-night scene now revolved around Canters, a deli on North Fairfax, where Frank Zappa and his musos congregated with Vito's "Freakers," whose ranks included Bob Roberts, better known as Beatle Bob, due to his pageboy haircut. Bob spent many evenings rapping with Burt there, as he scribbled on napkins using his Pentel pen. "Everyone knew about Burt. He was a genius artist and a forward thinker. He really was ahead of his time. He'd come by Vito's and they respected each other as artists. Vito had a lot of his work but Vito was anti-drugs, so if you were high on acid… Burt said once, 'You've got a look like an American Indian!' and he drew a visualization of me like that. He'd take you on his trip; he was very focused. He didn't make small talk. When you sat down with him he'd tell you stuff, not converse. He was pointed and direct. I was living in Laurel Canyon and I would see him walking along and talking up in the air to the Indians, doing an Indian chant to them. The last time I saw him was on Sunset, and we were both on acid. We looked at each other and he communicated telepathically that he wanted to be left alone, so I kept on walking."

Burt was now living just around the corner from his old place on Kirkwood, in a new pad on Ridpath Drive, which became a drop-in centre for young artists, like the painter John Boyce, who looked up to him: "If you were an artist Burt would take time with you. Young artists, not knowing what to do, would gravitate to him. Without being the centre of attention, he attracted creative people to him because we had questions and no answers. And he enjoyed it and encouraged it. I had little confidence in my figure work. I lost it in art school because others there were better and it fell away. But Burt caused me to navigate to what I was doing – I drew people and situations on the street in front of me, which was an aesthetic I was interested in. The experience I was having, while I was drawing, was a direct influence from Shonberg. If you're an artist, you ask yourself: What am I gonna draw? But you're answering those questions by doing the work. It's not about shows or personalities or movements but doing the work, and I was a very arrogant guy. I'd just gotten a degree in philosophy and had a background in academia and painting and I had my own attitude about what I wanted to do and Shonberg had that too, but he didn't talk about it, he just did it, which affected me. He was the most interesting of all of us. He was one of a kind. He didn't do work like anyone else. He was into his own thing, pure line drawings, which no one else was doing. I brought my friend Walter Teller, an excellent artist and actor, to meet him and I remember him showing us his new work, without talking. We were just sat there, the three of us, and he picked up one of his notebooks and began showing us the contents without explanation. I looked at it for what seemed like hours, and I was totally overwhelmed by his work and he recognised it. He would just hand me a drawing and sit and wait, watching me respond to it. Then he'd take it and give me another one to look at. Communication was through the drawings. He had an effect on you without making any effort, and the impact was meaningful. He didn't have an attitude about what should or shouldn't be done. He made no effort to impose a style. He was probing and experimental, and I saw him doing a manifestation of himself through his work, in a direction no one else was going in. He wasn't looking for the perfect picture or a great composition but a manifestation of a scene in front of him. It made him unique and it gave me the confidence to do what I would do – go out on the streets and paint what I was seeing. I have nothing but love and respect for him because his work had the most influential significance on me." Boyce also agrees that, as artists, they couldn't have asked for a better setting: "Laurel Canyon was an incredibly magical place. I lived on Grand View Drive, on top of Ridpath. Lenny Bruce had a place a few houses down from me and Frank Zappa was just down the street from Burt. The Barrere brothers, Rob and Michel – their other brother Paul later joined Little Feat – were two houses from him, and in every apartment, somebody was doing something that was wonderful, and we'd stay for a period of time because something amazing and compelling was going on."

Such sentiments are echoed by Walter Teller: "Laurel Canyon was a seminal, remarkable place, with such a great social scene. I was up the hill from Burt's pad, and Canned Heat were just around the corner. You'd roll a joint and say, 'Who am I gonna listen to tonight!?' I was studying acting and it was my early beginnings as an artist, and if you lived in Laurel Canyon back then you knew who Burt Shonberg was. He was *the* artist. Burt was older than me, and I discovered we both grew up in Massachusetts: I was from Swansea, just below Rhode Island. I told him I saw my first UFO in the early-'40s when I was 10-years-old, and we talked all about it. He was at the tail end of the smokestack series: a cynical way of depicting the pollution of the atmosphere, and he took the polluters on, as an artist. I started to work in casein because of him. Burt was truth! I don't know anyone who you can be put in the same category as him. He was pushing through to something new, that he knew was available, and he was faithful to it his whole life."

On September 8th, 1966, the debut episode of *Star Trek* aired on American television, scripted by Burt's chum George Clayton Johnson. As he lived without a television set, Burt mostly likely watched the tele-series at Bob Storr's apartment on the northwest corner of De Longpre and Fountain Ave. It was a place he would visit regularly to get high and watch TV or listen to music. "Burt would hear messages in music," Storr explains. "He'd approve if he liked the lyric of a song. He liked Simon and Garfunkel's The Sound of Silence. The title itself appealed to him, as did lyrics like *'The words of the prophets are written on the subway walls.'* But he'd jeer at lyrics like *'Bright, elusive butterfly of love'*

(Elusive Butterfly by Bob Lind) and snarl at Cherry Pink and Apple Blossom White by Pat Boone. We listened to The Beatles but mostly I had the dial tuned into KKGO radio station, playing West Coast jazz 24 hours a day: Miles Davis, Brubeck, Coltrane, Cannonball Adderley etc. We stayed mellow. He'd come up when I was practicing triads on the piano, or I would watch him paint; he painted in rhythm, to the beat. He loved all that."

At Storr's apartment, the two friends made a 55-minute tape recording in which they delivered a spontaneously improvised – "very Zen space-age dissertation," under the grandiloquent banner: "The Surrealistic Broadcasting System of Radio Free Twilight Zone, in conjunction with the Armed Forces Network of the True Secret, Mysterious Atlantis, is on the Air." Burt set the tone of the symposium by quoting lyrics to the Johnny Rivers hit Secret Agent Man: "*Be careful what you say, you may give yourself away, the odds are you may not live to see tomorrow,*" before he and Storr celebrated the invention of television as a "world-changing development in the history of mankind." Extrapolating on Marshall McLuhan's observation, on how the capacity of telecommunications had shrunk the world down into a "global village," Burt envisioned its future potential to bring ever remoter civilizations, like those existing on other planets and in distant galaxies, directly into people's living rooms. This segued into their mutual admiration for *Star Trek*, and the praiseworthy performances of the show's leading actors, Messrs Shatner and Nimoy, with Burt singling out Spock as an inspiration. He was equally impressed with the prevailing ethos of the Starfleet's Prime Directive, which stated that the U.S.S. Starship Enterprise could not interfere "with the natural evolution of any planet" it encountered during their weekly adventures, but felt the directive needed to be clarified, as it often put the crew at a distinct disadvantage when combating hostile inhabitants on alien planets. The two men echoed each other's belief that a supreme intelligence; a creator of life and the universe, lorded over each planet and every man.

They then moved on to more spiritual matter, and after Storr outlined that the purpose of life was to strive to attain the perfection of life, Burt responded with an appreciative "Bravo." Though he invoked Aleister Crowley's "Love is the Law" dictum, Burt strayed away from its original meaning, and reapplied it as "The law of the Creator himself," adding how this law "is in existence everywhere in the universe," where it is upheld by a government of the universe as a statute against any outside interference. In a jovial moment, both men mused about how their stimulating conversation could perhaps inspire future episodes of *Star Trek*, and Storr chuckled at the dichotomy of how their discussion was both very "in" and, at the same time, very "far-out."

Storr then quizzed his friend about the meaning of the term crime in "occult terminology," to which Burt opined: "What is called crime is any active participation – knowing, wilful and deliberate – or involvement with *any* form of what is written to be forbidden, evil, criminal, occult practices. Any type of black magic, witchcraft or any of that garbage is called crime in this sense." (A statement that may have gone some way to explaining why and he and Cameron could never quite work it out.) He then held forth about the structure of earthbound governance, and though cynical about The United Nations, he claimed a true U.N. of the world existed behind the scenes, which he described as a mysterious powerhouse consisting of an occult brotherhood, who would eliminate all the corrupt regimes in the world.

Under Valerie's auspices, Burt's artwork was brought to the attention of George Greif, a music business impresario with an eye for original talent (he previously represented Lord Buckley), who was looking to expand his roster of clients, which until now consisted exclusively of musical acts like the popular folk choral group The New Christy Minstrels and the jazz bandleader Stan Kenton. Greif admired what he saw and recognised the potential of aligning himself with someone who seemed to embody the (psychedelic) spirit of the times. Hoping to capitalize, Greif and his business partner Sid Garris signed Burt on to a contract that paid him $150 a week to create new works for a forthcoming exhibition.

The Greif-Garris firm was presently preoccupied with their latest enterprise, Go Go Records, a label created in order to discover newfound acts, as well as license hit singles by already popular international artists. Their first signing was the local outfit Dr West's Medicine Show and Junk Band, whose minor hit, The Eggplant That Ate Chicago (a whimsical ditty about an invading aubergine from outer space) was produced by Tony Marer, who was also the vice-president of their record company. Marer was already on friendly terms with Burt; they'd ran into each other at parties over the years, and in hangouts like Pandora's Box, where Marer bashed away on bongos. In fact, he and his actress wife Judith (who worked under the stage name Eve English) were part of the same tourist group, that included Burt and Valerie, who visited Salvador Dali's chateau in Port Lligat. "Dali came down the staircase and put a scarf around my neck," Marer remembers fondly. To capture the memory of that trip, Marer offered Burt $5,000 to create a large nine by three-foot *Magic Ship* painting, and he threw in free room and board at his house on 15631 Meadowgate Road in Encino so that he could complete it at his leisure. The two men would sometimes spend their down time dropping acid together, and Marer recounts how, on several occasions, Burt flipped out and began ranting about the Holocaust and how the Nazis worshipped those ovens: "He was very scared of them and had bad things to say about forces of evil." Working only in spurts of activity, the picture wound up taking four months to finish, but the result was especially arresting, given that the enlarged panorama brought the subject matter into a sharper focus than previous versions, though all the regular features: the ship(s), the olive tree, and the candy-striped lighthouse remained in place. Although its given title, *The Morning of the Magicians*, was quite obviously a take-off on the bestselling book of the same name (an anthology of mostly apocryphal arcana), Marer contends his houseguest meant it as a personal tribute: "Burt said I was a magic man who had influenced his work." There's little evidence of this in the picture itself, however, as it features known Shonberg symbols, like the Hamsa amulet, which graces the main sail, encircled by the suits from a deck of playing cards, which Burt painted years ago on the windows of his former address at 2222 Laurel Canyon Boulevard.

Despite Marer's generous, one-off payment, Greif soon realized it was going to be difficult to set a market value for Burt's work as he'd given so much of it away over the years. So, to counter this, he advised him to repossess as many pieces as he could, which Burt surprisingly went along with, albeit in a half-hearted fashion. One of the first places he visited was the Nazarians' pad, as Eve recollects: "When Burt took back his work it was very difficult for him, but together we stripped the drawings from the walls. He voiced his concerns of having management, but he was receiving a steady income from them and for that he was grateful. Though he really didn't care about money. He just used it for supplies and as a means to hang out in coffeehouses."

To showcase Burt's brilliance, Greif rented a space from the gallery owner Ernest Raboff in the Clear Thoughts building, located at 651 North La Cienega Boulevard, in West Hollywood, which was renamed the Gallery Contemporary. The exhibition covered the last three years of Burt's output, encompassing some of the work he completed in Ibiza, and 49 pieces were shown in total, with prices ranging from $3,500 for the *Seated Figure and a Cosmic Train* canvas to $150 for an untitled drawing. The exhibition was given the screwball title *This Are Burt Shonberg*, and a handsome poster was printed to publicize the event. It featured a photograph of Burt, wearing shades and sat next one of his featured pieces, *16*, a montage of sixteen panels dominated by examples of dark architecture that so intrigued him. The largest image revealed a skull, captured by the lens of a spyglass, lurking behind the metal mesh facade of a stark, forbidding structure. And Baphomet made a cameo appearance, holding a trident, captured in an oval frame that was superimposed on an image of a clifftop fortification. The poster also carried a quote from the artist: "LSD and other mind-expanding drugs are not a way of painting, but certain experiences in time and space which have been achieved can become subjects for the artist." Valerie was also pictured on the poster, admiring the "heroic-sized" terracotta clay bust of Burt she'd sculpted especially for the event, while the back of the poster bore a Xeroxed image of *Seated Figure and a Cosmic Train*. Valerie's sculpture was actually her second attempt at capturing Burt's face, as Szou Paulekas confirms: "Her first head of Burt collapsed on the floor because she put too many wet rags on it. She'd spent a long time making it, and when it was destroyed she came back and Vito said, 'Don't worry about it, we'll get another one going.'" For Valerie, this was the final straw, and she abandoned clay sculpting for good, declaiming, 'Clay is like shit!' The bust, however, became one of the main focus points of the show, and it remained there permanently throughout the exhibition's four-month run, as did Valerie, who worked tirelessly to drum up support.

The grand opening took place on Tuesday, April 4th, and though it was meant to kick off at 5 p.m., the start was delayed due to Burt's late arrival when the car Greif rented to ferry him to the gallery in style careened into a ditch en route. Ira Odessky was dispatched to salvage his friend and transport him the rest of the way, and when Burt eventually pitched up, he looked unruffled and dapper in a tuxedo and black bowtie, making good on an earlier promise he made to Bob Storr, that he was "ready for anything and could mingle with anybody: from warpaint to tux and tails." And yet, although he made an effort to socialize with all the invited guests, on what was, after all, his big night, Eve Nazarian could sense that Burt felt "tight and uncomfortable," especially as the evening drew on. "Burt just wanted to disappear into his shoes. It wasn't where he wanted to be – he wanted to be back at his studio."

The exhibition aroused the interest of Art Seidenbaum, a columnist at the *L.A. Times* with a penchant for the offbeat, who profiled Burt in his Spectator column, describing him as a painter whose brush is "dipped in mixed mysticism." And in his only known public interview, Burt extolled the merits of his new management team: "The artist is supposed to suffer and all that crap – the stuff of pulp magazines. An organization that supports him is a beautiful set-up." George Greif was also quoted throughout the piece and, at one point, he likened the launching of his exciting new artistic discovery to the way a music group, like the Tijuana Brass, found success by creating their own record label: "... we're putting a new sound to art... just have one of these become a hit painting and Burt will get the recognition he deserves."

And yet, tellingly and perceptively, Seidenbaum intuited a philosophical ambivalence in Burt's attitude to the whole venture, relaying his contention that artistic and commercial success were often mutually exclusive, and to emphasize this Burt quoted a line from the *Tibetan Book of the Dead*, "Be not attracted to, nor repelled by, anything." Before adding, with a smile, "Let it all be news."

Sadly, despite all the promotion and effort that was poured into the show, it was a similar story to the New York exhibition, in that most of the pictures on offer went unsold. Sometimes it doesn't pay to be in the vanguard of an artistic revolution, as few were willing to pay money for such radical new art. One exception was *Out Here*, a sublime self-portrait capturing the artist as he sat on a mountain slope in Joshua Tre, in a blissed-out, transcendent state, under a starburst sky. It was imbued with an extra radiant luminescence, due to the thick coating of Krylon fixative spray that Burt used on most of his larger paintings, and it consequently fell into the hands of Arthur Lee, frontman for the rock group Love, who related intimately to the sensation it evoked. Though it's unclear whether its original buyer bought it during the exhibition or post, it didn't really matter, as they were in the minority at the time; and, to all intents and purposes, Burt's relationship with his management team ended, though Greif remained in contact and continued collecting canvases that took his fancy. Burt's friends were not at all surprised; to them, the very idea that someone as freewheeling as Burt could ever work with "handlers" was doomed to failure, and Joe Steck, who also attended the opening, remained sceptical of his managers' motives: "I was not happy with Burt's relationship with them. I thought they were taking advantage. I don't think he was being remunerated well for his work, and I insisted that he should holdout for twice what they were offering. In my estimation, they were pretending to know what Burt was trying to do, for commercial reasons, because there was a lot of interest in him. Burt had so much energy in his heart that he was vulnerable. He knew his pieces were valuable because of the work that went into them, but he had no sense when it came to commercial business." A sentiment re-amplified by Bob Storr, who confirms that "Burt disdained the commercial art scene, and considered money in and of itself a 'crime.'"

Although Burt's artwork became synonymous with psychedelia, and he was, to be fair, the very definition of a psychedelic artist, it was merely one aspect of his artistry, and yet it became the all-encompassing tag that he was branded with. "Psychedelia has too much lurid, sensationalist baggage, Joe Steck argues. "It psychologically muddied the waters and it's not settled down yet. Burt was taken as a spokesperson for the Psychedelic Age; people who turned on and saw his work knew it was influenced by psychedelia. He was a mediator and interpreter of that world. Burt called himself a magical realist, and it's an accurate description, as it was realism painted by a magician, and we talked a lot about magic. Burt was the Rimbaud of the West Coast. I would have long conversations with him and, even in his psychosis, there was a poetic, organized, beautiful

Rimbaud quality which brought deeper understanding, not confusion. His influence was much subtler and pervasive. Sometimes it can mask an artist's talents, but with him, it didn't. He was ushering in the New Age. He influenced painters, writers, actors; graphic artists especially liked Burt. I know he helped inspire the psychedelic poster art of Tom Wilkes because Tom acknowledged it to me. [1] He synthesized, in a classical manner, the inchoate sounds being made by the hippy generation and distilled a system that connected to the artistic current of the time. He was way more influential than the people who collected him knew. He had transmissions of attitude that had his sweetness about it. And Burt's was crystallized into objects – not form. And he worked on an instinctual level; not an intellectual one. He was a true artist."

Burt's *The Morning of the Magicians* Magic Ship painting for Tony Marer. (Photograph courtesy of Dylan Marer.)

Burt's sixteen-panelled montage created in Ibiza. Mixed media on canvas. (Courtesy of Ledru Shoopman Baker.)

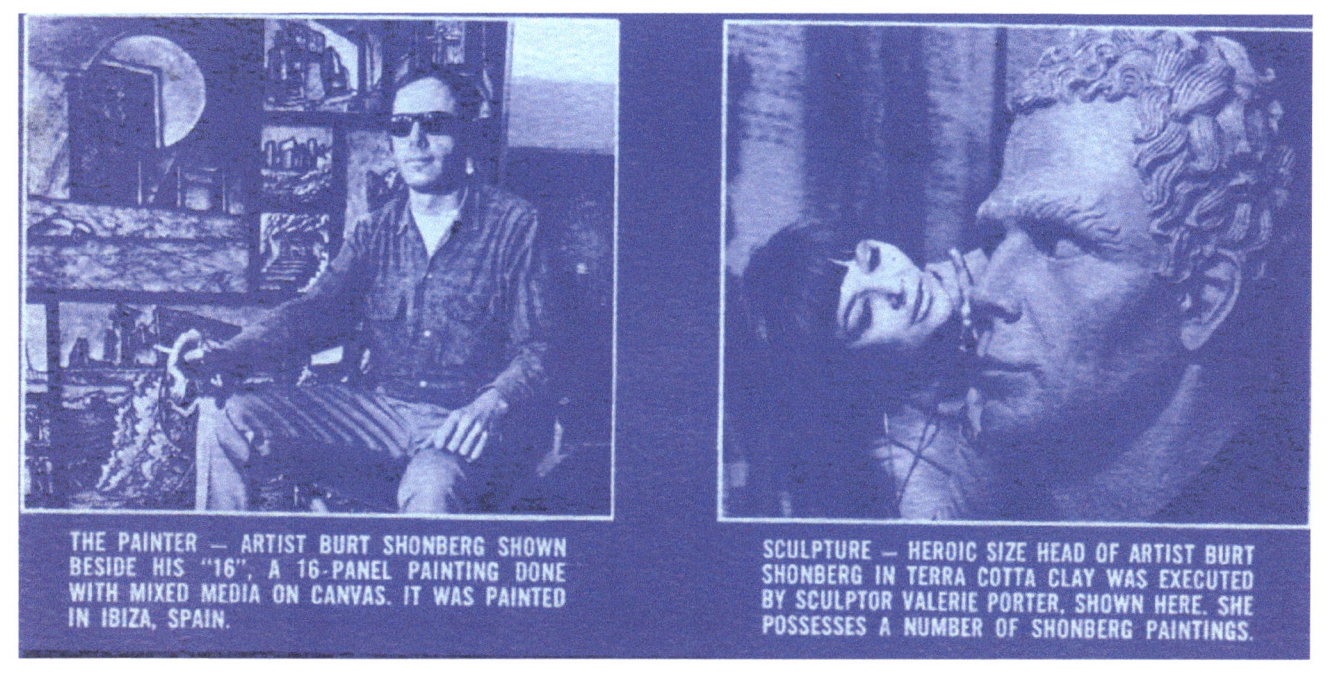

BURT SHONBERG ➡ OUT THERE

THE PAINTER — ARTIST BURT SHONBERG SHOWN BESIDE HIS "16", A 16-PANEL PAINTING DONE WITH MIXED MEDIA ON CANVAS. IT WAS PAINTED IN IBIZA, SPAIN.

SCULPTURE — HEROIC SIZE HEAD OF ARTIST BURT SHONBERG IN TERRA COTTA CLAY WAS EXECUTED BY SCULPTOR VALERIE PORTER, SHOWN HERE. SHE POSSESSES A NUMBER OF SHONBERG PAINTINGS.

Burt and Valerie pictured on the poster for the *This Are Shonberg* exhibition.

Burt explains his work to the actor David Hedison at the *This Are Shonberg* exhibition.

Valerie with her "hero-sized" bust of Burt at the *This Are Shonberg* exhibition. (Courtesy of Julian and Louis Porter.)

The poster for the *This Are Shonberg* exhibition. It includes a list of artistic styles associated with the artist: Impressionist, Realist, Surrealist, Experimentalist, Abstractionist, Cubist, Magicalist (sic), Mystic, but teasingly puts a ? under Psychedelist (sic). (Courtesy of Marshall Berle.)

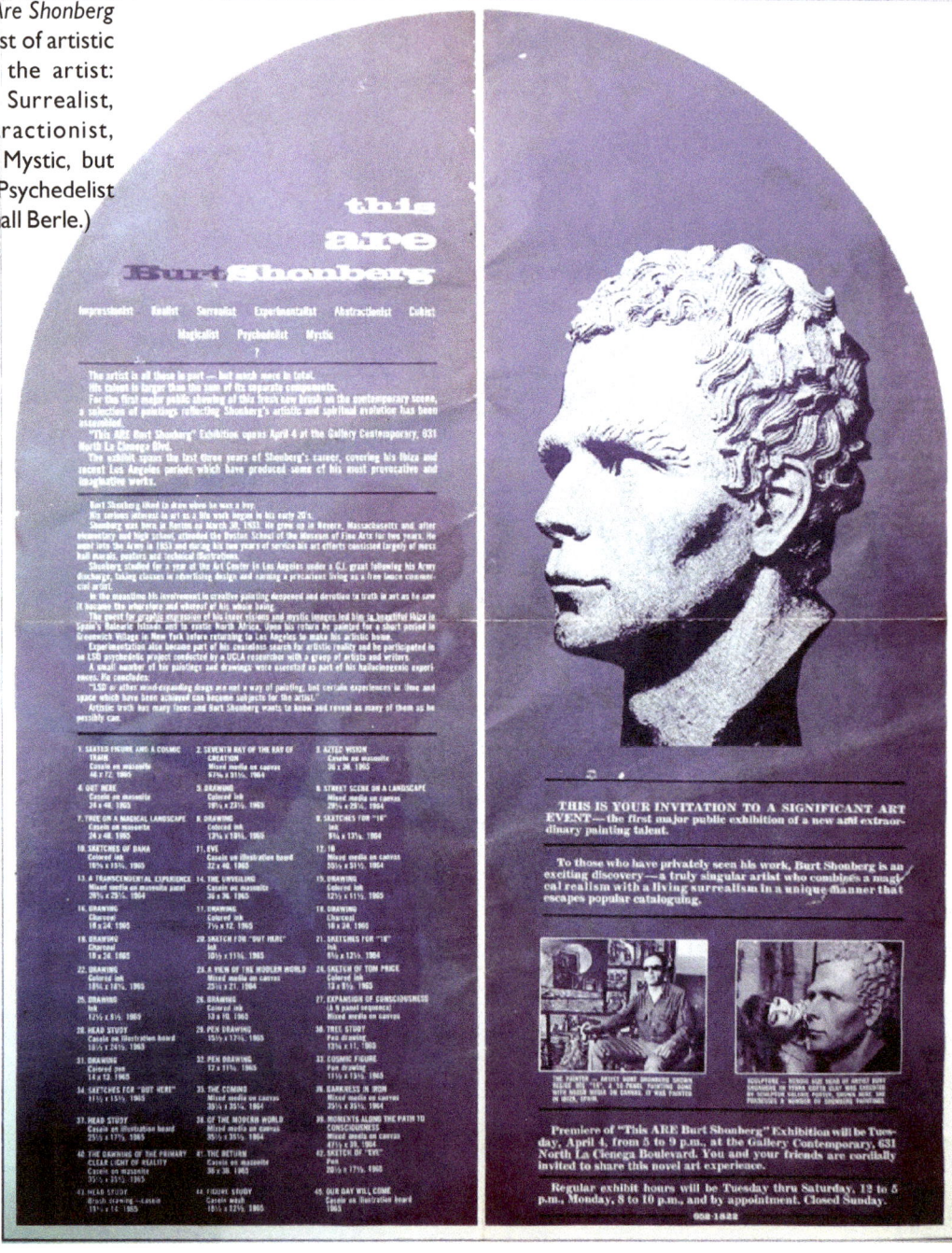

SPECTATOR, 1967

An Artist Who Has It Made

BY ART SEIDENBAUM
Times Staff Writer

"This are Burt Shonberg," says the poster in a burst of grammar that may have been dropped by Alfred Hitchcock's birds.

Taking Burt Shonbergs, one by one, the basic ingredient is an unknown painter who likes to call himself a "magic realist" or a "living surrealist," his brush dipped in mixed mysticism.

The display Shonberg is a La Cienega first — a whole gallery opened for the single purpose of bringing one man's work in front of the passersby.

The corporate Shonberg is a man with a patron-manager, public relations firm, gallery director, legal consultant. He is supposed to be the new working model: how to magnify a modern painter so the world will know he exists. Mass communicate him.

The personal Shonberg is a man who welcomes the retail retinue because it leaves him free, theoretically, to paint. "The artist is supposed to struggle and suffer and all that crap—the stuff of pulp magazines," beams Shonberg behind a few five-o'clock shadows. "An organization that supports him is a beautiful set-up."

The beautiful set-up is Gallery Contemporary, a place that would not have existed if there were no Shonbergs to sell. In space rented from longtime gallery-owner Ernest Raboff for at least four months at $350 per month, Valerie Porter sits among 49 hung-up Shonbergs which range from $150 to $3,000.

Valerie is a sculptor when she is not ornamenting the shop. The heroic clay head of Burt Shonberg that stares out the front window in fact, is a Porter work. She has been an admirer of Shonberg, been collecting his paintings for some time.

Pasted on the other side of the front window are various press clippings to prove that Shonberg's name is already dropping in public. This suggests a somewhat show-business approach to the visual arts and the impression is absolutely correct.

For behind the assorted Burt Shonbergs stands George Greif, music manager, recording guru and one-time manufacturer of the Christy Minstrels. Greif is patron and producer of the "This are Burt Shonberg" package. Greif and partner Sid Garris are the management team presenting a painter to the world.

George met singular Burt a couple of years ago, when the 34-year-old artist returned to Los Angeles from Ibiza. Collector Greif immediately liked what he saw and decided that Shonberg only needed some subsidizing to become a modern master.

So Greif-Garris became the business half of Burt Shonberg and it was their decision to open a new gallery in his honor.

"Our idea is not to foist some junk on the public with good merchandising and public relations," explains George. "But we're putting a new sound to art. Like it or not it's a new sound. And we've opened our own avenues."

George does not tell Burt what to paint, unlike the music business where a smart manager picks his artist's materials. But he does set the financial tone for the operation and masterminds promotion.

He likens having his own gallery to the success of the Tijuana Brass in launching their own record label. "All of a sudden, just have one these become a hit painting and Burt will get the recognition he deserves."

Greif-Shonberg will divide the proceeds from this revolutionary technique.

But the serious side of the magic realist admits that artistic success and commercial success do not necessarily happen together. As guidance for critics and audience alike, the incorporated creator offers a line from the Tibetan Book of the Dead: "Be not attracted to, nor repelled by, anything."

Then, nodding, smiling, the artist advises, "Let it all be news."

The *L.A. Times* article about the *This Are Shonberg* exhibition.

Chapter 10
Hollywood Babylon

Carol Green first met Burt when her artist boyfriend, David Bialle, brought him to meet her at the pie stall she ran at the Farmers Market. He made a memorable first impression: "Burt screamed and yelled about 'fucking Nazis!' It was part of his psychosis. You didn't have normal conversations with him because he was not of this world. But he liked me because I fed him; he was a good eater, but other than that he spoke with David. I was just a girlfriend making a living." Bialle – a lofty, Jewish guy from East L.A., had been a gunner in the army, where, after befriending a nurse, he gorged himself silly on emergency packets of morphine syrettes until he became addicted. Back on civvy street, he moved to Mexico and became a bullfighter, then returned to L.A. where he reinvented himself as an artist.

Through Green and Bialle, Burt was introduced to Ledru Shoopman Baker III, his very own fairytale giant. "Ledru was a one-night paramour," Green recollects, "but he then lived with me for a while. I met him through Fred, his cousin, who dumped me." Standing at a towering 6 foot and 7 inches, Ledru's height helped him dominate on the basketball court at school, and thanks to his mother's Mormon faith, he was offered a scholarship at Bingham Young University. But in true, rebellious style, he turned the offer down once he found out about the school's strict no-smoking edict that was part of its honour code. Though he was in his early 20s, and ten years Burt's junior, Ledru was struck by the beneficent attitude the artist exhibited towards him: "Fred, a cousin of mine, raved about how intelligent and talented Burt was, and when I met him I was blown away because he treated me with dignity, as though I was someone." Though Ledru was already studying The Fourth Way system, Burt guided him along his path and became his mystical role model. "Ledru became a carbon copy of Burt," Bob Storr explains. "In the Far East, a fakir will strike a pose and people will be so struck by it, they'll adopt it also, and that's what happened to Ledru. He adopted Burt's mannerisms and strut and spoke in the same tone."

It had been nearly three years now since Dolly Schrater had last seen Burt, and while she was in town, visiting a friend who lived in Van Nuys, she looked him up and they spent the day together: "I asked him if he was happy and he said he loved California and would never come back. When his mother couldn't get him on the phone there, I'd track him down by calling the LAPD to check that he was alright for her and the police would do it. They were wonderful."

According to Judy Shevin, Helen Shonberg even made a trip out to the West Coast to visit her son, but it was an awkward, tense affair: "We picked his mother up at the airport and she looked and seemed like an old school Jewish immigrant mama. Although you could tell she loved her son very much, she didn't know what to make of him. Burt felt he didn't belong with his family and he was very aware of it… always. He didn't fit in with them and couldn't wait to get out of there. He felt very separate and felt they had no idea who he was." And even for the brief duration of her stay, Burt used Ledru as a buffer and had him deal with his mother instead.

"Burt did have some respect for his mother and father," Joe Steck explains, "which sounds strange because he had such a distant relationship with them and never wrote or called them, but there was no animosity or disrespect, it was just an estrangement. If he hated his parents it would've shown in his work, not in his talk. He internalized everything. Burt would listen and smile and nod his head and offer a comment, but he'd only become vociferous when he was explaining cosmic concerns."

August 1967 saw the theatrical release of *Mondo Hollywood*, the latest project from the noted film documentarian Robert Carl Cohen. Filmed in L.A. between September 1965 and May 1967, it was conceived as a quirky divertissement from his overtly political films, for which he'd travelled to Red China, East Germany, and post-revolutionary Cuba, to capture the realities of life under a communist dictatorship. "*Mondo Hollywood* is a field study in social psychology," Cohen explains. "I make no commentary; just let people speak for themselves. I just asked them: 'What do you want me to film?' There were three criteria to be in my film: 1) Be a typical Hollywoodian – someone who was born somewhere else but came to Hollywood to realize their dreams and be themselves. 2) Be unusual, not a 9-5 desk job person. 3) Be 1 and 2. I put the word out at Barney's Beanery and had lots of volunteers." Vito, Szou and Franzoni were handpicked for the film, however, as they were obvious choices, and the resulting documentary could have featured Burt too, as Cohen met him and Valerie while visiting Vito's studio, but the filmmaker found he was just too far-out, even for him: "Burt was a good artist and produced interesting compositions, but he was borderline catatonic. He seemed preoccupied with this black cube he was holding, that he said was inhabited by Satan. He had a disjointed gait; almost robotic. He was very thin and I don't think he slept very much. He seemed very much alone. Vito delighted in visitors and speaking but Burt lived in his own mind and paintings, so I never filmed him. Plus, he never showed an interest. He wasn't very Hollywood."

Valerie, on the other hand, was super-keen to be a part of the shoot: "She told me she was a B-movie actress who had been given six electric shock treatments, and also claimed she was the niece of Draža Mihailoviæ, the Serbian war leader in World War 2, who led the loyalists until the anti-communist and Tito captured and executed him, so I had to put her in the movie." Cohen filmed Valerie sculpting in the garden of a girlfriend's home (where one of Burt's streetscapes is visible in the background), during which she mentions "a very strong LSD experience" she endured in Spain, presumably with Burt: "I can see why it could be dangerous because you see too much; you have super-vision; you have super-hearing; you have super-insight, and you start suffering like Christ did, because you think, my God!" Cohen also shot footage of Valerie enjoying a bubble bath with her gal pal's young daughter, in a scene where her perversity is played up for the camera: "I get very perverted at times because it's exciting. I think most sophisticated people do." But this was tame compared to what Valerie actually wanted to do. "I was being discreet but Valerie wanted me to get the camera into her vagina and I had to tell her 'This is a real movie. We can't show frontal nudity!' So, she said why not film me taking a bubble bath and her girlfriend, the artist Mary Ewart Guggenheim, said, 'Can I be in the movie too? I have a French maids outfit.' And I said, 'Do you do that normally?' and she said 'Yes.' Her daughter Monseratt wanted to be in the movie too, and said, 'I'll take a bubble bath with Valerie!'"

Vito and Szou were featured throughout the film, basking in their newfound glory as the crowned chieftains of the LA underground. But the appearance of their darling son Godot struck a devastatingly sad note, considering he had died tragically the previous winter as a result of medical malpractice. [1] To seal their status, the documentary ends with them throwing mad shapes on the dance floor of a nightclub (joined by Valerie and Shelley Jaman), where Szou is wearing an outfit decorated by Burt. "I'd planned my outfit: an ecru, flesh-coloured top, and tights. Then Burt painted an eye on the top and painted the tights, so it looked like I had no clothes on, just body painting. It gave the impression of nudism,"

Mondo Hollywood also featured footage of Richard Alpert from the LSD debate he conducted with Vito, and although Vito isn't actually shown, he hammers home his opposition to the drug in a fervid voiceover: "(LSD is) being treated as though it was something fresh and new; as though it was an intellectual experiment; as though the taking of drugs, somehow or other, broadens, expands man's consciousness, which is a lot of nonsense. The Chinese of 100 years ago got loaded on opium; had the most fantastic kind of fantasies that LSD never will touch upon. I'm particularly disturbed by the rationalizations taking place because in some of the so-called best intellectual circles there are discussions about taking LSD in order to make a special kind of person out of you. This is degrading!"

Vito expanded on this discourse further when he was interviewed by the BBC's globetrotting broadcaster Alan Whicker, who was in California to investigate the hippie phenomena for an episode of his popular television travelogue. During his diatribe, Vito referenced Burt as an example of the pitfalls that can await even the most enlightened artists: "I think getting loaded behind any kind of junk like that is to evade your responsibilities as a human being. Listen, if you're loaded behind LSD or any other of those, what I consider hard junk, you don't want to do anything except just sit back and contemplate something else. I have paintings around here by a guy who's a very dear friend of mine, and he's a groovy artist when he's straight, and he'll tell you, if you ask him, he'll say, 'Oh yeah, man, I really found those new kind of things' – and it isn't true! Because when he is loaded behind that stuff he doesn't do anything! He just stands there looking into space, man. You could push him and he might fall down, but he isn't doing anything! People who are loaded behind that kinda thing really don't do anything! This heavy kind of insistence, every place you go, with all the media about, 'Wow! Look at the colours, look at the lights, look at the strobe blinking, man, you can really find a trip if you get loaded behind this stuff.'. There's a lot of that kind of thing; insisting we become aware of it, that we become sensitive to it. And a lot of the young people are sensitive to it, and they become curious about it, so they say, 'Which of it is bad?' and I say, 'Man, *all* of it is bad!"

Szou, who was currently pregnant with her second child, was also interviewed on the subject (while swinging to and fro in a hammock), and she condemned LSD as a "military plot." This was a standpoint echoed by a growing number of anti-war activists, including Yippie leader Abbie Hoffman, who began to view the dissemination of LSD as a CIA-backed strategy to stupefy and ultimately neutralize the anti-war movement, by turning any would-be angry radicals into harmless hippies and docile flower children. In a highly contentious letter they wrote to the *LA Free Press,* Carl Franzoni went so far as denouncing Timothy Leary, the very public face of LSD, as an undercover CIA agent. But Robert Carl Cohen is not so sure: "I think the CIA was interested in using LSD, but Leary and Alpert refused to join them." One thing Cohen noted with some surprise was that unlike the majority of the anti-war protesters and peaceniks around him, Burt appeared to be quietly rooting for an American victory in Vietnam. "He would wear uniform parts, like a military cap or pin, but he didn't beat his drum for it." This could be viewed as a perfectly understandable reaction by a military veteran, who was merely showing his solidarity with returning troops, who were sometimes greeted with vitriol and abuse. But Hampton Fancher suspects there were other, deeper, contrarian motives behind it: "Burt was proud not to be involved in politics – none of us were. Nobody read newspapers. You'd only read *Time* if you were in the dentist's office. But by the time of Vietnam, it was a different case. Vietnam was crazy as crazy can be, and Burt being jingoistic suits his mad purpose for the moment; being perverse and rebellious. Especially for him; being a nonjoiner. He's a rock n roll guy. It's the twists and turns of his psychotic syndrome."

While Joe Steck asserts: "Burt appreciated his country. He was aware of its history and the more positive attributes of American democracy. We all had mixed feelings about authority, but I love the

Republic. And think about it: here Burt is, living in Laurel Canyon, spending his life painting pictures."

Szou, however, blames Burt's LSD usage for his outlook, as well as the wider cultural ramifications of the time: Burt was from a different era, and being a part of the military himself he thought of himself as a hero, and was so consumed with LSD he had no way of consuming information of what the US was doing in Vietnam, as it was very censored in the news and people were brainwashed by the media. You had to figure it out. Vito had a sensibility about it and knew about the underhand corruption of big bosses in America. His father had been in the Wobblies (Industrial Workers of the World), a labor union formed to stop the factory bosses ripping off their workers, so Vito was ultra-left-wing and he would sway everybody. We were the first peace protesters, hitting the streets with signs. But Burt was never around for these talks, so he couldn't be swayed. There was no opportunity to change his viewpoint."

On October 6, 1967, the Drug Enforcement Administration outlawed the use of LSD in California, and subsequently the rest of the country, in reaction to medical reports (many real, some ginned up) detailing the drug's adverse effects, ranging from panic attacks to profound psychosis. Of course, this didn't mean the drug wasn't still freely available to those who knew where to find it and, to stock up, Ledru made a special trip up the coast to San Francisco where he scored a thousand hits of "windowpane" (acid sealed inside a gelatin tab). "I gave a hundred to a friend and Burt and I did the rest," he recollects. Ira Odessky, who was a dependable connection for pot in the canyon, kept the trips coming in too, having found a reliable source at The Brotherhood of Eternal Love: a band of surfers turned longhairs who manufactured and distributed their own patented brand of "Orange Sunshine" LSD from their headquarters in Laguna Beach.

Meanwhile, Burt's reputation as one of the poster boys for the psychedelic revolution continued apace. He was namechecked in issue 9 of the bimonthly *Psychedelic Review*, that was edited by Ralph Metzner, PhD, who further cited his artwork in his 1968 book *The Ecstatic Adventure*, which featured Burt's potted bio and a reproduction of *Seated Figure with a Cosmic Train*: "Burt Shonberg is a Los Angeles artist, whose paintings and drawings express mythic and magical dimensions of inner space." Metzner described another artwork, entitled *A Transcendental Experience*, as "suggestive of the kind of opening and fluidizing of time and space that occurs in psychedelic states. It combines archetypal imagery and a visual mosaic which permeates the total field, breaking down the usual distinction between objects and backgrounds." At the behest of its editor Joe Dana, who was a big fan of his work, Burt also contributed artwork to the *Southern California Oracle*, the LA-based version of the original and more popular underground newspaper the *San Francisco Oracle*.

Carol Green adored Burt's artwork too, and when she opened her boutique, Sandwich, on Sunset Boulevard, in 1968, she asked him to design the 2 by 2-inch labels that were sewn into the garments she sold. "Burt used the image of the tall Vedra rock in Ibiza. A place where, according to local legend, sirens would lure sailors to their doom." Even though the store was located three blocks away from the main shopping area, its wares still enticed celebrity shoppers like Joni Mitchell and the wives of The Beatles, and Arthur Lee was a regular visitor to the store, as he was David Bialle's best friend. "Arthur hung out with us a lot; we had the best Afghan hash," Green explains. "But then he got into speed and David wasn't much of a speed freak." Bialle and Green were aware that Lee owned Burt's *Out Here* painting, and that he was planning on using it as the cover image and title for the band's next album. "We went to Arthur's beautiful house in the Valley – not the band house, "the castle," and he had art all over the place. We were walking around and David said, 'Where's Burt's artwork?' and Arthur said he'd hidden it under his bed because there were people hanging out at the house that he didn't trust. He then reached under the bed and pulled Burt's picture out and our mouths fell open because every other painting became insignificant." (2)

The prevailing climate of sexual permissiveness, particularly in a modern-day Babylon like Hollywood, led, inexorably, to some extremely dark consequences. It was now de rigueur for rapacious rock stars to screw sometimes underage groupies, and the erasure of sexual mores emboldened paedophiles to ply their perversions, sometimes in full view. When John Boyce orgied at Harbinger, a "clothing optional" commune at Harbin Hot Springs in Northern California, he grew uncomfortable with the lack of sexual barriers between the adults and children living there: "It went beyond what people could handle – me included," Boyce recollects. "I backed off because kids were being exposed to very aggressive, unhealthy sex. There were people there with money and academics who wanted to be part of the movement."

This unsavoury, shadow side of the sexual revolution fell on the Porter household, too. Considering how they'd borne the brunt of their highly-strung mother's violent mood swings throughout their blighted boyhoods, it wasn't entirely surprising that, though they were barely out of junior high school, Louis and Julian Porter were already skipping classes, smoking pot, popping pills and dropping LSD. "Me and my brother were too cool for school," Louis Porter explains. "Mom got us into pot. We were smoking weed in the 6th grade. I took LSD at 13. I was all too willing. I was a disturbed kid and pissed off at my mother and father. LSD gave me a lot of empathy and ethics. It changed my life. Without it, I'd be a sociopath. My mother was so self-centred. She was certain the sun rose and set on her. But Burt was really solid. He spoke to us like we were equals and most adults aren't like that." Valerie's laissez-faire attitude to drugs was an extension of her polymorphous sexuality that also knew no boundaries. Even her son's schoolmates were not off-limit; she considered them forbidden fruit and seduced them without qualms. Valerie's degenerate behaviour was shared with certain pederasts in the arty crowd she knocked around with, who felt no shame in targeting her boys with their unwanted attention. "Tony was part of my mother's crowd," Louis Porter recollects. "He smoked weed and made sculptures using a blowtorch and an airbrush. He put lights inside them so they looked like aliens; unworldly and ethereal. There was a big disparity in age: he was 38, I was 14, and scared of him. He was a pervert. He wore a floppy robe, like a woman's bedroom robe, with nothing underneath it. He was effeminate but not weak. You'd take him for a bear not a fairy or a dirty old man. I wasn't raped but molested. I hate it when people get bullied. I felt so embarrassed and helpless and worried things would go too far. You feel guilt like it's your fault. Anyway, he said to me, 'If you tell anybody, nobody will believe you.' And when I told my mom she minimalized it and said, 'He'd never do that!' But Burt heard me, and he knew this guy, and there was something about him he hated."

Although Burt still hadn't learned to drive properly, he borrowed one of Valerie's cars and drove the short distance to where the molester lived. "Tony lived near the top of Lookout Mountain, near Blue Jay Way where The Beatles once stayed. He owned the house but others lived there too. It had a big driveway. Burt was more into peace but he could be a cold-hearted guy if he needed to. He wasn't afraid of anything. He was a fearless person and could get heavy in a second. He could be steel, and he went and gave him a good talking to. I was waiting and watching in the car. Burt beat on Tony's door and he came out; Burt didn't hit him, but he put a shotgun under his chin – you could easily get a shotgun in those days as there was no gun control. Burt told him what time it was and what would happen if he even looked at me again. He pointed at me and made him know he'd get it real bad. He drove him into fear and panic and he didn't touch me again. This guy had gotten his way out of it by lying, but Burt knew I wasn't lying. I was so happy because someone was championing me and it made me feel so good. Burt was like a demigod. He was my hero."

Burt's righteousness was reflected in the cinematic heroism he and Bob Storr savoured in picture houses like the Toho La Brea and the Kokusai theatre on Crenshaw Boulevard, where they sat engrossed watching Akira Kurosawa's samurai sagas *Rashomon*, *Yojimbo*, and *Red Beard*, starring Toshiro Mifune. Burt just loved the alpha-male actor, and dubbed him "The Japanese Superman," in recognition of his triumphs over crime lords and evildoers. Like many cinemagoers at the time (especially those buzzing on a stimulant or two), Burt was equally captivated by *2001: A Space Odyssey*, Stanley Kubrick's cosmic conundrum, tracking a lone astronaut's interstellar journey to Jupiter. He found the cinematography and visual effects so believable that when the credits rolled he commented to Storr how "It looked like it was filmed on location." Compared to Kubrick's masterwork, the grainy black and white footage beamed back to Earth during the actual Moon landing appeared unremarkable, even though the technological achievement was epoch-making. It's unknown where Burt was during the historic event, but his ecstatic reaction to it was literally spelt out on one canvas, the triumphant *From Here To The Moon*, along with the words "Bravo Apollo 11." For Burt, the fact that this was an audacious *American* accomplishment heightened its appeal: "Burt was so patriotic," Stanley Dyrector attest. "He was like the John Wayne of painters. He raved about the astronauts and the moon landing." Another celebratory work, *Moon Prospector*, featured a boyish-faced astronaut, based on Neil Armstrong, inspecting a rock on the lunar surface. But Burt's most conspicuous tribute to the "Moonmen" was a three-panelled piece inspired by the famous photograph of Neil Armstrong traversing the Sea of Tranquillity, captured in the reflection of Buzz Aldrin's visor.

The triptych was commissioned by Frank Rowena, proprietor of the mod boutique Head East, and it hung high above his storefront on the northwest corner of Sunset and La Cienega where it became a much-admired focal point. [3]

Having enjoyed an intermittent love affair, that lasted most of the '60s, Burt and Valerie finally went their separate ways; provoked by an LSD session that went horribly wrong. "My mom told me she and Burt had a taken some tabs and the first ones didn't work, so after an hour, they took two more each" Julian Porter explains. "They thought the acid was weak or not working, so they took another and another; they kept eating them. And then, when she stood up, she said it all hit her like a truck, and over the course of the bad trip she apparently 'died a thousand times,' and had a horrid, life-changing revelation that LSD was poison. So, this overdose, unfortunately, provided the fuel for their breakup as a couple."

Valerie believed Burt's mind was now irrevocably damaged by LSD and she wasn't shy about relaying her feelings to her sons: "It's rotted his mind! That's why they call it acid because it eats away your brain!" But her boys, who idolized Burt, remained sceptical. "Despite what my mother said about Burt burning his mind out with LSD: you could see it had taken a toll on him, but not to the point of total damage," Louis Porter counters. "She was a total ballbuster; she destroyed men, and Burt didn't buy into it. She would not have been an artist if it wasn't for him. Burt called mom "Bunny," and she had a special place in her heart for him because he was a special man. I believe he was an angel. He made the world a better, more beautiful place. He was a shining light: an adult who wasn't an adult. He was deep and thoughtful and had a sense of humour, but there was no bullshit; he'd call a spade a spade. And he was the best advertisement for LSD. He went way beyond. He was out of this world."

Burt's artistry had a profound impact on the boys back then, and it remains to this day. "His work was spiritual psychedelia; it was something new like I'd never seen before," Louis Porter attests. "The territory was familiar because I'd been there. One painting looked like peyote, one looked like LSD – and he captured it! It was futuristic even by today's standards. He was our master, and my brother and I copied his work, although I later developed my own style." Julian Porter concurs: "I was in awe of what Burt did. His art did something to me. It took me to places, at an age when it was still very easy for me to get lost in them, and they did populate my mind and inflame my passion for art, and I wanted to be able to do that, just like him. It made me want to become an artist. Mom was a great artist and all, but her work didn't touch me like Burt's did. We both wished we could have spent more time with him."

In all fairness to Valerie, there were times when Burt appeared to be hopelessly unmoored from reality, and the hellacious thunderbolts, that so troubled the Shevins in the past, were back again, assailing him with a vengeance. It is worth bearing in mind, however, that such disturbing phenomena may have been rooted in Burt's youth, specifically the lightning bolts that heralded the physiological transformation of his favourite comic book hero, Captain Marvel. Also, Burt's favourite tarot card just happened to be the Tower trump, which symbolizes a sudden, intense, inner change from which a new identity emerges, through the demolition, by *lightning*, of the (Tower of) ego. And finally, let's not forget, it was a flash of lightning that initially fired up the electrical generator that sparked Frankenstein's monster into life. Now, in a not dissimilar fashion, a strange new being was rousing in Burt's febrile psyche; a visitor teleported down from the fourth dimension, whose identity would call into question whether Burt Shonberg ever truly existed at all.

BURT SHONBERG → OUT THERE

Burt's celebratory *Here to the Moon*. Pastel on paper. (Courtesy of Marshall Berle and LaughDome Records LLC.)

Moon Prospector. Burt's Astronaut is believed to be based on Neal Armstrong. (Courtesy of Marshall Berle.)

203

Burt's *Out Here* painting, formerly owned by Arthur Lee. (Courtesy of Marshall Berle and LaughDome Records LLC.)

Szou Paulekas dancing in her Burt painted top in a still from *Mondo Hollywood*.

The Super-Freaks: Szou with Carl Franzoni behind her. Vito holding Godot in his lap. Sheldon Jaman on the far left.

Chapter 11
Mysterian of the Cosmos

Valerie Porter wasn't the only one who feared Burt was now Bedlam-bound. He certainly looked like a man who was mentally unravelling, though it wasn't easy to delineate whether he was actually in the throes of an acid trip or in the midst of a psychotic episode triggered by the drug. That dividing line was now irretrievably blurred. Worse still, his disturbing behaviour was increasingly exhibited in full view of the public, and several of his friend's recount harrowing last glimpses of him.

While driving alone in traffic one day, Sally Kellerman spotted Burt as he shambled along the Strip in high dudgeon. Having lost touch over time, she was naturally excited to see him, but when she yelled out his name, Burt roared "barghhh!" back at her, like a monster, swatting a clawed hand in her direction. Kellerman was dismayed: "He didn't acknowledge me at all. He was just kept walking and looking straight ahead. I was scared because I thought he'd gone mad."

Though their friendship had strayed in the intervening years, Hampton Fancher also caught sightings of his old pal in that neighbourhood: "From Fairfax to Crescent Heights and Sunset, it was not uncommon to see guys you'd known earlier who were now nuts, taking off their clothes or flailing their arms. The area was a magnet for crazies. They were now wrecks and twisted but they had a community there. I took LSD *a lot*, but never went crazy. But Burt and others... it did tip them over the edge because he was crazy to begin with – genetically. I'd seen him on the street before and knew he was on acid because he'd be staring at a fireplug or whatever. Then, on this occasion,

I saw a group of crazies being led by a guy in a white coat and Burt was part of the group."

Although Judy Shevin had long been worried about Burt's progressively unhinged state, she was still not prepared for the reality of it. During her daily drive down Laurel Canyon Boulevard, she spotted Burt by the side of the road, screaming and waving up at the sky: "I pulled over and let him in, but I was frightened because he didn't say a word. I'm convinced he didn't know who I was. He was holding it in – the schizophrenia. He was being haunted by violent voices, and I was young and it was frightening to me. I had no experience under my belt."

Staging an intervention was a foreign concept back then, and Judy feared Burt's delirium left him even more open to exploitation: "Wherever Burt went, people took advantage of him. He was like a child, naive and innocent, and in other ways, he was a macho guy – 'Don't mess with me!' But it was to cover up his vulnerability. And in Laurel Canyon, in those days, people were feeding off each other, and he was a sitting duck for that. But unlike him, they didn't have any talent." Reports of Burt's aberrant behaviour were broadcast beyond the boundaries of Laurel Canyon and they reached his former roommate Joe Steck: "I'd heard about him yelling on street corners, but you could always get Burt to drink a cup of coffee; sometimes he'd drink 30 cups in a day. I felt he was getting estranged from all his old friends. I was disturbed because the problem was progressing, He was too full of the intergalactic battle. Burt had a clean slate, psychologically, but he was also potentially certifiable as anyone I've ever met, and I knew some who *did* end up in the lockdown ward. He was not a psychotic but a victim of the psychedelic generation, who stayed open to those influences even though they took grotesque forms. And he paid a heavy price with his mental stability." Steck also believes that Burt's decade-long exposure to the highly toxic fumes in the Krylon fixative spray he applied to his pictures, without wearing a mask, exerted a deleterious effect on his mental wellbeing.

Still, the sightings continued. While cooling off from a month-long bender in Palisades Park, Walter Teller spied Burt, who seemed to appear out of nowhere, tilting at windmills: "He was flapping around the green, dressed in a raincoat and brandishing a trash can lid, which he seemed to be using to ward off evil spirits." Bob Storr witnessed such spectacles both up close and from afar: "Burt was bombarded with visions. He was going through a *War of the Worlds* scenario about visitors who should and shouldn't be here, and he would speak with a stentorian voice and people would flee the restaurant." One such incident took place at the Yellow Submarine, a Beatles-inspired pizza parlor, on the northwest corner of Santa Monica Boulevard and N. Harper Avenue. Burt was a semi-regular there, having sign painted the joint in return for some free food. One day, Storr arrived there just as some commotion was breaking out inside. "Some guy had slapped Burt because he had taken something he said personally. Burt had been holding forth and speaking, and although his language was clothed in objectivity if the shoe fit than a person could take offence at what he was saying. Burt was not in a good place physically; he didn't know how to box or fight, so I calmed this guy down by putting my arms across his chest and bustling him back into his booth." Storr confirms that many of Burt's disturbing dialogues centred on his ongoing psychic battle with f.o.e: forces of evil, disordered personalities who were causing all the wrong in the world. "Burt would march down Sunset; his spine would straighten and he'd lift off on one foot and strut in a parade stance like a British Beefeater, mumbling to himself about 'The filthy f.o.e.' – saying they're piss, shit and corruption in human form. He spoke metaphorically and parenthetically. He'd never really elaborate, just that they had to be destroyed. He never mentioned exact people but he identified the f.o.e. – he spelt it with small letters because he said, 'there was nothing GREAT about the forces of evil' – as those who knowingly do harm to humanity. Those who treat others in a manner that they themselves would not like to be treated, and who have incurred a debt to be repaid. He would say, 'They know who they are!' And 'Them's gonna pay for the crimes they've committed!'"

To Hampton's mind: "The whole forces of evil thing was total paranoia. Burt felt the world was conspiring against him, and he was walking a fine line trying not to be destroyed by it. He would act like that: 'Watch out for that guy, he's checking us out.'" And for Stanley Dyrector, Burt's current state was a sobering reminder of the fallibility in us all: "People have feet of clay, and my idealism in him disintegrated when I saw him talking to himself. I didn't like the forces of evil talk and the thunderbolts coming down and hitting him; these other worlds coming after him. It could be heart-wrenching, but he functioned well with a lot of support, though his body was a bag of bones. It's interesting, in some of his paintings, like *Out Here*, you see great white sparks coming out of him, and in my reading of Chekhov's *Marriage Proposal*, it mentions 'the spark of man,' a patchwork quilt of metaphysical cosmic consciousness. He suffered the slings and arrows but without the fortune."

When Morgan Ames found out about Burt's plight she was concerned but not entirely surprised: "Burt wasn't stable enough for LSD. He wanted more and more and he was fearless and would try anything. It was The New Frontier and he was first in line to go too far. We thought he killed himself after one acid trip. The level of awareness for drug issues was non-existent, and so there were lies, and most didn't know how to use it. But doing acid was a prestigious thing, especially for Burt, it made him feel special. I think he was manic-depressive and very unhappy. It was a gloomy atmosphere and we feared that a veil of darkness had fallen upon us."

This shared sense of foreboding materialized that summer, when genuine forces of evil terrorized Los Angeles in the malignant guise of Charles "Tex" Watson and his young, pliant, hippie henchwomen; perpetrators of the horrific Tate-Labianca murders. These amphetamine-amped, amateur assassins were groupies of Charles Manson, a recidivist robber turned minstrel who'd been able to inculcate his minions with a manipulative line of psychedelic-inspired mystification. [1] The gruesome slayings served as a reality check for many famous ravers whose "open house" policy – fostered by the egalitarian ethos of the Love Generation – was abandoned overnight, and drawbridges were raised, guns were swiftly purchased, and security systems installed. Despite some shoddy police work, the rippers were eventually apprehended that December, and by the time they were brought to trial the following summer, Ledru had already lured Burt out from his Laurel Canyon lair, where he was behind on his rent, and moved him into his new, two-bedroom apartment on 403 Ocean Avenue, in the Seal Beach community of Orange County. The multidwelling unit in which they lived was tucked back away from the main street, where only a row of houses separated them from the Pacific Ocean.

One of their first visitors there was Marshall Berle, nephew of the popular entertainer Milton Berle, who worked in rock management; first at the William Morris talent agency, looking after such headlining acts as The Beach Boys, Little Richard, Marvin Gaye and Ike and Tina Turner, and then under his own flag as the head of the Carma Booking Agency. Although he'd met the flatmates a few months earlier, he was first drawn into Burt's orbit back in the mid-60s, when he cruised past the Purple Onion mural one day, high on peyote: "When I saw that mural, I stopped the car, jumped out, gazed at it and thought, how does this guy know? How can this painter capture what we're seeing?"

Wonderstruck by the imagery, Berle endeavoured to track down the artist but hit a dead end until a few years later when he wandered into the Indian Trading Post store in Hollywood one day. "While I was in the store, I asked this hunchbacked guy where I could buy some peyote, which I didn't quite realize was not the done thing to do, and he pointed me to this Indian guy who was sat on the sidewalk outside. It was Semu, who was currently living in a crash pad beneath the store. He knew where I could buy peyote and, it also turned out, he had a drawing by Burt, which he sold to me for $75. I then saw another Burt drawing at Steve Ross' house, who was a mutual friend, and I asked him if he'd introduce me to Burt because I wanted to commission a painting from him, and he arranged for Burt and Ledru to come over to my apartment. I was expecting these wild, way-out freaks, but they show up and I think they're cops because they've got short hair and shades and have their pants tucked into their boots. I found out later this was their tribute to Captain Kirk and Spock from *Star Trek*. They were on this big science fiction trip. After that, we became very close and saw each other every day."

On the surface, Burt and Ledru made for an eccentric double act, and Berle was tickled by their comical customs and interactions, as well as their quaint modes of expression. Dextroamphetamine was now a major part of their vast pharmacological intake, and when Ledru would offer some from his pillbox, he'd say, 'Vitamins?' And Burt would reply, 'Don't mind if I do!' And whenever they were introduced to an attractive female, Burt would gush, 'How lovely,' to which Ledru would retort, 'Indeed.' Like an old married couple, they even picked up each other's eating habits. Ledru was a big man with a hearty appetite and, living with him, Burt couldn't help but pile on the pounds; and so, as a consequence, he lost his slimline frame and developed a potbelly. They even homed a stray moggy together, when it wandered into their lives one day, on which they bestowed the honorific title "Special Cat."

In exchange for a reduction on the rent, Ledru carried out odd jobs around the apartment building, as an unofficial maintenance man, but despite this and the patronage of Marshall Berle, money was still tight, so he found some steady work driving a "steel steed" auto transporter for a trucking company. Although it paid well, Ledru didn't like the work much and spoke of it disparagingly. It carried too much responsibility; there were tight schedules to meet, and although he was a good driver, there was always the threat of an accident occurring while navigating such a big rig. Plus, his real pleasure in life centred around getting high and painting with Burt, and under his tutelage, he created several Shonberg-inspired abstracts and a pleasing portrait of a blue-faced reptilian alien.

He also witnessed first-hand how Burt, aided and abetted by the astronomical amount of drugs he'd consumed over the years, became so disconnected from reality, his very identity was called into question. He was now claiming the artist known as Burt Shonberg was a complete fabrication, a cover story, and his real identity was Jack Bond, an intergalactic agent hailing from Time Coast, a realm outside of "moving time," located in the 4th Dimension. "Burt was Burt until he was abducted," Marshall Berle explains helpfully. "He was put here and given the identity of an artist called Burt Shonberg, but then he awakened and realized he was actually Jack Bond from the 4th Dimension."

Though a psychiatrist would have doubtlessly diagnosed him as suffering from a dissociative fugue state or an identity disorder triggered by his drug use, a clinical observation was never going to happen. "Burt hated psychiatrists," Berle confirms. "He thought they were a bunch of quacks!" Furthermore, Burt believed his new persona was the specially chosen receiver of transmissions emitted down from the exosphere by the Mysterians, an extraterrestrial force of "space brothers," who protected him karmically from the invisible government agents that were spying on him, trying to discover what he'd been writing and drawing. "It was all about the crimes of industry; the crimes of business, and corruption in government," Ledru explains. "He felt government people were after him and said someone had actually shot at him." Bob Storr confirms: "Burt believed the FBI thought he was an alien, and the way he spoke to strangers – his manner – aroused suspicion. He'd say 'I knew they were sent over to me,' as a private joke."

Burt was particularly obsessed with the plight of a Mysterian spacecraft that had recently crash-landed in Alaska, due, he claimed, to illegal sound wave technology operated by the same shadowy government agency, who were operating in the region. Like Burt's previous extraterrestrial scenarios, this one also had its origins in a favourite film: the 1951 chiller *The Thing from Another World*, whose plot pivots when U.S. air force pilots, stationed at a remote research base at the North Pole, recover the body of a humanoid found frozen in a block of ice near a crashed flying saucer. And, naturally, all hell breaks loose once he thaws out.

Ledru was as invested in this scenario as Burt was, and felt vindicated one evening when they left a restaurant in Huntington Beach, after discussing the Mysterians over a meal. As they walked to their car (parked at the intersection of Charing Cross Drive and Coventry Lane), a loud voice came thundering down from above. "We both heard this one-word communication: 'Roger,'" Ledru recollects. "As in 'Roger that'! A term uttered during radio transmissions. I looked at Burt and he looked at me and I said, 'Did you hear that?' and he affirmed he did, and we realized it was confirmation of his Alaskan dissertation, and his belief that the Mysterians were in telepathic contact with him."

Burt's resulting napkin art was plagued with Mysterian-related symbolism, including the letter R for Roger; the numbers 403; relating to his earthly address, and 22, his cryptic personal number that he began signing everything with, which correlated to Mars. Consequent communiqués were scrawled across pages of sheet music, and in his *Mysterian of the Cosmos* portrait, he depicted a black, ominous, Gort-like droid named M-20 (M20 is the astronomical name of the Triffid Nebula in the Sagittarius constellation), shadowed by his flying saucer, in a galaxy ruled by pewter-coloured planets.

Though Ledru was a true believer, George Clayton Johnson remained sceptical of Burt's startling claims, and he recounts a drive he and the two men took along Pacific Coast Highway: "It was the last time I saw Burt. He told me he was now Jack Bond, an intergalactic spy menaced by all manner of things. I immediately thought of James Bond and told him, 'Aren't you afraid it'll be seen as derivative?' And he said, 'No, no, no.' He was having this interplanetary adventure and living this sci-fi creation. I thought it was trite and unoriginal; a story I'd seen before." Marshall Berle, however, remained intrigued by the drama, though it was tempered when Burt, in either a moment of candour or cognitive dissonance, admitted to him "This is all science fiction."

As well as commissioning personal artworks from Burt, Marshall Berle began exploiting his music business contacts and managed to place several Shonberg's on album covers. It started with the fearsome self-portrait *Waking State of Consciousness*, that depicted Burt's malformed face twisted in a rictus grimace. This unflinching attempt to exteriorize his split-personality was couched in comic book luridness and was redolent of the acid-scarred Batman villain Two-face. The image was revealed in the inner sleeve of the 1972 LP *Crazed Hipsters* by the psychedelic blues-rock outfit Finnegan and Wood, and although it certainly complimented the album's title, the duo apparently hated the image so much it was struck from subsequent reissues. Then in 1976, again through Berle's largess, *Seated Figure and a Cosmic Train* become the arresting front cover for the self-titled debut album of country-rockers The Curtis Bros. But it's his pivotal role in another album cover, created a year prior to this, for which he remains most rightfully proud. At the time, he was managing the affairs of the reformed rock band Spirit, fronted by hotshot guitarist Randy California. Although the group was currently without a record contract, they'd spent five weeks recording new material at Studio 70 in Tampa, Florida, and on hearing the quality of the new songs, Berle was able to ink a deal with Mercury Records.

Randy envisioned the album as a celebration of the country's bicentennial, the following year, and when he mused about an appropriate album cover, Berle suggested they enlist Burt to create one, and he readily agreed, having met Burt previously, through Marshall, at a friend's peyote party in the Hollywood Hills. Marshall immediately contacted Burt, and they made arrangements, out of their own pockets, to fly him down to Tampa to meet the group and hopefully collaborate.

While waiting for his flight to depart from LAX airport, Burt was thrilled to spot the actor Christopher Lee, whose minacious portrayal of Dracula in the British Hammer Horror film series met with his full approval. In fact, he considered him a worthy successor to Bela Lugosi. But when Burt arrived at the studio, things did not go smoothly, initially. After Randy relayed the title and concept of the album – how he wanted *Spirit of '76* to represent Old Glory and the 200th anniversary of the country – Burt rebuffed the notion declaring: "I'm an artist, not an illustrator, and I don't get involved in politics!" On the surface, this seemed a strange thing to say given Burt's patriotic sentiments in the past, but it would become evident in the fullness of time, that he was only masking his true intentions. Despite this less than promising start, Burt felt a rapport with Randy California, upon whom he conferred the spiritual nickname "Rama," While Randy was totally sold on Jack Bond, Burt's alter-ego; so much so he invited him into the vocal booth to deliver some bulletins. Strained through an effect unit, Burt's phased-out voice ended up being showcased twice on the album. Although the Jack Bond Part 2 cut was so swamped in delays and reverb it made it unintelligible, Part 1 was fathomable, if arcane:

> "*Introducing Jack Bond of Miami 1992 A.D.* (a place that existed on Time Coast.) (Unintelligible) *Contralto*. (Unintelligible). *We are located in different places, in more ways*

than one. One juxtaposition to another. There are those situations that are worlds apart, there are those that are situations that we relate to, travel to, journey to, and get involved with. We're located in another type of distance away from each other. (Unintelligible) *Some are located in the past, some are located in the present time dimension and others are located in the future. Zing Zang* (a term used by Jack Bond when he was traveling along the Time Coast, outside of moving time). *Creatures from the camp of* (unintelligible) *in the year of 1976 A.D."* [2]

The band's newly acquired bassist, Barry Keene, was also fascinated by their new arrival: "When Burt showed up it was like having an E.T. around, as you never knew what he was going to say. The things he said were so enlightening; there was an attractive power to them. He was a completely unique person. He was an artist through and through, always thinking about painting. I never detected any off-the-wall behaviour with him. The only thing was when he got excited, he'd make a noise and do that thing that horses do when they exhale and their lips blow out. He'd do it five, six, seven times, which I thought was unusual. He seemed utterly introspective and let things be, just soaking the whole thing up." Coincidently, Keene was currently undergoing psychiatric therapy with Dr. Oscar Janiger, and when he later mentioned Burt's name, the headshrinker lit up: "He thought Burt was the greatest." But not everyone in the group was so enamoured. Ed Cassidy – Spirit's powerhouse drummer, as well as Randy California's stepfather, was put off by Burt's peculiar quirks, and the two did not gel at all. "Burt would sit in the studio and when someone would approach him, he'd say, 'Who goes there?' Marshall explains. [3] "He had weird ticks and would talk to himself. People got nervous but it didn't bother me at all. Cassidy later said in an interview that Randy and I brought in a 'whack job' to do the artwork, but Ed came to a bad demise. People who criticised Burt often did." Marshall, by now, was used to Burt's aberrant moments, though he remained concerned by the endless speed pills his friend popped as he soaked in the atmosphere. Although he wasn't necessarily a fan of rock music, Burt appeared to enjoy the studio environment, and for nine of the ten days he spent there, he stationed himself with a black pen and restaurant napkins engaged in, what Berle describes as, "air drawing." For no matter how long he sketched, nothing seemed to materialize on the sheets. It wasn't until the tenth and final day of his stay that Burt actually produced some artwork, but when he presented it to Marshall and Randy, they weren't exactly sure what to make of the Stygian mishmash. There were two intricately decorated 5 by 5-inch napkins, mired in Jack Bond jargon. One of them, which was subsequently used as the album's front cover, read:

Tampa Jam

Electro Jam

From The Time Coast

Spirit of '76

While the other napkin listed, amongst other things, names of the rulers and chiefs of "Space Action Agency," including Rama. It wasn't until months later, after the *Spirit of '76* album was released, that Berle and the band discovered that Burt had fulfilled Randy's remit in the most ingenious way. Forr under close inspection, and with the aid of some stimulants, they realized that both images did indeed depict the American flag, most notably the second image used on the back of the album cover, where there was enough white space between the graffiti to resemble the 13 stripes on Old Glory, while an idyllic snapshot of the Sunshine State – palm trees overarching a swimming pool, most likely inspired by Burt's hotel digs – was sketched in the top left canton where the 50 stars would normally be.

In order to promote the album, Spirit embarked on a nationwide tour and Burt attended several memorable shows, including one at Gulfstream Park in Hallandale Beach, Florida. On June 22nd, Ledru took the wheel of his red Ford Mustang and drove Burt and himself down to Diablo Stadium in Tempe, Arizona, to watch Spirit supporting British prog rockers Yes. Marshall recalls that the groupies were plentiful at the show, and with no woman in his life, Burt was ready to get it on with them. However, more often than not, he felt more comfortable just keeping company with Berle's girlfriend (and future wife), Paula.

For the special hometown show held at Santa Monica Civic Center, on August 15th, Burt appeared through the gap in the stage curtain and, with a spotlight on him, introduced Spirit in his heavily-modulated Jack Bond voice. He dressed up special for the occasion, too, wearing a white t-shirt bearing the cryptic lettering: Miami 1992 A.D., and wore a sailor's cap that partially concealed the strands of his now thinning gray hair. [4] When the tour ended, Burt hung out at Randy California's pad in Topanga Canyon, sharing the fruits of his latest interplanetary visions, like the painting *Starships of Tarot One*, showing a fleet of flying saucers slaloming between the spheres of Earth and the Sun.

Meanwhile, back in Revere, Burt's parents were living out their peaceful retirement in a modest apartment they'd moved into at 106 Elliot Road. For the rest of her life, Helen remonstrated with herself over that original bust-up with her beloved son, rueing the hard line she'd taken over his relationship with Connie all those years ago; tortured by the thought that if she'd allowed their love to develop, he probably would have settled down and started a family by now. Instead, he went his own unique, solitary way, leaving the two of them estranged and Helen without grandchildren. Looking back, Dolly recalls a bittersweet moment when Helen, wracked with guilt, half-jokingly quipped, "It's too bad they don't offer a course at Harvard on how to be a good mother!" On August 16th, 1975, Helen Shonberg died of a heart attack and was buried in Sudilkov Cemetery, in Everett, a small town bordering Revere to the west. Burt did not attend the funeral. "Burt would say 'my family' in a scoffing tone," Bob Storr recollects. "He'd say, 'I didn't come from there – that's not my real family.' He made his break from them after (the LSD experiments with) Janiger. They become a *historical family.*" Regardless of Burt's attitude, Helen bequeathed a tidy sum of money to her brother in her will, so that he could continue the monthly stipends to her son in the event of her demise.

When Marshall Berle visited Burt in Seal Beach that summer, he found him in a dishevelled state, his hands shaking as he worked obsessively on some napkin sketches. "Ledru told me Burt had been up three weeks, without sleeping, doing those drawings. He looked a mess." It was a sad, unsettling scene, and as if triggered by a premonition, Marshall promised his friend that he would preserve his body of work, but Burt just chuckled and shook his head, bemused by the very notion.

Several months later, Berle was hanging out at the Whiskey a Go Go, where the new, high-energy rock combo he was managing, Van Halen, were in the middle of a residency and about to sign their first major record deal. It was there, in the midst of all that excitement, that Marshall received a phone call from Ledru, who, having managed to track him down to the venue, conveyed some godawful news: Burt had passed away. "The call was a huge bring down for me," Marshall recollects. "I was devastated."

On the evening of September 16th, Ledru returned home to find Burt laying on the couch, with one eye open and the other eye closed. It was later established that he'd died alone at approximately 5:00 pm of a heart attack, aged just 44-years-old. "Death was not a surprise to Burt," Ledru explains. "He *knew* where he was going. He'd found answers to the existential questions and he'd completed what he'd come here for. His works were in the world so he was ready to go. He'd scoff when I would say he should protect these paintings. He said, 'I'll try and have my body disappear when I leave.' He had a way of lightening up a situation."

Though grieving, Marshall Berle could also see a positive side to his friend's passing: "Burt's death freed him," he contends, philosophically. He also believes Burt depicted his earthly exit in one of his final paintings, *Outer Cosmos #22*. "It was commissioned by a drug dealer in LA. He gave Burt $500 but the guy hated it, so I paid him $500 for it instead. It's abstract but you can make out his head, so it's a self-portrait where he's leaving the world and his human role behind to become a super-agent."

There then followed a huge brouhaha over what to do with Burt's body, which needed to be buried in a timely manner, as per Jewish custom. Burt's uncle Harry flew out to Orange County to take charge of things and favoured burying Burt in a plot somewhere in his adopted California. Dolly, however, was adamant: Bitsy had to be returned to Massachusetts, to be buried by his mother, because even though she was now in the great beyond, Dolly feared Helen would never forgive her if she didn't make this happen. Ultimately Dolly won the day, and Burt's corpse was flown back to his home state, but there were further recriminations at the funeral when Dolly discovered Harry hadn't arranged to have a rabbi present to officiate the committal, provoking a family rift that hasn't healed to this day. Louis Shonberg was not informed of his son's passing, and just seven months later, on April 15th, 1978, he bid his own final farewell to the world and was laid to rest next to his wife and son. Dolly subsequently arranged for a brass plaque to be fixed to the flat marker on Burt's grave, to commemorate his brief but not uneventful military service.

Burt sat beneath his *Seated Figure and a Cosmic Train* masterpiece, in the Northern California home of Gary Groom, a collector of his artworks. 1973. (Courtesy of Marshall Berle.)

Burt and Marshall in Tampa 1975. (Courtesy of Marshall Berle.)

Mysterian of the Cosmos. 1973. Casein on canvas board. 14" x 18". (Courtesy of Marshall Berle.)

Burt's *Waking State of Consciousness* painting that featured on the inside sleeve of *Crazed Hipsters*, the 1972 album by Finnegan and Wood.

Burt's *Cosmic Notes* napkin art. Circa 1973. (Courtesy of Marshall Berle.)

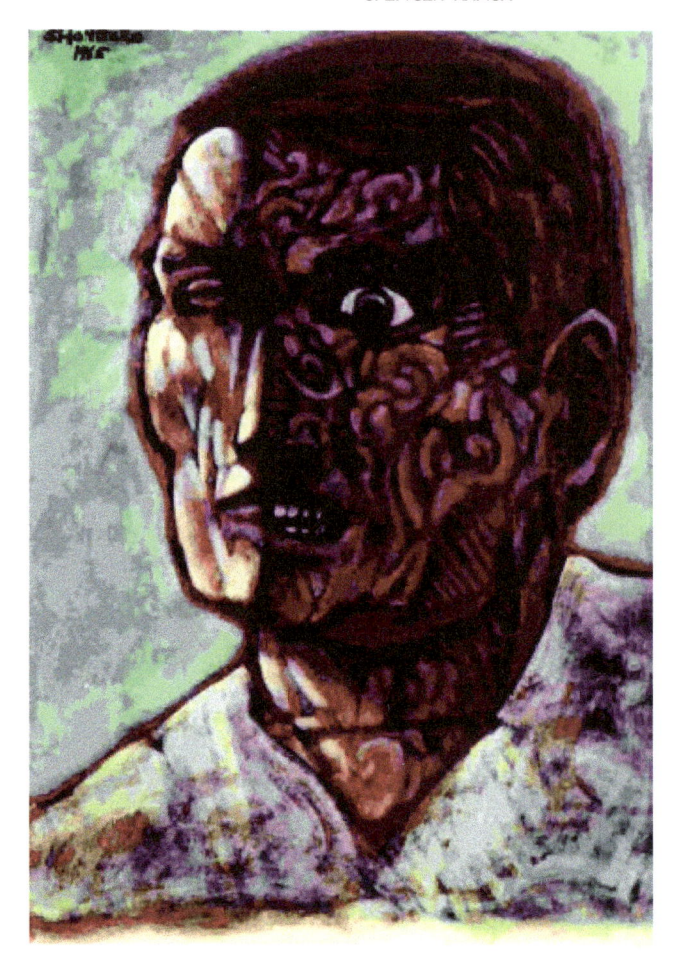

Spirit of 76 front and back cover images.

The Starships of Tarot One. Casein on Masonite. 4 ft x 4 ft. This is believed to be Burt's final painting. (Courtesy of Marshall Berle and Laugh Dome Records LLC.)

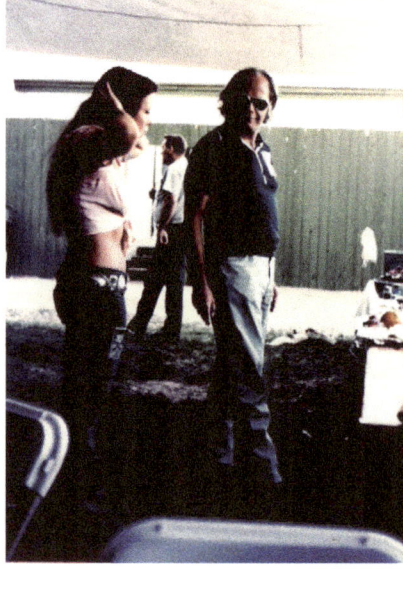

Burt attending a Spirit gig at the Gulf Stream Racetrack in Florida. (Courtesy of Sherman Keene.)

Burt with Marshall Berle's girlfriend (and future wife) Paula, backstage at the Spirit gig in Tempe Arizona. (Courtesy of Marshall Berle.)

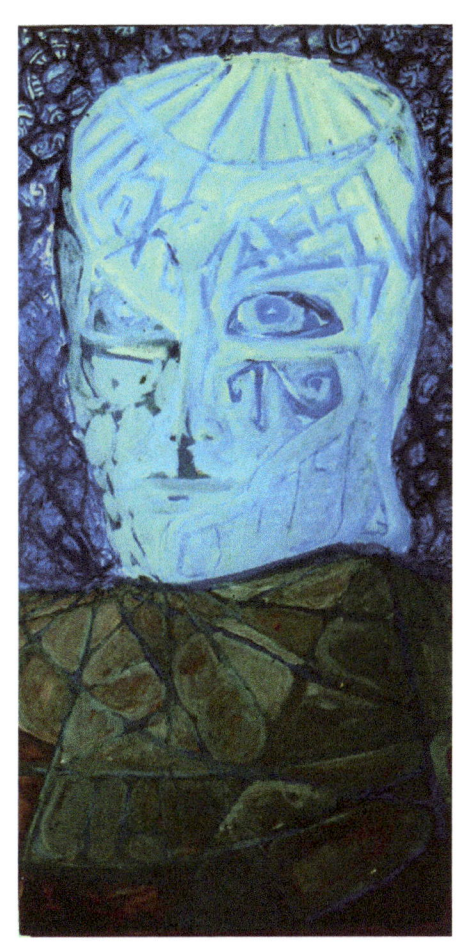

Ledru's reptilian alien painting. (Courtesy of Marshall Berle.)

Ledru and his Mustang, Arizona Desert. (Courtesy of Sherman Keene.)

The Mysterian. 1974. Watercolour on Bristol Board. In memory of Joseph Jay Dekeyser.
(Photographed by Raphael Hernandez. Courtesy of Marshall Berle and LaughDome Records LLC.)

Burt with Randy California and Marshall Berle backstage at Spirit's Santa Monica Auditorium gig. (Courtesy of Marshall Berle.)

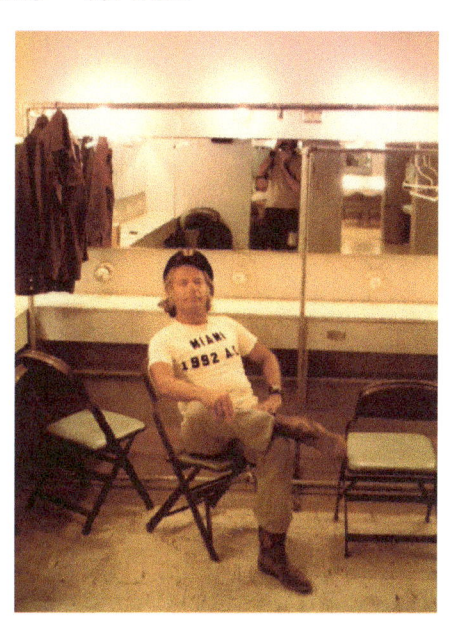

Burt with Barry (now Sherman) Keene and Marshall, backstage at Spirit's Santa Monica Auditorium gig. (Courtesy of Sherman Keene.)

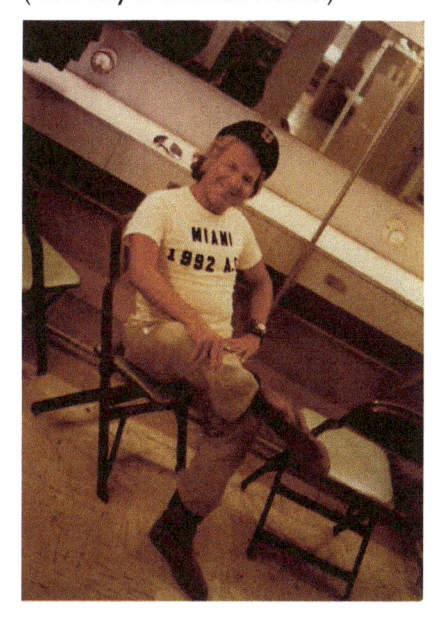

The smile's back. Burt backstage at Spirit's Santa Monica Auditorium gig. (Courtesy of Sherman Keene.)

Burt's *Occult House* napkin art. Circa 1974. (Courtesy of Marshall Berle.)

Zing Zang napkin art. 1976. According to Marshall Berle: "Zing Zang was a term often used by Burt when he was "outside of moving time" traveling along the Time Coast. He gave this to me for my birthday, one year before he died. (Courtesy of Marshall Berle.)

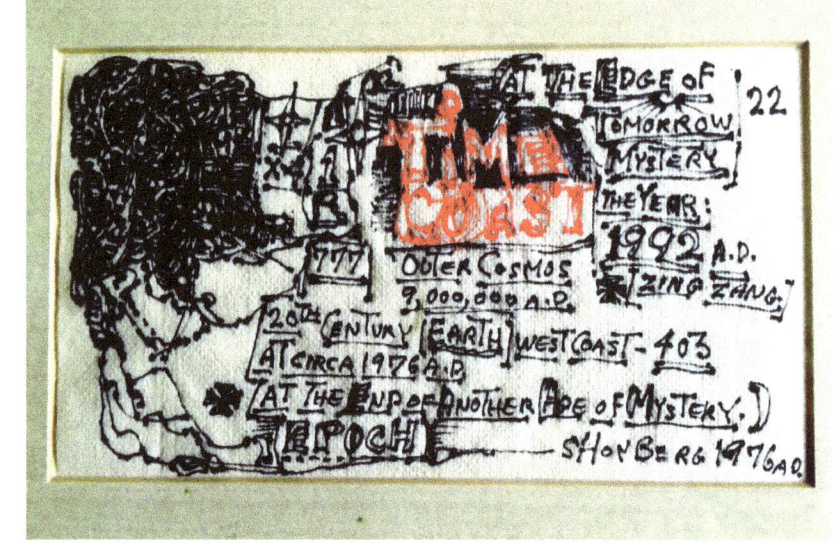

BURT SHONBERG ➥ *OUT THERE*

Outer Cosmos #22. Marshall believes the abstract depicts Burt's earthly exit and transformation into Jack Bond. (Courtesy of Marshall Berle.)

The last known photograph of Burt sat in Marshall's backyard in North Hills, L.A. (Courtesy of Marshall Berle.)

Burt's gravestone marker. The mention of Korea on the marker is a bit of a misnomer, of course, as The Korean War was over by the time Burt enlisted. (Photographed by Dorothy Slotnick Green.)

Epilogue

Having seen the progressive promise, exemplified by Martin Luther King and Bobby Kennedy, snuffed-out by assassins, and witnessed the appalling mistreatment of anti-war protesters by cops outside the Democratic National Convention in Chicago that August, Vito Paulekas foresaw a countrywide, state-sponsored crackdown on peaceniks like him, following 1968's "corrective" election of President Nixon. So, on December 2nd of that year, he and Szou fled the country and headed to the Caribbean. Despite prior warnings from Robert Carl Cohen, they washed up in Haiti and found out for themselves how scary it was to live under the dictatorship of Papa Doc Duvalier. "We lived across the street from his palace and locals would try and guess where we were from," Szou recollects. "They'd ask us, 'Are you from Cuba?' We'd take walks at night from our pensione until a mass of people closed in on us; it was very frightening." They then sought refuge in Kingston, Jamaica, but discovered it was just as dangerous: "Nobody got off the plane except us. There was a sugarcane strike and people were out of work and resentful against whites." By December 1969, they were back in California to attend the Altamont Free Festival, headlined by the Rolling Stones. In *Gimme Shelter*, the documentary film of the concert, Vito can be seen, in all his freak-out glory, dressed in long johns, dancing with ribbons in his hair on a platform behind the stage, whilst the Jefferson Airplane play their aggro-interrupted set. Afterwards, with their young children on board, they travelled north, across San Francisco Bay, to Cotati, in Sonoma County, where Vito bought a house for $8,000. Part of their belongings included artwork by Burt, but some of it ended up meeting a familiar fate. "We left LA with some of Burt's large pieces rolled up; we had a lot of his stuff," Szou recollects. "A small one of a house in a wooden frame; one of his car pictures, which is really dynamic. It captures the feeling you get – the movement. We had one of his palette knife paintings – he was so good with the palette knife – in the kitchen over the stove. We named them Starburst abstracts. But it was well known that there was a curse attached to Burt's work. They would burn up, and after we'd been here six months there was a fire in Vito's workshop, caused by the next-door neighbour, and some of Burt's paintings were destroyed."

In 1974, Vito nearly lost his life during a hernia operation, but it did little to diminish his boundless energy. With Franzoni, he created a new street theatre troupe called Freestore; they played live concerts and delighted the studio audience when they appeared on the bonkers, *Gong Show*. Vito built a bandstand in the park; taught dance classes at Sonoma State College, and carved an impressive wooden sculpture dedicated to the town's namesake, Pomo Indian Chief Cotati, which helped revamp the sleepy hamlet into the hippie outpost it is today. Following her divorce from Vito in 1977, Szou became a psychiatric technician nurse at the Sonoma State Hospital and remained working there all the way up to her retirement.

A few years before Vito died (on October 25, 1992, aged 79), he was visited by one of his former studio assistants, the muralist Kristina Rochelle Steinke, who was known as Marko back in the day. "It came back to me who he really was: the greatest of men. The way he treated people; he put you on a pedestal, he gave you the centre stage. He gave his unselfish affection and attention and energy to you – not himself. He made you feel good. He was an amazing person. He probably could've been a great political leader, if he didn't smoke pot! {laughs}

Shortly after she Burt went their separate ways, Valerie reverted back to her Serbian birth name Velinka and married Art Kunkin, the publisher/editor of the *LA Free Press*. Although she was not physically attracted to him, he was a powerful player in the political life of the city, and by luring him away from his wife and children, she hoped that part of his prestige would reflect onto her. When that marriage went south, she wed John James Stancin, an artist known for his neo-romantic style of painting. Together they moved to Maui, Hawaii and opened the Stancin Art Gallery in Lahaina, which showcased and sold their paintings and sculptures. They returned to the mainland sometime in the 1980s and lived out their remaining years in Palm Springs. After Stancin died, in 1990, Valerie visited Szou in Cotati, but the reunion was marred when she began hitting on some of Szou's friends, of both genders. "After John Stancin's death, she suffered from depression, and she ruined her liver by drinking paint thinner – turpentine, to kill herself. She then told me she thought she had leukaemia, but she went vegan and kicked the disease without taking the cancer medicine. She cured herself." Although she retained her raging libido well into her seventies, Valerie never remarried but found a new passion, flamenco dancing, which she performed for audiences up until the year 2002, when it became physically impossible. She died on February 4th, 2012, aged 84. Her sons Louis and Julian both live in San Francisco now, and though they have conflicted emotions regarding their mother, they've retained nothing but reverence for Burt, whose artistry continues to inform the digital art they create.

In 1977, Hampton Fancher purchased the film rights to Phillip K. Dick's science-fiction novel *Do Androids Dream of Electric Sheep?* with hopes of turning it into a movie. Five years later, he realized his dream, when *Blade Runner* was released, based on the screenplay he co-wrote. Although it was not commercially successful at the box office, it became a cult movie and is now regarded as a modern classic. Hampton agrees that its dystopian storyline about a detective hunting down escaped androids (known as "replicants") would have especially appealed to Burt, and for one section of the story, he reached back into their shared past and based the Methuselah Syndrome on the aging disease that prematurely killed Charles Beaumont. For years a follow-up to the film was mooted but, despite many abortive attempts, nothing materialized until July 2016 when it was announced that principal photography had begun on Hampton's co-written sequel, *Blade Runner 2049*, which is slated to be released in October 2017.

In the mid-1980s, Ringo Starr became a keen collector of Burt's paintings, thanks to his friendship with George Greif, who shared several pieces with him at a house party. In quick succession, he purchased several pieces, including *The Tree on a Magical Landscape* and *Unicorn*, and even came to the Greif house personally to collect them, stripping one painting straight off the wall and loading it into his vehicle. Although they were excited to have a famous Beatle in their home, Greif's now-adult daughters, Laura and Diane, grew up loving these paintings and were saddened to see them go. They were relieved, however, when their favourite picture, a Purple Onion-style vista of Monument Valley, entitled *The Moons*, remained untouched, as they derived such pleasure from it as kids, picking out and counting up the many moons it contained.

When asked in 2005 who his favourite artists were, the legendary drummer listed Burt alongside Rembrandt, Van Gogh, George Condo and Peter Max. However, ten years later he sold seven Shonberg pieces, including a superb *Magic Ship*, at an auction, as part of his drive to downsize his possessions. Coincidently, the front cover of Ringo's 1974 album, *Goodnight Vienna*, was an homage to the sci-fi classic movie *The Day the Earth Stood Still*, one of Burt's all-time favourites. It was one of those films that he could recite entire lines of dialogue from, and he regaled friends with his imitation of Gort the robot. When Sally Kellerman visited Ringo's house in LA, a few years ago, she was delighted to discover that he owned Shonberg's too: "I'm such a Beatles fan, and finding out that Ringo had these two, big paintings by Burt, I thought, Oh, how nice. I've got a painting by the same artist as a Beatle!" Taking a moment to look back, she has nothing but admiration for her old friend: "Burt was pre-*Star Trek* and pre-*Star Wars*. He was so ahead of his time."

In August 1986, Dr. Oscar Janiger hosted *The Enchanted Loom: LSD and Creativity* exhibition at his home in Santa Monica, California, as a celebration of his pioneering work back in the 1950s and '60s. Although he was now 68-years-old, and semi-retired, he expressed the vain hope of kick-starting some new trials with the drug again, feeling he'd "only just scratched the surface of the effect of altered states on the creative process." For he still maintained that LSD was a valuable tool in unlocking the mysteries of the mind. [1] The exhibit displayed testimony from some of Janiger's celebrity volunteers, such as Cary Grant and the conductor Andre Previn, and featured paintings made by 60 of the artists who took part in the original study, including Burt. Stanley Dyrector attended the show and was pleased as punch to see a couple of his friend's pictures on the walls.

On August 14th, 2001, Janiger passed away in his private hospital room, having dosed himself with 100 micrograms of LSD; departing the world in the same style as his friend and fellow psychonaut, Aldous Huxley. While his pipe dream of building a society where LSD is administered to citizens as rite of passage, based on the annual Eleusinian Mystery of ancient Greece, where the libation kykeon (that may have contained an entheogen agent like ergot or toadstool) was given to initiates at the climax of the ceremony, to induce a transcendental experience, remains just that.

In 1988, Ledru met a lovely lady named Joei (Joey) Underhill who worked in the banquet room of Acropolis, a Greek restaurant in Pacific Palisades. "His landlord and landlady and fellow tenants would bring him there and it was a fun place for both of us," she remembers fondly. "I found him fascinating, and he didn't let anyone get out of line with me. I was in an unhappy marriage, a bad situation, and even contemplating suicide when I met him, and he pulled me out of that and we fell in love."

In no time at all, Joei moved into the Seal Beach apartment: "I initially gave Ledru some money but he wouldn't accept it," Joei explains. "He was only into bare necessities; money meant nothing to him. It was nothing he strived for. Ledru was striving to be a good influence in people's lives, and he was. He was so good to me. He gave me so much."

Ledru enjoyed having company again. Burt's death had left a big hole in his life and he would wax nostalgic about him to his new love: "Ledru talked of Burt all the time and knew him better than anyone. He told me many stories about their times together. One very funny thing involved illegality. They were on their way to Hollywood and they got stopped and busted for pot and ended up in jail. Ledru converted Burt's bedroom into my closet and used the two garages downstairs to store his art, which I was privileged to see. Ive always been attracted to smart people, and Ledru had a photographic memory. He could quote from the Bible like no one else and I was raised in that atmosphere. Although I couldn't buy any of it at that point, Ledru felt I had met God himself and, through him, I found the answer to everything, and it changed my whole life. Like night and day. He had a good working knowledge of Christianity and other beliefs, but I couldn't fully grasp the outer space stuff he was describing. He said, 'We don't have the vocabulary.' He'd been studying esoteric beliefs long before me and was interested in things higher than this earth. So, I was very impressed."

Their bliss lasted until September 12th, 2008, when Ledru died from a massive heart attack, the same cause of death as Burt. Just as he had once returned home to find his best friend lying lifeless on the couch, now it was Joei's turn to make the same fateful discovery. "I came home and found Ledru on the bathroom floor and there was a little movement, so I called 911 but by the time the paramedics got there he was gone. I was in the hospital the night before, and if I'd been relieved earlier, I could have been home and got him to the emergency. I put my head on his shoulder and he didn't move. I didn't know he had heart problems. He loved to eat and weighed close to 270 lbs. He had to stop playing tennis, which kept him fit and trim because his leg hurt, and he'd gained quite a bit of weight in the front area, so getting him through those little apartment doors was difficult. He never wanted to be a burden to anyone."

Ledru was cremated and Joei and friends gave him a local Seal Beach send-off. "I was going to hire a boat and skipper and take the ashes out close to the inlet that leads to the inland waterway, but we couldn't get permission; so, in the end, we just walked down to the shore at twilight and scattered his ashes there. They were contained in a biodegradable container which would dissolve in the ocean water. What we did was still against law, but 'Screw the law!' as Ledru would say."

In January 1997, Randy California was dragged under by a powerful riptide off the coast of Molokai, Hawaii, while attempting to save his 12-year-old son Quinn from drowning. His body has never been recovered. He was only 45. John Boyce continues to paint and is represented exclusively by the Jean Marc Gallery in West Hollywood. Walter Teller, however, abandoned art to became a preacher. Cameron spent her dotage living in a bijou bungalow in West Hollywood, where she continued seeking new spiritual dimensions. Since her death from cancer in 1995, her artistic reputation has grown steadily. In 2011, her fascinating life was finally chronicled in the biography *Wormwood Star*, penned by your humble correspondent, and in 2014, a retrospective of her work entitled *Cameron: Songs for the Witch Woman*, was held at the MOCA Pacific Design Center in Los Angeles.

In 1999, Subterranean Press published *All of Us Are Dying*, an anthology of short stories by George Clayton Johnson, featuring a front cover illustration of a sax player moaning into his horn, courtesy of Burt Shonberg. In 2005, *The Fictioneer* was released, an audio book of his short stories, featuring the visage of Lucifer from Burt's *Magic Landscape* on the front cover. In 2012, George was invited to be the guest of honour at the San Diego Comic Fest. To celebrate his past, the organizers built a recreation of Cafe Frankenstein, a period of his life that he'd spoken about so warmly. Wendy All, a toy designer by trade, and a longtime friend of George (they first met at Comic-Con in 1975) was put in charge: "I began to research it, and what started as just a painting grew into an entire set. I recreated as much as I was able of the original cafe from pictures on the net and from George's personal files. There was a lot of art history research, set design and development, and the discovery that the "stained glass" window was not true stained glass but painted with casein paint on glass." The results were marvellous, and (with Barry Alfonso) All produced an accompanying chapbook about "The brief (but monstrous) history of Laguna Beach's notorious mecca."

All is currently involved with the Rock Art Archive at the Cotsen Institute of Archaeology at UCLA, and her studies of petroglyphs and pictographs, created by many cultures around the world, has shed some valuable insight on the glyphs that Burt created for his Long Beach joint. "For Burt, I think this script had meaning but it was personal, and not likely translatable. To generalize, you might call Burt's script or glyphs or symbols "cabalistic calligraphy." My best guess, having reproduced Burt's symbols for the set design, and enjoyed the sensuality of their shapes, is that they are Burt's take on meaningful symbols of power for him. This is why I relate them to petroglyphs and pictographs. For an ancient tribe, certain symbols pecked or painted on the rock were symbols of power. To capture the symbol on the rock face was to increase the individual's power or the tribe's power, or the power of the place. Perhaps Burt wanted to imbue Cafe Frankenstein with his personal sense of magic and power, so he covered it with symbols that were important and meaningful to him. If you think about Mary Shelly's themes in her book; Frankenstein's monster, and chemistry and alchemy and power over nature, like bringing a dead creation back to life, the dots begin to connect on why Burt might have been thinking the way he did with these symbols."

On Christmas Day, 2015, George Clayton Johnson died from bladder and prostate cancer at a Veterans Administration Medical Center Hospital in North Hills, California. He was eulogized as one of the seminal speculative fiction scribes of his era. Just four months later, Doug Myres, his and Burt's partner in fun at Cafe Frankenstein, also passed away.

In 1988, due to the family's history with arthritis, Dolly and her elderly parents relocated from Massachusetts to Las Vegas, to escape the bad New England weather. Living there meant Dolly was able to make good on her girlhood dream of buying a house with its own swimming pool. Although most of the individuals in this book are now enjoying their well-earned retirement, several continue to ply their trades. Marshall Berle has quit the rock business but runs the comedy website Laugh.com and continues to fly the Shonberg flag via Burtshonberg.com, where you can view many other examples of Burt's amazing artwork. In collaboration with Laura Decludt (George Greif's daughter), he has produced a documentary on Burt, entitled *Out Here*, that will hopefully be released soon. Stanley Dyrector is still a jobbing actor in Hollywood. He is also the author of *Shedding Light on the Hollywood Blacklist: Conversation with Participants*, and the forthcoming book, *Comedians Funny People Hollywood (V1)*. Judy Shevin remains a much-in-demand interior stylist in Los Angeles, and like her fellow contemporaries, she harbours inordinately fond memories of Burt, though some of her final thoughts on him are infused with a bittersweetness: "How blessed I was to know this person and know him so well, and be part of his life. What a mind! Burt was definitely an evolved being. Part of him was so developed but he could not handle it. It was happening too fast and it was not his time, and towards the end, he was gone. He was an innocent and such a fragile man; his only drive was making art. There was a part of him that wasn't touched by this life. He was not touched by the world or greed or negativity that was around him. He was connected to another realm. Once in a while, you meet someone like that; a purity quality, untampered by this life. But he was vulnerable because of that. Although we came from different worlds, I knew at the time that he was a special, interesting human being. I recognised his specialness and never took him for granted. t was a privilege to know him and I miss talking to him; his choice of words. He was a poet as well as a painter. He was an explorer and a magician. Just an extraordinary being and the heavens were opening up for him." When asked if she believes Burt's transformation into Jack Bond might have been a sci-fi-inspired, cosmic joke he was playing on people, she concurs: "Burt had this great wink when he'd say something, 'It's between us – it's our deal.' So, I'm not sure if he took Jack Bond totally seriously. It was tongue-in-cheek at first but it became the real deal. He was a great actor and he began to believe his own story. Knowing Burt, he knew the drama he could create. Maybe it was just entertainment. He loved an audience. He was a showman." When she read recently about the Austronesian Moken people, a tribe whose limited language has never developed words to convey "hello," "goodbye" or "time," Burt immediately sprung to mind. "Burt had his own language, too. He talked like the wind."

Finally, in a fitting coda, Bob Storr ruminates: "In Burt's case, many of the stories he told and statements he made merit profound contemplation. One is: 'There is no such thing as 'Conscious Evil,' because true consciousness would be a higher level and 'Evil' would seem to indicate an incomplete understanding. It was an aspect of the Fourth Way that he could use because later on, he and Ledru felt Gurdjieff *schools* were bullshit. Ledru even said 'Ouspensky's a loser!' I wish Burt could have seen *The Matrix* because it touched upon what he was delving into – the search for the miraculous. What he was seeking was the extraordinary reality beyond the veil of normal experience. He's the man nobody knew. Burt would say, 'I am that I am!', which is the name of God that God gives to Moses in the Torah. I think he was the man nobody knew. A very Zen person living in the Eternal Now."

The Moons by Burt Shonberg
(Courtesy of the George & Marzia Greif Family Trust.)

Burt's drawing adorning the cover of George Clayton Johnson's anthology *All Of Us Are Dying*.

Marjorie Cameron outside her home in West Hollywood in 1987. (Photograph courtesy of Robert Aiken.)

BURT SHONBERG ➥ *OUT THERE*

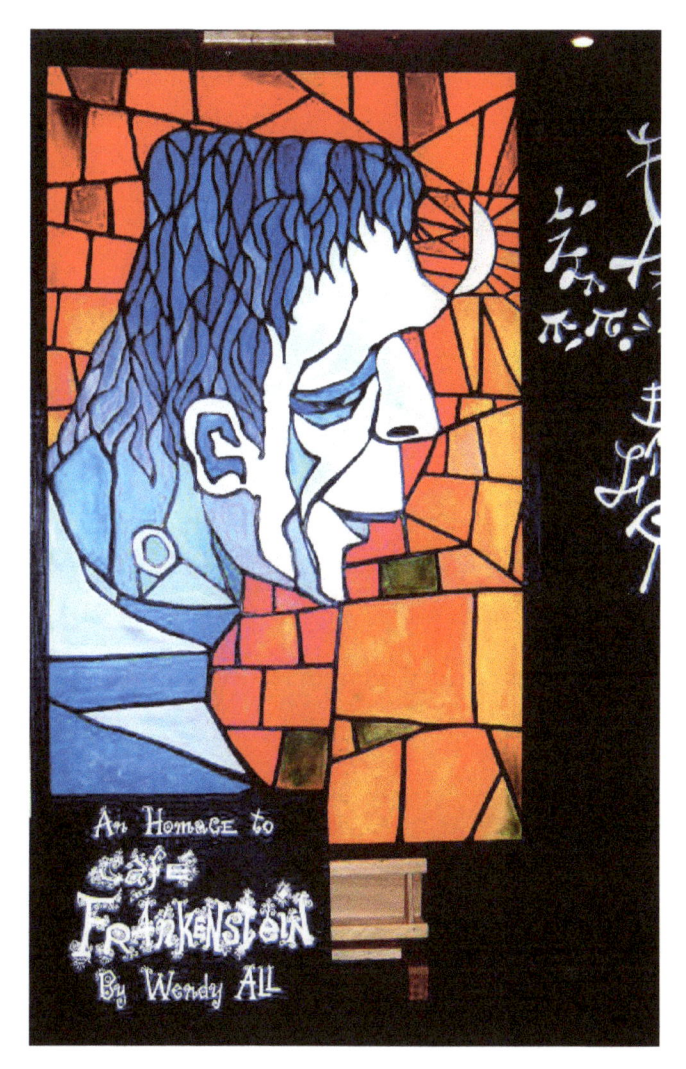

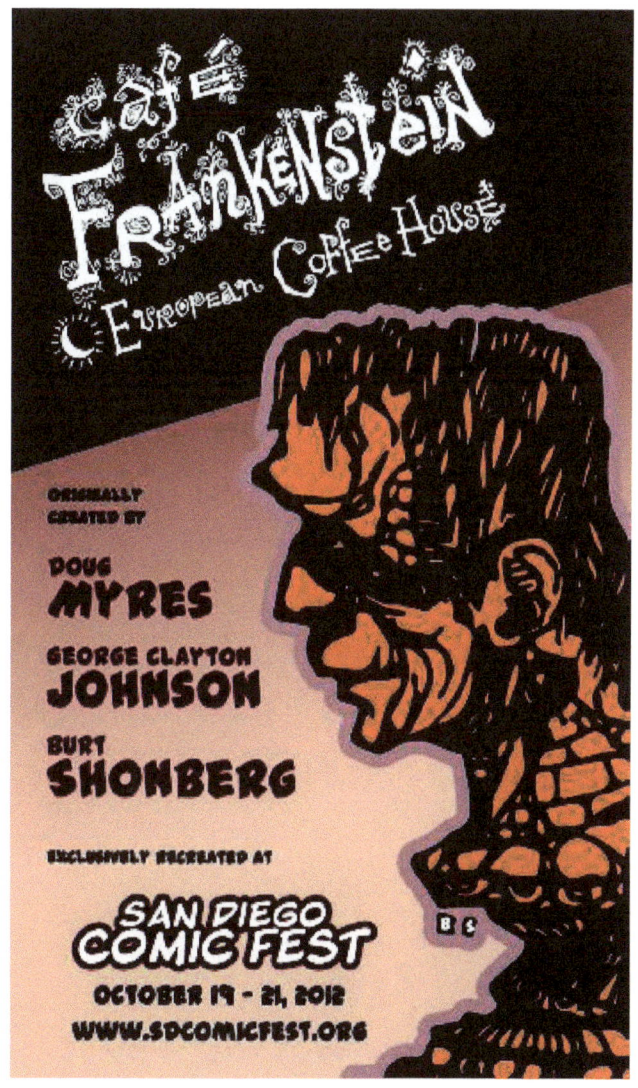

Poster for the Cafe Frankenstein recreation at the San Diego Comic Fest in 2012.

Wendy All's recreation of Burt's Cafe Frankenstein faux stained glass window. (Photograph courtesy of Wendy All.)

243

Wendy All's recreation of Burt's Cafe Frankenstein cartouche.
(Photograph courtesy of Wendy All.)

Wendy All at the entrance of her wonderful recreation of Cafe Frankenstein at the San Diego Comic Fest in 2012.
(Photograph courtesy of Wendy All.)

BURT SHONBERG ➥ OUT THERE

Ledru and Marshall pose with Burt painting *Aztec Vision*. Los Angeles, 1978. (Courtesy of Marshall Berle.)

Stanley Dyrector with his Shonberg *Who Am I? No Thing. Here. Now.* (Photographed of by Joyce Dyrector.)

245

Appendix

All of the quotes in this book derive from interviews that were conducted by the author, except for those listed below.

Chapter 1: Bitsy.
1) The different spellings of the Schreter/Schrater surnames are due to an Ellis Island misspell that was never corrected.

Chapter 2: Frolicking in Flickerville
1) Dean's iconic role in *Rebel Without a Cause* appears to have inspired an undated sketch of Burt's, part of his juvenilia, that depicts a cool dude, seen from behind, wearing turn-up jeans, with a ghoulish face emblazoned on the back of his windbreaker jacket. An early take on that new, mid-20th-century sociocultural phenomenon: The American Teenager.
2) In an interview with Barry Brown, conducted years later, Bruno VeSota claimed that Burt designed the costumes worn by the Vega-men monsters in his risible, 1962 B-movie *Invasion of the Star Creatures*. The costumes consisted of nothing more than dyed green burlap sacks with carrots for eyes, and it's difficult to imagine that Burt – who is not listed in the film's credits – would have countenanced such an artless job.
3) Although it's been reported that Burt's handsome, post-impressionist portrait of classical composer Pyotr Ilyich Tchaikovky was commissioned by Capitol Records for the cover of his sixth Symphony, an extensive search of Discogs.com yields no such album.

Chapter 3: Cafe Frankenstein
1) Bolstering his Beat bona fides, Burt supplied an ink wash sketch of a young urchin girl standing atop a rubble heap, to an anti-war anthology of poems by Elizabeth Case entitled *Pax and Dig*. Case, a former Disney animator who worked on *Sleeping Beauty*, became so popular reading her poetry in the many coffeehouses up and down the West Coast, she was unofficially dubbed "The Mother of the Beat Generation."
2) *Out Here: A brief account of how this all began for me* by Burt Shonberg with Ledru Shoopman Baker III
3) *Cafe Frankenstein: A brief (but monstrous) history of Laguna Beach's notorious beatnik mecca* by Wendy All and Barry Alfonso.
4) *Cafe Frankenstein, a brief (but monstrous) history of*

Laguna Beach's notorious beatnik mecca by Wendy All and Barry Alfonso.

5) There's every likelihood that the ERONBU ranch still stands today in the shape of Rancho Mojave, although the original quarters are long gone and have been replaced with a Southwest style casita.

Chapter 4: Firestarter

1) According to Hampton Fancher, the Kramer brothers relocated to San Francisco in the 1960s, where they both died at a premature age. After Jack Kramer's International closed, the premises became The Lamp and then a short-lived gay bar called The Macabre. But it only fully realized its potential when the jazz drummer Shelley Manne took it over and turned it into Shelley's ManneHole, which became a thriving jazz club until it closed in 1972. Interestingly, the venue was used in a scene in the film *Night Tide,* in which Cameron makes her dramatic entrance and gives Dennis Hopper's sailor character the evil eye.

2) Despite her adoration for him, Sally Kellerman regrettably rebuffed Brando's advances, feeling intimidated and out of her depth as a guileless ingénue.

3) 'A Declaration of Independents' by Brian Chidester.

4) Vincent Price's daughter, Victoria, has confirmed that there were no Shonberg paintings in her father's estate at the time of his death.

Chapter 5: The Experience

1 & 2) Excerpted from *Out Here: A Brief Account of How This All Began For Me* by Burt Shonberg with Ledru Shoopman Baker III

Chapter 6: Baphomet

1) Interestingly, the title of Bester's novel reportedly derived from a letter written in 1943 by Cameron's deceased former husband, Jack Parsons, to his then-wife Helen, in which he assures her: "*(rocketry) may not be my True Will, but it's one hell of a powerful drive. With Thelema as my goal, and the stars my destination and my home, I have set my eyes on high.*" It remains unclear how Bester came across this personal correspondence, although he and Parsons shared a mutual friendship with the author Robert Heinlein.

2) Lenny Bruce played sets at the Purple Onion and, according to Rosemary Vail, he admired Burt's artwork. The Purple Onion panels later fell into the hands of Jay Dekeyser, a friend of Marshall Berle's, who kept them in his storage garage in Las Vegas, until they became warped and were destroyed.

Chapter 7: Out (of) Here

1) Lou Adler has confirmed to Marshall Berle that he's owned several works by Burt over the years.

2) In a depressingly familiar postscript, a year later, the Domino Bar was snapped up by a new owner (an abrasive New Yorker named Harold) and one of his first decisions was to whitewash Burt's mural off its walls. Sally Enright was livid when she heard: "The ink wasn't dry on the contracts before he charged in with the buckets of whitewash and destroyed the lot." But there was

some payback: "The customers turned on Harold, regarding him as a vandal and a philistine, and he never got the bar back on track. It only lasted about six months."

3) Franco himself viewed Ibiza dismissively, as an impoverished backwater, and regarded its native Ibancencos, who'd rallied to the Republican cause during the Spanish Civil War, as nothing more than peasants. The dictator had so little time for the place, he used it as a dumping ground to offload bad cops and gave plum administrative jobs to his corrupt officials. "It was mainly an anti-Franco island, but it was divided along class lines," Sally Enright explains. "Franco put his stooges in at the government level and it was still technically against the law for the locals to speak Catalan. But nobody talked politics – it was too bloody dangerous. A couple of the fishermen would get drunk and start singing Republican slogans until their mates dragged them off."

Chapter 8: Super Chief

1) That year, after experiencing a spiritual awakening at an ashram in the Himalayas, Richard Alpert changed his name to the more Eastern guru-sounding Baba Ram Dass. In the title of his popular book, he distilled Gurdjieff's mental exercises for the attainment of super-consciousness to a three-word aphorism: *Be Here Now*.

2) Tragically, most of Ira's photographs documenting Burt's artwork, including the negatives, were lost years later after he was mugged by a junkie.

Chapter 9: Rimbaud of the West Coast

1) Tom Wilkes became the art director for the Monterey International Pop Festival, and he co-created Camouflage Productions with Burt's pal Barry Feinstein. He designed many famous album covers, like The Who's *Tommy* and the charity record of the *Concert for Bangladesh*.

Chapter 10: Hollywood Babylon

1) A pack of malicious lies, concerning the death of Godot, have been spread over the years, by paranoid and delusional conspiracy nuts, who believe the Laurel Canyon music scene was conceived and orchestrated by the CIA as a mind control experiment. (They seem unable or unwilling to ask themselves this simple question: What could have happened in the world between 1939 and 1945 to explain why so many fathers of baby boomer rock stars were enlisted in the military during that period?)

The tragic facts are that Godot was scampering around on the roof of the building above Vito and Szou's abode, with two older children, while their parents stood nearby, readying themselves for a photo session conducted by Ray Leong for the *LA Free Press*. Leong recollects that Godot accidentally fell through the transom of the broken skylight up there, but Szou contends that one of the other children, "an evil child," pushed Godot *onto* the skylight, and he fell 25 feet onto the floor of the stairwell below. He was rushed to the hospital, where his parents were told his injuries were not serious and he would be alright. The medical team then decided to perform a spinal tap on the child, to check the fluid; a highly dangerous procedure to carry out on a patient already suffering from a brain injury. According to Szou: "This student doctor carried out the spinal tap, which sucked his brain down into his neck and killed him. It was so painful for us. Nobody ever knew what happened to Godot, because it was such a shock to us – we couldn't talk about it. I was 6 months pregnant at the time and felt at risk over the grief, so we kept distracting ourselves and made sure we had a party planned every night." Although Szou and Vito sued the hospital for medical malpractice, as well as their landlord for the broken skylight, their inexperienced lawyer was no match for the medical profession's lawyers, and the lawsuit went nowhere.

2) In 1970, Arthur Lee sold Burt's *Out Here* painting to Jay Dekeyser, to help fund his heroin habit. According to Marshall Berle: "Jay was a lifelong friend and we went to Arthur Lee's house to buy it. Jay had $600 but Lee wanted $3500 for it, but Jay bargained him down to $700 cash."

3) According to Carol Green: "David got Burt's Head East wood panels and we kept them in the store for a while, but they must have subsequently been thrown out into the garbage."

Chapter 11: Mysterian of the Cosmos

1) In early December 1968, Vito and Szou vacated their Laurel Canyon headquarters for good. In their wake, a new crew moved into the area and took their run of the place. Like Vito, their leader was a pint-sized, seasoned ex-con, with a devilish look and a magnetic personality, as well as a penchant for young girls, but unlike Vito, he saw the world through the prism of a thoroughly malignant mind, Charles Manson. "We were sitting in our house in Cotati and Carl (Franzoni) visited us with his Italian girlfriend Basha when the news broke about the arrests made in the Tate-Labianca murders," Szou recollects. "And Basha said, 'Don't you remember these people, Szou? They were in the shop!' Well, I remembered Tex Watson, the tall one. I recall him standing over to one side with three or four Manson girls in the shop. And I remembered Bummer Bob, a.k.a Bobby Beausoleil, (responsible for the earlier Gary Hinman killing) because he had a striking appearance, and he'd just hang out at the front door of my shop with his white dog, but he never made an approach to me. I never spoke to him. Manson was new in the area and wanted to gain notoriety as a religious leader. I went to high school with one of the girls, Catherine "Gypsy" Share. We sat next to each other because our names were so close. I knew her background: she was orphaned during WW2 in France and was adopted by a blind psychologist and his wife. She seemed very lonely but lived too far away for us to socialise. She didn't talk much but was a nice person. Years later, after we'd done a dance at the Shrine Auditorium for 3,000 people, I saw her backstage and she looked so lonely, and I felt a heart tug. She was with a group of people. I heard Manson beat her up to within an each of her life – kicking her in the head. I never saw Manson hanging around the place but someone told me they saw him checking the shop out after we left."

2) A brief Jack Bond outtake from the Studio 70 sessions also appears on Randy California's 1977 album *Future Games*, but the voice is unintelligible.

3) *Who Goes There?* is also a science fiction novella, penned by John W. Campbell, Jr., on which *The Thing from Another World* is based on.

4) This show should not be confused with another Spirit gig held at the Santa Monica Civic Center, on August 28, 1976, when Dr. Demento introduced the group onto the stage.

Epilogue

1) Quoted from *Los Angeles Times* article by Alan Goldstein

Acknowledgments

It simply would not have been possible to write this book without the invaluable contribution of Burt's family and friends. At the top of the list, I am deeply indebted to Marshall Berle – a total mensch – whose patronage and friendship with Burt is celebrated throughout the final chapter, and Dolly Schreter, whose childhood memories illuminated so much of Burt's early life. I'm grateful to her son, Steven McCormack, for connecting us, and to Stephen Schrater, who provided further family insights, as well as the surviving examples of Burt's juvenilia.

I am incredibly grateful to all of Burt's L.A. compadres, his childhood playmates and his European acquaintances, who all generously shared their memories of him: Judy Shavin, Hampton Fancher, Robert Storr, Joe Steck, Stanley Dyrector, George Clayton Johnson (R.I.P), Ledru Shoopman Baker III (R.I.P), Doug Myres (R.I.P), Julian Porter, Louis Porter, Robert Carl Cohen, Sally Kellerman, Morgan Ames, Michael Greene, Jim Maxwell, Ira Odessky, Ed Fagen, Jeri Elam, Sheldon Weinstein, Eleanor Oliver, Danny Weinstein, Rochelle Weinsten, Sally Enright, Shep Sanders, Sherman Keene, Steve Ross, Daryll Copeland, Szou Paulekas, Tony Marer, Judy Chester (R.I.P.), Walter Teller, John Boyce, Jim Maxwell, Kristina Rochelle Steinke, Christina Rosenthal, Carol Green, Eve Nazarian, Sheldon Jaman, Jim Maxwell, Sydney Sencio, Carl Franzoni, Rosemary Vail, Bonnie Vail Sussman, Edward Vail, Bob Roberts (Beatle Bob), Wanda, Pete Hendleman and Richard Field Levine.

I would also like to thank those many people who contributed valuable testimony and/or cooperation: Roger Corman, Adrian Haller, Joie, Mildred Popovitch, Robert Janiger, Laura Decludt, Rod Salmons, Mercy Baron, Dorothy Slotnick Green, Ray Leong, David Del Valle, Dylan Marer and Omy Marer, Georgiana Steele-Waller, Darin Murphy, Seth Daniels, Lord Sydney, Kevin Sheehan, Larry Bell, Paul Barrere, Marc Mastey, Trent C. Hoskins-Kleinkopf, Marilyn Wenker, Tom Weaver, Victor Parra, Jerry Yester, Richard Carroll, and my fellow seekers on the Shonberg path, Wendy All and Brian Chidester. Finally, I'm grateful for the graft and cooperation of my publisher Mogg Morgan.

Index

A

Abrams, Isaac 143
Abrams, Rachel 143
Ackerman, Forrest J 39, 40, 41
Ackerman, Forrest J "Forry" 39, 40, 41
Adams, Fred 156
Adderley, Cannonball 178
Adler, Lou 135, 247
Adrian, Ruth 60
Aldrin, Buzz 200
All, Wendy 238, 247, 251
Allen, Steve 172
Alpert, Richard 145, 156, 157, 193, 195, 248
Altoon, John 72
Ames, Morgan 70, 71, 72, 208, 251
Andress, Ursula 137
Anger, Kenneth 55
Armstrong, Jack 7
Armstrong, Neil 200
Atwell, Allen 143

B

Bach 160
Baker, Chet 76
Baker III, Ledru Shoopman 190, 191, 196, 209, 210, 211, 212, 213, 216, 218, 235, 236, 237, 240, 246, 247, 251
Baphomet 114, 116, 126, 182, 247
Bara, Theda 28
Baudelaire 141
Beardsley, Aubrey 55
Beaumont, Charles 40, 234
Bengston, Billy Al 72
Berle, Marshall 55, 209, 210, 211, 213, 214, 216, 217, 218, 239, 247, 249, 251
Berle, Milton 209
Bester, Alfred 117
Beverly Hills 28, 29
Bialle, David 190, 197
Bikel, Theodore 52
Bogart, Humphrey 33
Bond, Jack 211, 213, 214, 216, 217, 240
Boone, Pat 178
Bow, Clara 28, 102
Boyce, John 175, 198, 237, 251
Brando, Marlon 36, 39, 70, 247
Brennan, Walter 36
Brooks, Louise 28
Brubeck, Dave 178
Bruce, Lenny 59, 155, 172, 176, 247
Buckley, Lord 42, 101, 179
Bummer Bob, a.k.a Bobby Beausoleil 249
Burnham, Patrick 141, 143
Burroughs, William 52

C

California, Randy 213, 214, 215, 217, 237, 249
Cameron, Crystal 53, 60, 79
Cameron, Marjorie 52, 53, 54, 55, 56, 58, 60, 61, 62, 69, 75, 78, 79, 97, 122, 124, 125, 126, 127, 179, 237, 247
Campbell, Connie 14, 217
Canned Heat 177
Captain Marvel 8, 9, 32, 58, 122, 202
Case, Elizabeth 246
Cassidy, Ed 215
Chekhov 208
Clifford, Irving 137
Coburn, Beverly 158
Coburn, Charles 121
Coburn, James 158
Cohen, Herb 11, 52, 123, 124, 172, 192, 195, 231, 251
Cohn Jr., Harrison (Harry) 164
Cole, Nat King 98
Coleman, Ornette 137
Coltrane, John 137, 178
Copeland, Darryl 76, 162
Corman, Roger 42, 77, 115, 251
Corso, Gregory 52
Count Dracula 34
Crocker, Clive 136
Crowley, Aleister 53, 55, 58, 71, 115, 179
Crumb, R 144

D

da Vinci, Leonardo 75, 94
Dalai Lama 158
Dali, Salvador 140, 180
Dana, Joe 197
Davis, Miles 137, 178
de Hory, Elmyr 137
Dean, James 34, 71, 246
Decludt, Laura 239, 251
Dee, John 55
Dekeyser, Jay 247, 249
Dick, Phillip K. 233

Dr West's Medicine Show and Junk Band 180
Dr. Demento 250
Dracula 9, 39, 41, 59, 214
Duncan, Isadora 174
Duvalier, Papa Doc 231
Dylan, Bob 141, 172
Dyrector, Stanley 28, 120, 121, 155, 200, 208, 235, 239, 251

E

Elam, Jack 144
Elam, Jeri 144, 251
Elliot, Denholm 137
Elvis 146
Empey, Marguerite 72
Enright, Sally 70, 71, 136, 137, 142, 173, 205, 234, 247, 248, 251
Escapade 38, 72, 73, 74

F

Fabares, Shelley 135
Fagen, Ed 18, 251
Fancher III, Hampton Lansden 30, 32, 33, 34, 36, 37, 38, 39, 40, 41, 42, 43, 56, 58, 59, 61, 69, 72, 74, 75, 78, 93, 98, 99, 114, 116, 122, 124, 125, 126, 127, 195, 205, 208, 233, 247, 251
Feinstein, Barry 70, 123, 248
Fonda, Jane 172
Fonda, Peter 173
Forry. See Ackerman, Forrest J
Fowley, Kim 173
Franco 142
Frankenstein 9, 37, 39, 40, 41, 51, 57, 58, 59, 60, 61, 69, 72, 73, 74, 75, 80, 123, 202, 238, 239, 246
Franzoni, Carl 172, 195, 251

G

Garris, Sid 180
Gaudi, Antoni 139
Gaye, Marvin 209
Ginsberg, Allen 51, 59, 101, 144
Godot 174, 193, 248
Gordon, Al 161
Goya 79
Grady, Art 72
Grant, Cary 101, 235
Green, Carol 190, 197, 249, 251
Greene, Michael 100, 124, 125, 126, 156, 251
Greif, George 179, 180, 181, 182, 183, 234, 239
Guggenheim, Mary Ewart 193
Gurdjieff, George Ivanovitch 75, 94, 116, 118, 119, 120, 155, 164, 168, 174, 240, 248

H

Haller, Daniel 77
Harvey, Laurence 164
Heard, Gerald 54
Henske, Judy 59
Hinman, Gary 249
Hitchcock, Alfred 43
Hoffman, Abbie 195
Hoffman, Albert 101
Holiday, Billie 137
Hopkins, George 174
Hopper, Dennis 125, 247
Hubbard, L. Ron 53
Huntington, Joan 135
Huxley, Aldous 54, 100, 235

J

Jaman, Sheldon 8, 9, 10, 12, 15, 119, 140, 174, 193, 251
Janiger, Dr. Oscar 100, 101, 102, 103, 104, 114, 116, 122, 145, 158, 215, 218, 235, 251
Jefferson Airplane 231
Jesus 117, 121
Joan of Arc 55, 76
Johnson, George Clayton 39, 40, 57, 61, 73, 76, 79, 116, 120, 177, 213, 237, 239, 251
Judith 180
Judy 27, 28, 29, 37, 55, 59, 93, 94, 117, 118, 126, 164, 191, 205, 206, 239, 251
Julian 99, 198, 201, 202, 233, 251

K

Karloff, Boris 9, 58
Keene, Barry 215
Kellerman 70, 71, 72, 173, 205, 234, 247, 251
Kennedy, Bobby 231
Kennedy, President 125
Kerouac, Jack 51, 172
King, Martin Luther 126, 231
Klix, Richard 156
Kramer, Harry 28, 30, 31, 59
Kramer, Jack 28, 29, 30, 31, 34, 51, 69, 249
  and Harry 28, 30
Krishnamurti, Jiddu 118, 163
Kubrick, Stanley 200
Kunkin, Art 232
Kurosawa, Akira 200

L

Laura and Diane 234
Le Petit Sphinx 69, 75, 80
Leary, Timothy 145, 146, 195
Ledru. See Baker IIILedru Shoopman
Lee, Christopher 41
Lee. Arthur 14, 121, 183, 197, 214, 249
Leong, Ray 75, 78, 115, 118, 126,

253

136, 164, 248, 251
Levi, Eliphas 115
Levine, Walter 36, 38
Lewin, Max 70
Lewis, Edward 119, 156, 251
Little Richard 209
Lorre, Peter 9
Lugosi, Bela 9, 34, 214

M

Mancini, Mary 97
Manne, Shelley 247
Manson, Charles 209, 249
Marer, Tony 180, 181, 251
Marvin, Lee 121
Marx, Groucho 96
Matisse, Henri 75, 94
McBean, Angus 40
McCormack, John 15
McLuhan, Marshall 178
McNabb, Joann 30, 31, 32, 33, 43
Meredith, James 125
Metzner, Ralph 197
Michelangelo 164
Mifune, Toshiro 200
Mihailoviæ, Draža 192
Milland, Ray 115
Miloskovich, Velinka Lubitsa 98
Mitchell, Joni 197
Mix, Tom 172
Modern Folk Quartet 124
Monseratt 193
Montejo, Mario 30, 32
Moore, Henry 120
Mosco, Boyce 121
Motherwell, Robert 162
Mozart 160
Mulligan, Gerry 76
Myres, Doug 57, 60, 62, 69, 239, 251

N

Nazarian, Eve 165, 180, 181, 182, 251
Nazarian, George 165
Nazis 122, 180, 190
Nicholson, Jack 173
Nico 137
Nietzsche 69
Nimoy, Leonard 178
Nurmi, Maila 34

O

Odessky, Ira 94, 135, 162, 182, 196, 248, 251
Oliver (nee Cohen), Eleanor 11, 251
Ouspensky, P. D. 75, 94, 116, 120, 240

P

Parsons, Jack 53, 54, 56, 247
Paulekas, Szou 97, 119, 157, 172, 174, 182, 192, 193, 195, 196, 231, 232, 233, 249, 251
Paulekas, Vito 95, 96, 97, 119, 157, 172, 174, 175, 182, 192, 193, 194, 196, 231, 232
Pentland, Lord 118
Pertwee, Jon 137
Phillips, Jack (aka Philipo) 72
Picasso, Pablo 75, 141
Pittman, Tom 71
Pollock, Jackson 162
Porter, Louis A. 98
Porter, Valerie 98, 99, 100, 102, 124, 138, 139, 141, 143, 160, 165, 174, 179, 180, 182, 192, 193, 198, 199, 201, 202, 205, 232
Posner, Arlene 98
Price, Vincent 77, 78, 247

R

Raboff, Ernest 181
Ramos, Johnny 121
Rembrandt 234
Reynolds, Burt 121
Rice, Don 161
Rimbaud 141, 172, 184, 248
Rivers, Johnny 178
Robbins, Freddie 73
Roberts, Bob 175, 251
Robson, Dame Flora 40
Rolling Stones 145, 231
Rooney, Mickey 172
Ross, Steve 210
Rouault (Georges) 100
Rowena, Frank 201
Rublev, Andrei 100

S

Salmons, Rod 139, 251
Sanders, Shep 116, 251
Sartre, Jean-Paul 69
Satan 192
Schley, Michael 74
Schrater, Dolly 6, 11, 13, 15, 191, 217, 219, 239, 251
Schreter, Dolly 6, 8, 9, 11, 12, 146
Schrater, Harry 219
Schrater, Stephen 146, 251
Seeger, Pete 59
Seidenbaum, Art 183
Seley, Stephen 142
Semu 164, 210
Shaffer, Sueanne 97
Share, Catherine Gypsy 249
Shatner, William 178
Shevin, Judy 85, 91, 117, 118, 164, 170, 191, 202, 206, 239
Shevin, Ray 75, 78, 94, 118, 140, 164, 202

Shonberg, Bill 6, 11, 15, 27, 117
Shonberg, Helen 5, 6, 13, 15, 191, 217, 219, 247
Shonberg, Louis 5, 13, 98, 99, 198, 201, 202, 219, 233, 251
   Louis and Helen 5
Shonberg, Louis Jr. 99
Simon and Garfunkel's 177
Sklar-Weinstein 143
Smith, Bill 117
Smith, Jimmy 137
Soffer, Sid 60
Sonny and Cher 173
Spence, Ivan 136
Spirit 162, 213, 214, 215, 216, 217, 250
St. John, Jill 172
Stancin, John James 233
Starr, Ringo 234
Steck, Joe 157, 159, 160, 161, 162, 163, 164, 166, 167, 184, 191, 195, 206, 251
Steinberg, Saul 35
Stewart, Jimmy 44
Stoker, Bram 9
Storr, Robert 121, 122, 123, 155, 177, 179, 182, 184, 191, 199, 200, 207, 211, 217, 240, 251

T
Tchaikovsky, Pyotr Ilyich 246
Teller, Walter 176, 177, 207, 237, 251
Terry-Thomas 137
The Beach Boys 209
The Beatles 145, 173, 178, 197, 199
The Brotherhood of Eternal Love 196
The Byrds 141, 172
The Mothers of Invention 172
Toulouse-Lautrec 141, 161
Turner, Ike and Tina 209
Turner, J. M. W. 79

U
Underhill, Joei (Joey) 235, 236, 237

V
Vail, Bonnie 119, 251
Vail, Rosemary 119, 155, 247, 251
Valentine, Elmer 173
Vampira 34, 61
Van Gogh 141, 234
Van Halen 218
Van Tassel, George 163
Verlaine 141
VeSota, Bruno 38, 42, 246
Vining, Constance 74
Vogel, Ron 73

W
War of the Worlds 10, 207
Warhol, Andy 144
Watson, Charles Tex 209
Watt, Judy 27, 37, 55, 93, 206
Weinstein, (nee Gauvin) Rochelle 13
Weinstein, Danny 12, 15, 251
Weinstein, Sheldon 8, 251
Welles, Mel 42
Welles, Orson 10, 42
Wells, H. G. 10
Werner, Oskar 36
Whicker, Alan 194
Wilde, Cornel 29, 38
Wilkes, Tom 185, 248
Wolf Man 9, 37, 39, 41, 58

Y
Yasuda, Robert 143

Z
Zappa, Frank 172, 175, 176

Lightning Source UK Ltd.
Milton Keynes UK
UKHW051900010321
379600UK00005B/258

9 781906 958794